Advance Praise for *If You Will It*

"Elliott Abrams' passionate new book is a vital message for American Jews about Israel—and about their own future."

–Natan Sharansky

"American Judaism is in crisis. In this deeply insightful and important work, Elliott Abrams comes to grips with the difficulties we face and points the way forward."

–Rabbi David Wolpe

"At an inflection point such as ours, we need deep thinkers like Elliott Abrams. *If You Will It* surveys the landscape of American Jewry, its challenges and opportunities, and provides a vocabulary to build a bright Jewish future. Thoughtful, provocative, and crisply written— this volume is required reading for anyone wondering how we got to where we are and, more importantly, where we should go from here."

–Rabbi Elliot Cosgrove,
Park Avenue Synagogue, Manhattan

If You Will It

If You Will It

Rebuilding Jewish Peoplehood for the 21st Century

Elliott Abrams

Wicked Son

A WICKED SON BOOK
An Imprint of Post Hill Press
ISBN: 979-8-88845-553-1
ISBN (eBook): 979-8-88845-554-8

If You Will It
Rebuilding Jewish Peoplehood for the 21st Century

Cover Design by Jim Villaflores

Post Hill Press
New York • Nashville
wickedsonbooks.com
posthillpress.com

Published in the United States of America
1 2 3 4 5 6 7 8 9 10

To Rapha, Maya, Samson, Levi, Lily, Shiloh,
Noah, and Alma—and their parents.

Table of Contents

Introduction

On October 7th, 2023, I woke up early and glanced at my iPhone. I had a brief but anguished message from a friend: "Can you believe it? It's too awful." I went to the website of an Israeli paper—and that's how I found out about the massacres that began the Gaza war.

Soon—like so many American Jews—I was texting with my children and with relatives in Israel. My nephew and my niece's husband were in the reserves and were quickly called up for active duty in the IDF. That Saturday, which was the holiday of Shemini Atzeret, the battles with terrorists inside Israel continued. Throughout America's Jewish communities, there was fear, anger, sorrow—and soon disbelief and then outrage as the real details of what Hamas had done to children, women, and whole families emerged. Soon, Jews and Jewish organizations were asking what they could do. Donations? Meetings? Marches? Demands on the president and Congress? Solidarity visits to Israel? I spent hours replying to media queries about the war, doing interviews, writing articles—and continuing conversations with Jews here at home and around the world as we coped with the savage assault, the loss of life, the number of hostages.

At the Tikvah Fund, the Jewish educational NGO that I chair, we started a series of forty classes over the following weeks. These classes were aimed at high school students and their parents to help them understand what had happened in the broadest context—Jewish history, Israeli history, Middle East politics, the laws of war, Judaism, the rescue of hostages, and much more. We began to plan a new day school where Zionism (and teaching Hebrew) would be central in the curriculum, as well as new college programs and tracks for Jewish students. In the face of tragedy, we thought, *How can we build more? Do more?*

Within days, the shock and horror that American Jews felt at what Hamas had done was deepened by watching people *cheer* for Hamas's actions. This happened widely in the Arab world, and all of a sudden, the sweet idea that Israel had been accepted once and for all, that the Abraham Accords would quickly encompass more and more Arab countries, was gone. Then 100,000 people demonstrated against Israel and for Hamas in London, while bodies were still being found in the destroyed kibbutzim. In other parts of Europe, the slaughter of Jews was met with obvious approval. Our comfortable conclusions that Israel was now, finally, safe and secure were gone too.

We had come to think that the struggles of past decades were over. The wars of 1956, 1967, and 1973 were ancient history, and Israel was the Start-Up Nation. Zionism was a movement started in the 1800s and completed in 1948. But in October 2023, we saw that the struggle against the Jewish state had not ended—so the struggle to defend the Jewish state could not end either, and American Jews had to be part of that struggle.

Worse yet were the reactions here at home. Students at some of the most prestigious American universities joined campus marches to "Free Palestine," unmoved even slightly by Hamas's inhuman, savage killings of Jewish babies, children, and elderly men and women, or by the mass hostage taking. There was violence against Jews on campuses, followed by advice not to display obvious signs of Judaism such as Stars of David; on Halloween three weeks after the massacres, Jews wondered about taking down or covering the mezuzahs on their doorposts for the night. Police seemed unable to restore a sense of security to many American Jews as anti-Semitic incidents skyrocketed. On campuses, especially the most famous places, the leadership was very often cold. Deans and provosts and presidents who leapt into action to support fashionable and "progressive" causes and punish "microaggressions" could not find their voices now in the face of murder. Instead, they issued morally blind calls for "peace" and wrung their hands about "all forms of violence." Others, including the Secretary General of the United Nations, "contextualized." You see, Hamas's actions "did not happen in a vacuum,"[1] and one must understand the complex background. Hundreds of college professors signed petitions condemning Israel's self-defense. All those campus offices of inclusion and diversity were dead silent when it came to the safety of Jews.

All of this left American Jews with two contrasting emotions: a deep connection to Israel, where Jews had been so brutally attacked, and a fraying connection to just about everyone else. Who were these friends and allies and partners of ours if they could not see that hundreds of Jews had been slaughtered without mercy simply because they were Jews? What was being taught, and what was being learned, in the "best" colleges if thousands and thousands of professors and students could argue that this was "a reaction to settler colonialism" or some form of "legitimate protest" against the lack of a Palestinian state? I kept watching those marches and thinking *CHILDREN WERE TAKEN HOSTAGE. FORTY BABIES WERE MURDERED. WHAT IS WRONG WITH YOU?* But there was a simple answer. Nothing can explain cold indifference to the suffering of Jews except hatred of Jews. And for the enlightened, educated "leaders" who issued carefully balanced statements of regret about "violence on all sides," it was clear that other audiences, other groups, other pressures outweighed whatever was troubling the Jews.

For American Jews, these were new challenges. My daughter told me of her discussions with other Jewish parents about what to tell their children. The weekend after the Hamas terror attacks, while their kids attended Hebrew school on Sunday, she and the other parents met in the synagogue. One mother summed up the discussion: We all try to tell and show the children that being a Jew is a joy and a gift, from the Bible stories and the history to the songs and prayers, to Hanukah and Passover, to Israel. How do we now tell them that there's just this one other thing: people want you dead and will try to kill you. That is also your fate as a Jew.

This is a book about the past and future of American Jews and our relationship with Israel. There has been a lot of what I'd call happy talk about the situation of the American Jewish community—about our history and today's demographic trends, about our support for Israel, and about how we are mobilizing ourselves to prepare the next generation of Jews who will have to lead us. Will our children have the knowledge and the will to defend Israel and defend our own community here? Will they feel the deep connection to other

Jews, the sense of Jewish identity and peoplehood, that has lasted for a hundred generations but is clearly weakening among American Jews today? Will the crisis Israelis and all Jews faced after October 7, 2023, lead to changes in the way we teach our children, live our lives, or target our charitable giving as Jews? Will we confront anti-Semitism by arguing with anti-Semites or by building the strength and commitment of new generations of American Jews?

In the past, we have responded to crises energetically—but briefly. After the Holocaust, American Jews strongly supported the establishment the State of Israel. But once it was founded, our attention wandered to our immediate concerns: social and economic mobility, and assimilation in America. The great sociologist Nathan Glazer wrote in his 1957 book *American Judaism* these almost shocking words:

> The two greatest events in modern Jewish history, the murder of 6 million Jews by Hitler and the creation of a Jewish state in Palestine, had had remarkably slight effects on the inner life of American Jewry.... The establishment of Israel meant little for American Judaism specifically...."[2]

But then came the great Israeli triumph in the Yom Kippur War of 1967, and it awakened Jewish pride and great enthusiasm about Israel. One of America's leading rabbis of those years, Arthur Hertzberg, wrote in *Commentary* magazine soon after the war that "the mood of the American Jewish community underwent an abrupt, radical, and possibly permanent change...far more intense and widespread than anyone could have foreseen."[3]

"Possibly permanent." But like the intense support for Israel in 1948, it was not permanent. In the half century since the 1967 War, we have seen that Jewish education changed little; most American Jews know little of their religion and little of Israel because so many have never set foot there even once. In 1957, Glazer wrote that "Most American Jews are incapable of giving a coherent statement of the main beliefs of the Jewish religion and tend to call 'Judaism' whatever views they happen to hold today."[4] Is that any less true now, more than 65 years later?

Whether we measure the strength of American Jewish "Zionism" or the strength of our own sense of community, identity, and peoplehood, there's plenty of evidence of weakness. In the decades since the 1967 war, we have seen affiliation rates fall and the intermarriage rate skyrocket. The data shows that hundreds of thousands of American Jews are not raising their children as Jews in any meaningful sense, and hundreds of thousands more have simply left the community.[5] When it comes to the education of (non-Orthodox) American Jews, have we changed things in the last few decades and moved away from the largely failed synagogue "Hebrew school" model? I attended a pretty standard Hebrew school in a Conservative synagogue in the 1950s and learned next to nothing. Are we doing much better in Hebrew schools today? Is anyone learning Hebrew?

Never in Jewish history, which is saying a lot, has there been a community with such secular educational achievements but that is so uneducated in Jewish history, language, and religion. American Jews visit Israel far less than Jews from any of the other large Diaspora communities—less than French, British, Canadian, or Australian Jews. If it weren't for Birthright's free trips, the numbers would be even more dismal. We should be immensely proud of the American Jewish community's contributions to the United States; they have been extraordinary. We have been the model minority or immigrant group in so many ways. But our record as a *Jewish* community is different.

It does not need to be this way. There are concrete—even obvious—steps the American Jewish community can take to increase the odds that more American Jews remain Jewish and raise their children as Jews so that those children view themselves as a part of the Jewish people. Some of these steps will seem easy and would meet little resistance except for their expense; others will strike some American Jews as against their secular principles or their foreign policy views. The role I propose for Israel will seem obvious to some and objectionable to others. For in my view, a relationship with the Jewish state is an essential aspect of Jewish peoplehood, without which no diaspora community can thrive—or perhaps even survive.

The essence of my argument is simple. Jews of the immigrant generations and their descendants, until around the 1960s, lived in an immersive Jewish environment that is gone today for all but Orthodox Jews. Those earlier generations lived as my immigrant grandparents did—in dense Jewish neighborhoods among Jewish friends and relatives. To them, the world they had left behind in Europe and the world in which they lived now were both divided into two groups: Jews and non-Jews. My parents grew up speaking Yiddish at home, and all their friends were Jewish. It's hard to describe this environment to younger generations today, but this story will help. I distinctly remember an event that occurred in 1959, when I was a small boy. My father decided to sell our car, and he put an ad in the *New York Times*. The buyers, a husband and wife, agreed to the price and came to our home to present the check and take the car and the title. Why was that a memorable moment? Because it was the only time I can ever recall gentiles entering our home—except as plumbers, electricians, or other workers. Jews and Christians did not socialize; even in the Boy Scouts, there was a Jewish troop and a Christian troop in our area.

So Jewish identity wasn't a problem or a construct; it was the natural product of the way Jews lived (enforced to some degree by anti-Semitism, which helped keep Jews in Jewish neighborhoods, hotels, clubs, and even out of certain jobs). But today the sense of Jewish identity, of belonging to the Jewish people, has broken down for so many American Jews. Far from living in a dense Jewish environment, American Jews and their children are scattered among the 97.6 percent of Americans who are not Jewish. Today a Jewish environment must be created *intentionally* if it is to be experienced, whether in Jewish schools, in Jewish summer camps, or through time spent in Israel—places where Jews live together as Jews.

Will the emotional reaction among American Jews after the tragedy of October 7, 2023, result in lasting changes—or ephemeral ones as happened after the triumph of 1967? The many problems in the American Jewish community in recent decades are a cautionary tale, but decline is not destiny. We have choices to make. We have the ability to change the future path of our community, and in this book, I will try to explain what I think we—as a community, as families, as parents and grandparents—ought to be doing. Our situation is changing and our actions and ways of thinking must change too. What we need to do isn't impossible, and the obstacles can all be overcome. That's why I took the title of this book from Theodor Herzl: "If you will it, it is no dream; and if you don't, a dream it is and a dream it will stay." We can do better than dreams.

Chapter One

How Are We Doing?

AMERICAN JEWS TODAY: GROWTH OR DECLINE?

American Jews have typically been a self-satisfied group, and our success in America is the obvious explanation. Our numbers grew steadily into the millions after 1880, and the children of the immigrant generations found America a congenial haven. We moved from unskilled labor to skilled, and then into business and the learned professions such as law, medicine, and university teaching. We got advanced degrees. Especially in the years after World War II, we built many new and mostly suburban synagogues. Intermarriage rates were low, whether that reflects Jewish choice or Christian unwillingness to marry Jews. There are many reasons to say we are thriving today. But we are not, and we will never act to change negative patterns until we recognize what is going wrong.

The analysis of "Jewish Americans in 2020" by the Pew Research Center[1] claims to reveal an American Jewish community that is growing and now totals 7.5 million people—an all-time high. The figures are not technically wrong, but they are, if not meaningless, misleading.

In 1951, *TIME* magazine put Rabbi Louis Finkelstein, chancellor of the Jewish Theological Seminary, on its cover. And *TIME* described American Jewish life in glowing terms: "The old, half-deserted synagogues are filling up again, new congregations are forming, new synagogues are being built."[2] But in 1964, *Look* magazine published a cover article on "The Vanishing American Jew," forecasting the demise of North American Jewish communities by the end of the twentieth century.[3] As many critics have noted, instead it was *Look* magazine that vanished while the American Jewish community is still here.

But as these two cover stories suggest, the fortunes of American Jewry have long been a source of interest inside the Jewish community and well beyond it. Moreover, predictions of doom and arguments against it are very far from new. In 1967, the Jewish scholar Simon Rawidowicz published a famous article entitled "Israel: The Ever-Dying People."

> As far as historical reality is concerned, we are confronted here with a phenomenon that has almost no parallel in mankind's story: a people that has been disappearing constantly for the last 2,000 years, exterminated in dozens of lands all over the globe, reduced to half or third of its population by tyrants ancient and modern–and yet it still exists, falls, and rises, loses all its possessions and reequips itself for a new start, a second, a third chance—always fearing the end, never afraid to make a new beginning, to snatch triumph from the jaws of defeat, whenever and wherever possible. There is no people more dying

> than Israel, yet none better equipped to resist disaster, to fight alone, always alone.[4]

Decades later, is our community vanishing or getting larger and stronger? That depends not so much on whom you ask as on what definitions you use. Pew has divided the Jewish community into two groups: "Jews by Religion" or JBRs and "Jews of No Religion" or JNRs. But this description or division can be misleading because it tells us little about the Jewish *community* and its size and health; instead, it gives us numbers (which may, in any event, not be meaningful) about the Jewish *population*. Counting the number of individuals who say they are Jewish in some sense but are entirely unaffiliated with the community is still a useful activity. But we must be careful in judging what those numbers tell us.

A Look at Pew's "Jewish Americans in 2020"

"Jewish Americans in 2020" tells us that there are 7.5 million American Jews. Of these, 4.2 million are adults who say they are Jewish by religion, and 1.5 million are adults who say they are Jews of no religion. These JNRs are individuals who had at least one Jewish parent or were raised Jewish, but say they are now atheist, agnostic, or nothing in particular—*but* they consider themselves Jewish in some way, such as culturally or ethnically.

In addition, Pew has some other categories of what I would call "used to be Jews." In fact, the pattern of loss, of people disaffiliating from the Jewish community, is striking. As Pew puts it,

> Overall, 68% of those who say they were raised Jewish or who had at least one Jewish parent now identify as Jewish, including 49% who are now Jewish by religion and 19% who are now Jews of no religion. That means that one-third of those raised Jewish or by Jewish parent(s) are *not* Jewish today, either because they identify with a religion other than Judaism (including 19% who consider themselves Christian) or because they do not currently identify as Jewish either by religion or aside from religion.[5]

By any definition, a loss of one-third is a major weakening for any population group, and it is especially dangerous for a minority group. Such losses among Jews created a new group, which Pew describes as people of "Jewish background:"

> An additional 2.8 million adults...have a Jewish background. These adults all had at least one Jewish parent or a Jewish upbringing, but most people in this category, 1.9 million, identify with another religion, such as Christianity. About 700,000 have no religion and do not consider themselves Jewish in any way.[6]

These individuals are not counted by Pews as Jews, and rightly so. This category is again a reflection of losses to the American Jewish community.

Pew provides figures on Jewish children, adding to the 4.2 million adult Jews by religion and the 1.5 million adult Jews of no religion.

> There are an estimated 2.4 million children living in the United States in households with at least one Jewish adult.... This includes 1.8 million who are being raised Jewish *in some way*, such as 1.2 million who are being raised exclusively Jewish by religion, and an additional 400,000 who are being raised as Jewish but not by religion. It also includes roughly 200,000 who are being raised both as Jewish by religion *and* in another religion. About 600,000 U.S. children live with a Jewish adult but are not being raised Jewish in any way.
>
> Meanwhile, approximately 1 million children live in a household without any Jewish adults but with at least one adult of Jewish background, although 900,000 of these children are not being raised Jewish in any way.[7]

Thus does Pew reach its total Jewish population of 7.5 million.

> Combining 5.8 million adult Jews...with 1.8 million children (living in a household with a Jewish adult and who are being raised Jewish *in some way*, including those who are being raised both Jewish and in another religion) yields a total estimate (rounded to the nearest 100,000) of 7.5 million Jews of all ages in the United States...."[8]

Let's do the math. To reach 7.5 million, Pew had to include not only the 26 percent of adult Jews who say they have no religion, but also the 200,000 children being raised in another religion as well as Judaism.

These numbers tell a tale of loss, not of vitality. Think of the children: of the 2.4 million children Pew says are "living in the United States in household with at least one Jewish adult," *only half, 1.2 million, are being raised exclusively in the Jewish religion.*

More math: In my 1997 book about the American Jewish community, *Faith or Fear*, I wrote that "*Roughly 12 percent of Americans of Jewish heritage are now Christians.*"[9] If one adds up the 7.5 million people Pew says are Jews today and the 2.8 million people it says are people "of Jewish background," the total is 10.3 million people. If Pew is correct in saying that 1.9 million are now in other religions, which in the United States will most often be Christianity, approximately 18 percent of all people of Jewish background in the United States—however strong or weak—are probably now Christians.

The Pew numbers also tell us that if there are 10.3 million Americans of Jewish background and 5.4 million Americans who say they are Jews by religion, a remarkable *48 percent of all Americans of Jewish background no longer report Judaism as their current religion or are raising their children in that religion.*

That is a grim statistic. Of course, one can play with these numbers and definitions endlessly, but this is not a numbers game. More important is the *meaning* of the terms—and what we can learn about the Jewish community and its future.

The Pew survey, which is arguably the best data available, is based on the self-identification of the individuals who were contacted. Thus the famous JNRs are "people who describe themselves (religiously) as atheist, agnostic or nothing in particular, but who have a Jewish parent or were raised Jewish, and who still consider themselves Jewish in any way (such as ethnically, culturally or because of their family background)."[10]

Who is that individual? Think of a young man born to two parents who were born Jewish. The parents are themselves practitioners of no religion and there is no religion in the home, nor did the boy receive any religious training. When he grows up, he considers himself an atheist. He marries someone raised as a Christian but who, like him, practices no religion, and they raise their children without religion. The couple is not in any way part of any religion community; there is complete disaffiliation. Along comes Pew, which asks him "Aside from religion, do you consider yourself to be Jewish in any way (for example ethnically, culturally or because of your family's background)?"[11] He answers "yes," thinking that because both his parents were Jews, he is Jewish "in some way."

He is now part of Pew's 7.5 million Jews in America, but this example should make us wonder if that number has much meaning. Professor Leonard Saxe of Brandeis, one of the most distinguished students of the American Jewish community, likens such Americans to what are called *hiloni* or secular people in Israel; they are still Jews and not lost to the community, nor are their children, he argues.[12] But that comparison of Israelis to Jews in America, a country that is less than 3 percent Jewish, is not persuasive. Secular Jews in Israel live in a society marked by the Hebrew language and calendar, public celebration of Jewish holy days, and an extremely low intermarriage rate. The children and grandchildren of those secular Israelis will remain Jews; the children and grandchildren of unaffiliated, atomized "Jews of no religion" in America may very well not. Pew counts them as part of the Jewish *population* now, but they are already lost to the Jewish *community*.

And then there is the Orthodox community. We relearn from the Pew 2020 study what was obvious decades earlier, in the Pew 2013 survey and in the 1990 National Jewish Population Study, about the strength of Orthodoxy in the United States. This is widely understood today, but it is extraordinary: as Nathan Glazer noted in his introduction to the 1989 edition of *American Judaism*, "this generation is the first in two hundred years in which Orthodoxy has not declined."[13] For two centuries, roughly 1750 to the end of the Second World War, what would today be called Orthodoxy declined: Jews practiced Judaism less strictly, other forms of Judaism captured some portion of the Jewish population, and in the Holocaust many of the centers of Orthodox learning and population were destroyed and many key leaders were murdered.

But today, Pew reports that while 9 percent of American Jews are Orthodox, among Jews age eighteen to twenty-nine the figure nearly doubles to 17 percent.[14] This is primarily the product of natural growth: Orthodox Jews are more likely to get married, marry younger, marry Jews, and have more children than other Jews, and they are better at keeping their children in their religious communities. Orthodox couples have 3.3 children on average, while Reform Jewish couples have 1.8 (the replacement rate is 2.1) and Jews who report they belong to no denomination have a 1.2 percent fertility rate. The population growth of the Orthodox community makes it crystal clear that they will play a greater role in the American Jewish community in the future.

Jews In Name Only?

In the Pew survey, an Orthodox Jew whose life is built around Judaism and the Jewish community in which he or she lives is counted exactly as is the young man I described above—one is a JBR and one is a JNR, but both are counted equally as American Jews. The problem is that this equivalence is completely misleading as a description of Jewish life in America and in what it portends for the future of the Jewish community here. The leading Jewish demographer of our day, the Israeli Sergio Della Pergola, explains why in his critique of Pew:

> Crucially, the definitions adopted—especially in the case of children—include persons absolutely marginal or absent in terms of the meaning of being Jewish. The bottom line in the screening questionnaire is persons who consider themselves Jewish because of their family background. Jewishness is defined fundamentally as a property that once acquired can never be lost. This contradicts the precepts of sociology and demography, neither of which follows a deterministic approach, seeking instead to ascertain facts empirically.
>
> Listen to the following example: I was born in Trieste in Northern Italy. I left the place when I

> was 11 months old. My birthplace is an indelible detail in my ID document. My children can declare a Trieste-born father, and my grandchildren have a Trieste-born grandfather. None of them has ever visited the place (to which I returned myself five or six times since I left), most of them don't know or care where the city is located. How significant is this type of ascription?
>
> From a social scientific perspective, it is better to consider the Jews as a *socially meaningful collective* rather than a *random aggregate of people with an indelibly ascribed trait.*[15]

A "socially meaningful collective," Della Pergola's useful phrase, requires for membership what Jack Wertheimer has called "intentionality."[16] Once upon a time, Jews were born into a natural community whose boundaries were enforced both from within and without—by everything from rabbinical power to residential segregation to anti-Semitism. Jews were born and lived their lives largely within those boundaries, even in the United States until about seventy-five years ago, but now they barely exist if they exist at all. Today's Jewish community is an intentional community, made up of individuals and families that mindfully choose to stay within it.

Those community boundaries were sometimes physical or nearly so: there were thick Jewish neighborhoods. As the historian of American Jews and Judaism Jonathan Sarna wrote, there was a

> widespread belief during the interwar years that Jewishness (*Yiddishkeit*) could thrive in America even in the absence of such standard components of religious life as synagogue attendance, ritual practice, and Jewish education.... Simply by living there they experienced, absorbed, and in many ways internalized that Jewishness. Even if they neither practiced it nor trained their children in its precepts, they assumed that it was well-nigh inescapable—as inescapable as the neighborhood atmosphere itself.[17]

The dense physical nature of Jewish life counted a great deal: as Sarna also wrote, "For Jews, the migration to the suburbs posed particular challenges. Outside the protective womb of the urban Jewish subculture, Judaism could no longer be absorbed, like sunshine, from the surrounding atmosphere. "[18]

And that is why Pew's count of American Jews can be accurate and inaccurate at the same time. It measures a *descent* community, when the more important number is the size of the *intentional* community.[19]

What Pew calls JNRs, Jews of no religion, might better (to borrow from a comment made to me in conversation by the sociologist Dr. Steven M. Cohen) be called JINOs: Jews in name only. As the authors of *Saving Remnants: Feeling Jewish in America* concluded in 1992, whatever the total numbers given for the number of American Jews,

> approximately half this group are not part of the American Jewish community. They are

> "unaffiliated": although they may be classified as Jewish, they are not members of the organized community. They do not practice Judaism as a religion, although they may occasionally attend a Passover Seder or light Hanukkah candles. They make no special effort to associate with other Jews, and they belong to no Jewish organization or group. Many would marry or have married non-Jews. They know very little about Jewish history or culture...and they are not inclined to learn. They do not give their children a Jewish education. They do not contribute regularly to the local federation of Jewish charities.... They will not deny that they are Jewish, but this may be their only act of Jewish identification.[20]

This is a new phenomenon. In shtetls and even in large cities in Europe before the twentieth century, and in the United States until the Second World War, the number of Jews and the size of the Jewish *community* were pretty much the same; disaffiliation was not easy. Today it is, which means that people must have reasons to affiliate. In the great melting pot that is America, most pressures push Jews to join the national mix rather than to stay out of it.

The most common example of this phenomenon is the decline of inmarriage. From Marshall Sklare's April 1964 *Commentary* article "Intermarriage and the Jewish Future" to the discussions of intermarriage in Seymour Martin Lipset's edited 1990 volume *American Pluralism and the Jewish Community* and in innumerable books, articles, and studies since then—intermarriage has become an issue of wide discussion as the numbers rose and rose. The 52 percent intermarriage rate found in the 1990 NJPS was shocking to people back then; Pew now reports that "among non-Orthodox Jews who got married in the last decade, 72% say they are intermarried." (Pew also reports that "Intermarriage is almost nonexistent in the Orthodox Jewish community. In the current survey, just 2% of married Orthodox Jews say their spouse is not Jewish.")[21]

This isn't an exclusively Jewish phenomenon: as another Pew study headlined, "Interfaith marriage is common in US, particularly among the recently wed."[22] In 2015, Pew found that four in ten Americans who had married between 2010 and 2015 "have a spouse who is in a different religious group." On the other hand, Pew found that intermarriage rates were considerably higher for Jews than for Muslims, Hindus, or Mormons. A 2022 report from the American Enterprise Institute found the same trends:

> The institution of marriage is evolving in important ways. Religion, which at one time was at the center of much of American family and married life, has become less prominent. Not only are interfaith unions increasingly common, so are marriages among people who have no religion....
>
> Today, a majority (59 percent) of married Americans report having a spouse with the same religious affiliation. More than one-quarter of married Americans are in an interfaith marriage (14 percent)—a union between people who have

> different religious traditions—or a religious-secular marriage (14 percent), in which one person identifies with a religious tradition and the other does not. Secular marriages, in which both people are religiously unaffiliated, have become increasingly common; 12 percent of marriages are among people who are both not religious.
>
> Fifty years ago, same-faith marriages dominated the religious landscape. Over eight in 10 (81 percent) couples married before 1972 share the same religious affiliation with their spouse. More recent marriages reveal a distinctly different pattern. Among Americans married in the past decade, just over half (52 percent) are among couples who belong to the same religious tradition.[23]

All of this reflects a wonderfully open and fluid society—the most open to Jews that they have ever experienced in the diaspora. As Irving Kristol wrote, "a high rate of intermarriage testifies to the ever-fuller acceptance of Jews by the non-Jewish community. Is that not what American Jews have always wanted? Is that not what America has always promised? How fortunate American Jews are to be living in such a wonderful country!"[24]

Yes and no, Kristol then argued. Whatever the impact of religious intermarriage on other faith communities, intermarriage is significant for Jews because of its typical effects on the Jewish community. Decades ago, the individual involved in out-marriage in the American Jewish community was often in many ways expelled from it and might even have been shunned by his or her own family. The act was often seen as a rejection of Judaism and Jewishness, of community, even of family—and sometimes it was. That period of American Jewish life is over for non-Orthodox Jews. So what are the effects that create concern?

The greatest worry is about continuity: "Will the children be Jewish?" With a non-Orthodox intermarriage rate of 72 percent, if all the children of intermarried couples left the Jewish community and religion, the demographic impact would be catastrophic. Intermarriage is a chain phenomenon. As the Pew report states:

> Intermarriage rates also have an intergenerational component: Adult Jews who are themselves the offspring of intermarriages are especially likely to intermarry. In the new survey, among married Jewish respondents who have one Jewish parent, 82% are intermarried, compared with 34% of those with two Jewish parents. Similarly, intermarried Jews who are currently raising minor children (under age 18) in their homes are much less likely to say they are bringing up their children as Jewish by religion (28%) than are Jewish parents who have a Jewish spouse (93%).[25]

Those are very large gaps. And it goes both ways: intermarried Jews are far less likely to raise their children as Jews by religion, and Jews of no religion, Pew's "JNRs," are far more likely to intermarry. The Pew data shows that "Among all Jews by religion who are married, 68% have a Jewish spouse. By comparison, 21% of Jews who have no religion who are married say their spouse is Jewish, while 79% report that they are married to someone who is not Jewish."[26]

Intermarriage has other effects as well. Jack Wertheimer noted that "intermarriage is strongly related to attachment to Israel: 26% of Jews very attached to Israel are intermarried versus more than twice as many (66%) among Jews who claim no attachment to Israel."[27] We will look more deeply at issues of group solidarity and "peoplehood" in the next chapter, but it's clear that intermarriage plays a role here. A child raised in a home with two religions, or none, is far less likely to develop a feeling of community with other Jews, in the United States, Israel, around the world, or even next door. Even in the case of conversion of the non-Jewish spouse to Judaism, there will be a non-Jewish half of the family with beloved grandparents and other relatives who are not Jews. None of this is surprising, but its impact on one of America's smallest religious communities can be enormous.

Jonathan Sarna suggested the centrality of intermarriage for the Jewish community: "more than we realize, the whole question of the division among young Jews is a division between those who have two Jewish parents and those who do not. I think we have not fully come to grips with the vast impact that intermarriage is having. Increasingly, the Jewish community, I think, is seeing what Steven M. Cohen years ago called a tale of two Jewries—the inmarried and the outmarried."[28]

But some of these conclusions are in dispute. It's obvious that if two Jews marry and have two children, they maintain the number of Jews in the population. Conversely, if a Jew outmarries and has two children who are not raised as Jews, on the parent's death, the number will have gone from one Jew to zero. But what if a Jew intermarries and raises his or her two children as Jews? Then the numbers go from one to three; the Jewish population increases. The variable is whether the children of intermarriage are raised as or identify as Jews.[29]

For many years, the assumption was that loss of population was inevitable, and the Pew data still suggests that it is happening. But some sociologists claim that the trend is changing: Professor Leonard Saxe argues that, among millennials (born after 1981), the majority who are children of intermarriages identify as Jews when they turn eighteen. He states that more than 60 percent of millennial Jews born to intermarried parents choose to identify as Jewish, versus fewer than 30 percent in the previous generation.[30]

The Pew report makes the same claim:

> People with two Jewish parents are more likely than those with just one Jewish parent to retain their Jewish identity into adulthood. However, among people who have just one Jewish parent, younger cohorts are more likely than those ages 50 and older to be Jewish as adults, suggesting that the share of intermarried Jewish parents who pass on their Jewish identity to their children may have increased over time. Or, put somewhat differently, the share of the offspring of intermarriages who choose to be Jewish in adulthood seems to be rising.[31]

Rising, perhaps—but low. The Pew 2020 report finds that of individuals over age fifty who were raised by one Jewish and one non-Jewish parent, a very high 79 percent say they are not Jewish in any way. Of the 21 percent who say they *are* Jewish, only 9 percent say they are Jews by religion while 12 percent say they are Jews of no religion. Pew says that for those under fifty, 53 percent say they are not Jewish in any way, a significant reduction from 79 percent for those over fifty. But the percentage who are Jews by religion rises (from 9 percent) only to 16 percent, and those who say they are Jews of no religion goes up (from 12) to 31 percent.

Why might even this small increase of Jews by religion be occurring? We can only speculate. One factor might be a sense of security over recent decades: Americans Jews have usually not (at least until the wave of anti-Semitism that arose during ghe Gaza war) feared that if their children are Jews, they will face dangerous anti-Semitism that may blight their careers and futures. Those who ran from a Jewish identity in past generations or tried to ensure that their children fully assimilated into a majority-Christian America might be less inclined to do so today. This means there is less energy pushing people away from Jewish identity—while at the same time there is more effort being made to pull them towards it. Synagogues, religious denominations, federations, and other Jewish community organizations now engage in outreach programs designed to attract the intermarried couple, the non-Jewish spouse, and especially their children. Active engagement has replaced exclusion. The Reform movement eliminated the ancient requirement of matrilineal descent and now accepts individuals with patrilineal descent (that is, their father but not their mother was Jewish) as fully Jewish.

It is impossible today to know whether the optimism of a scholar like Professor Saxe, or the doubts expressed by Dr. Cohen and Professor Sarna, will prove to be correct. The issue about continuity will not be resolved, however, even if a greater percentage of the children of intermarried couples "identify" as Jews as Saxe suggests—because the critical question is whether they pass on that identity to their children.

For those under fifty who are children of one Jewish and one non-Jewish parent, to repeat the Pew numbers, 53 percent say they are not Jewish at all, and 31 percent say they are Jews of no religion—and only 16 percent adhere to the Jewish religion. What is the substance and meaning of the Jewish "identity" of the 31 percent who are Jews of no religion? Is their reply to Pew their only act of Jewish self-identification, without further meaning in how they live their lives or raise their children? If so, that "uptick" that Pew notes and that made Saxe less pessimistic about the impact of intermarriage will be mathematically accurate—and largely meaningless.

It is worth adding here a word about conversion. "Intermarriages" or "mixed marriages" are marriages between a Jew and a non-Jew. So if the non-Jewish partner converts to Judaism before the wedding, there is no intermarriage. Pew's data rightly counts converts to Judaism as Jews, as Jewish law also requires. Moreover, the data show that converts to Judaism act and think like their born-Jewish spouses (with exceptions worth noting).

An analysis of Pew data conducted by Dr. Steven M. Cohen for the author looked at non-Orthodox converts to Judaism married to individuals who were born Jewish and are still Jewish. Here are some of the findings:

- ☆ 46 percent of born Jews and 42 percent of the converts are members of synagogues
- ☆ 58 percent of the born Jews and 55 percent of converts say caring about Israel is an essential part of being Jewish
- ☆ 42 percent of born Jews and 48 percent of converts say being part of a Jewish community is essential
- ☆ 64 percent of born Jews and 72 percent of converts say they care a great deal about belonging to the Jewish people
- ☆ 33 percent of born Jews and 41 percent of converts say they are very attached to Israel

That positive pattern is not found in answer to one question in Cohen's analysis: Are most of your close friends Jewish? While 44 percent of born Jews say yes, only 17 percent of converts give the same response. That answer is logical, especially considering the typical age of marriage nowadays: the non-Jewish spouse (or fiancé) who is converting will have lived as an adult for years, perhaps over a decade, and will have a pattern of friendships that reflect living in American society generally and not as a member of the Jewish community.

This is encouraging data about conversion if one is concerned about Jewish continuity. But it is worth noting as well that conversion rates are very low: in the last two decades, under 10 percent of non-Jews who marry Jews convert, which is lower than in the preceding two decades. There is no great effort or pressure by the Jewish community to convert the non-Jewish spouse in new intermarriages. Often that pressure is viewed as unwelcome by the Jewish spouse and family as well as by the non-Jewish spouse, and it can be seen as offensive. Instead, efforts made by the synagogue, rabbi, or other Jewish organizations will be directed toward involvement in the synagogue or community despite the decision not to convert and especially toward the children: having them raised as Jews and engaged in various Jewish activities.

It's fair to say, then, that conversion is the product of the most intimate decisions by the couple that are marrying and, of course, especially by the non-Jewish spouse. If the individual chooses to convert, much follows from it. Unlike the moment in which an individual tells a caller from Pew or some other survey that he or she does or does not "identify" as a Jew, conversion is life-changing. That alone may explain why the numbers are low compared to the number of those who say they are "Jews of no religion." JNRs may live their lives as members of the Jewish community in meaningful ways, but most often, they do not.

Pew's data shows precisely this. The Pew study is voluminous, but here are some important numbers: only 27 percent of JNRs think "caring about Israel" is essential to being Jewish; only 12 percent think being part of a Jewish community is essential; 79 percent report being married to someone who is not Jewish; 4 percent say it is very important to them that any potential grandchildren be Jewish; 2 percent say it is very important to them that their potential grandchildren marry someone Jewish. Additionally, 61 percent of Jews by religion say they feel "a great deal of belonging to the Jewish people," while only 13 percent of JNRs agree; 61 percent of JBRs have contributed to a Jewish charity in the past year, while only 11 percent of JNRs have.

These responses suggest that Pew's JNRs are mostly individuals who are members of a "descent community" and for whom that is a unchanging but barely relevant fact about their lives. Pew asked them if they consider themselves Jewish "in any way" and they responded "yes," but they are generally not part of any Jewish community or of the American Jewish community as a whole.

Are You Part of the Jewish People?

Pew did not ask a related and perhaps even more complex question: do you consider yourself part of the Jewish *people*? Recall Sergio Della Pergola's comment that "From a social scientific perspective, it is better to consider the Jews as a *socially meaningful collective* rather than a *random aggregate of people with an indelibly ascribed trait*."[32] Is that meaningful collective the Jewish *people*—and what does that expression mean? When American Jews are asked whether or how much they care about other Jews, especially about Jews in other lands, and whether or how much they care about Israel and Israelis, this is the question being asked. Jews in Israel, Canada, France, or Brazil, and Jews in America are not part of the same community. Do they view themselves as part of the same people? As Dr. Shlomo Fischer of the Jewish People Policy Institute wrote, "The Jews of no religion do not seem to carry the 'sacred' commitment, or sense of obligation, to Jewish continuity and solidarity."[33]

It is not that Pew's uninvolved Jews or JNRs are energetically *rejecting* any association or affiliation with Jewishness or Judaism; the better term is drift or indifference. Seymour Martin Lipset and Earl Raab argued in 1995 that Jews in the United States were not "willfully abandoning" their identity to escape the effects of anti-Semitism. Instead, "erosion of identity is mainly a natural product of living in America...."[34]

In 2000, Dr. Bethamie Horowitz wrote about the meaning of assimilation in a paper on Jewish identity for the UJA Federation of New York.

> The typical image of assimilation involves people abandoning Judaism for a society that accepts them. As identified in this study, however, assimilation differs from the popular conception in that it no longer involves a conscious *rejection* of Judaism or of being Jewish, rather it results from a basic indifference about the subject. After all, rejection is a pattern that requires some previous involvement so that one has something to reject. This was a phenomenon more characteristic of the children of immigrants in America fifty years ago, at a time when America was less tolerant of group distinctiveness and Jews themselves were less secure in their American-ness. For the younger Jews of today who are fully in the mainstream of American life, there is no longer

> a feeling of forced choice between being Jewish and becoming American. Being American has simply become the default position, and any active relationship to Jewishness requires either prior commitment (i.e. a history of involvement or prior socialization) or an act of will.[35]

Being Jewish, then, is an *option* for American Jews today. Never before in Jewish history has it been easier to turn away from that option than in America in the twenty-first century. To take up that option, as Horowitz says, requires a definite *act of will*. For most Orthodox Jews—raised in Jewish religious practices, in still-strong communities and neighborhoods, and with their own religious beliefs—it is still the case that opting *out* is an act of will or even a rejection of family practice. But for the great majority of American Jews, the opposite is true. What then would lead them to exercise that option to be Jewish, if not religious faith? Do they nevertheless, even without faith, believe themselves to be part of some great collective, some people, some glorious ancient entity?

Anti-Semitism

Perhaps anti-Semitism will answer that question for us. Whatever Jews think, the rest of the society will tell us where we fit—and where we don't. Will American Jews now be "saved" by a wave of anti-Semitism that reminds us all of our Jewish identity and collective destiny?

Don't count on it. *It's not the anti-Semitism that will decide the question, but how we in the Jewish community react to it.*

Historically, Jewish communities around the world were held together in good part by pervasive anti-Semitism. It threatened their livelihoods and their lives, was often religiously based and religiously sponsored, and was equally often a matter of state policy. There was no escape—except by literally escaping to America or other distant lands, which is precisely what millions of Eastern European Jews did. This kind of persistent, pervasive, and violent anti-Semitism also gave rise to the Zionist movement. Most European Jews experienced life as my grandparents had: there were Jews and there was everyone else, and everyone else constituted a never-ending threat.

The United States was different from the very start—when George Washington wrote his letters to the Jews of Savannah and Newport promising not toleration but freedom and equality. That did not eliminate anti-Semitism, of course, and once their numbers began to rise greatly after the Civil War, Jews lived separate lives. Yet that kind of separation had been imposed socially rather than by law or by physical threat. Many hotels and private clubs refused all Jews; neighborhoods were "restricted" against Jews; university quotas kept out all Jews above the set percentage; many top banks and corporations did not hire Jews or would not promote them to the top executive ranks. So even in the United States, Jews were a people apart, typically living in Jewish neighborhoods and marrying each other. I remember as a small boy listening as my relatives named country clubs and pointed out hotels that did not admit Jews.

Anti-Semitism declined after the Holocaust and the Second World War, and for decades had a declining influence on how American Jews lived. Where we lived, where we vacationed, where we studied, whom we married were all less and less affected by anti-Semitism. In the 1950s, for example, the intermarriage rate was estimated at 7.2 percent.[36] By the time of the National Jewish Population Survey of 1990 it had risen to 52 percent—a seven-fold increase in a few decades that measured not only Jewish conduct but the willingness of greatly increased numbers of Christians to marry Jews.[37]

But in recent years, perhaps the last ten, anti-Semitism seemed to be more apparent, and Jews thought there was more of it. In its 2020 survey of American Jews, Pew found that "three-quarters (75%) say there is more anti-Semitism in the United States than there was five years ago." And similarly, "slightly more than half of Jews surveyed (53%) say that, as a Jewish person in the United States, they personally feel less safe today than they did five years ago."[38] And that was before the outbursts of anti-Semitism that followed the Gaza war of 2023.

Certainly, prior to the 2023 war, whatever level of anti-Semitism existed did not much affect American Jewish behavior. In fact, Pew found that only 5 percent of American Jews said back in 2020 they "hesitated and *chose not to participate* in Jewish observances or events because of safety concerns."[39] In part, this is because the highest figures for perceptions of the dangers from anti-Semitism were those of Orthodox and other more observant Jews: Pew noted that "the overall pattern is that more observant Jews are more likely both to perceive that anti-Semitism has increased and to feel that their safety has diminished."[40] As Elliot Kaufman wrote in 2022 in *The Wall Street Journal*, "Americans Against Antisemitism has studied 194 anti-Jewish assaults...in New York City since 2018.... Of the 194 anti-Jewish assaults his group has tracked, three-quarters were in four Brooklyn neighborhoods, and 184 of the victims were Orthodox Jews, identifiable by their dress."[41]

This is not a surprise: "Jews who usually wear something in public that is recognizably Jewish (such as a kippa or head covering) are especially likely to feel less safe," the Pew study reported.[42] Pew also found that "Jews by religion are far more likely than Jews of no religion to say there is a lot of anti-Semitism today."[43] But the Orthodox are also the least likely to be prevented from their religious practices by such threats because they view those practices as obligations. Sadly, there has been remarkably little solidarity from less observant, richer, more assimilated Jews with poorer and Orthodox, often Hasidic, Jews who have suffered physical attacks in New York City. Every aspect of their lives is sufficiently foreign to the majority of Jewish Americans to have created a barrier that apparently prevents the kind of solidarity that existed when in the first half of the twentieth century almost every Jew faced pervasive anti-Semitism—at least of the social sort.

The lack of solidarity among American Jews extended beyond the Orthodox to Jews caught up in quota systems that kept them from schools and colleges their parents' generation had attended. The imposition of numerical formulas that sought to raise the number of non-white students in universities, for example, gave rise to lawsuits by Asian students who claimed their numbers were deliberately reduced as a result. Jewish attendance percentages were reduced as well in many colleges. One survey found that "self-identified Jews now number just 7% of Ivy League students, compared to 10% during the height of the antisemitic quotas" of the period before the Second World War—and down from perhaps 30 percent in the 1960s.[44] But the community was divided, and some of the best-known institutions, such as the Anti-Defamation League, the Reform movement, and the National Council of Jewish Women supported the universities rather than the affected students.[45]

Though there had been two horrifying and murderous attacks on synagogues in the previous decade, Pew found in 2020 that most Jews experienced anti-Semitism in much milder ways: by hearing or reading about an anti-Semitic remark not made in their presence while "reports of physical attacks are rare across the board."[46] In addition, the "vast majority" of American Jews who said in 2020 that there was more anti-Semitism then than five years before say this is because anti-Semites feel more free to express their views—rather than because there are more people with anti-Semitic views. Only 5 percent of American Jews said in 2020 that "the rise in anti-Semitism is taking place mainly because there are more people with anti-Semitic views."[47]

Then came the Gaza war of 2023 and a shocking increase in anti-Semitic, anti-Zionist, and anti-Israel activities in colleges and universities, on the far left, and in the left wing of the Democratic Party (exemplified by the so-called "Squad"). Suddenly, American Jews awoke to a kind of anti-Semitism that seemed to affect all Jews and our children. It wasn't primarily the Orthodox community who suffered from it, and it wasn't a mild, social anti-Semitism. On many campuses there was actual violence; on many more, administrators and professors condemned Israel and basically backed Hamas. We became used to headlines like these: "More than 100 Columbia University professors signed a letter Monday defending students who supported Hamas' 'military action' in Israel on Oct. 7...."[48] Or "Ethnic studies professors demanded the University of California stop referring to Hamas' attack on Israeli civilians as 'terrorism'...."[49] An associate professor at Cornell said "I was exhilarated" by what Hamas had done (before pressure made him apologize).[50] An associate professor at Yale said "Israel is a murderous, genocidal settler state and Palestinians have every right to resist through armed struggle."[51]

One can imagine what was being taught to undergraduates in their classes. And the bias certainly extended to Middle East studies: as the journalist Eli Lake put it, "Most universities today have purged from their Middle East studies departments anyone who believes the Jewish people have a right to a safe haven in Israel."[52] Even Jewish Studies departments are infected. After the massacres of October 7, the Executive Committee of the Association for Jewish Studies said in a statement that we "express deep sorrow for the loss of life and destruction caused by the horrific violence in Israel over the weekend. We send comfort to our members there and our members with families and friends in the region who are suffering. We offer support during these dark times." The Association for Jewish Studies couldn't even bring itself to mention Jews or to condemn Hamas. Like many organizations whose first statements were disgraceful and indefensible, the Association for Jewish Studies issued a second statement that did condemn Hamas; still missing was any recognition that the targets of Hamas were *Jews*.[53] And finally there came the appearance of the presidents of Harvard, Penn, and MIT before Congress. American Jews watched as none of the three were willing to say that calling for genocide against Jews was unacceptable and would be barred on their campuses.[54]

The explosion of campus support for Hamas and the pusillanimous reaction by campus authorities led to a mini revolt of Jewish donors, graduates, and board members, who had apparently not previously understood the rot setting in on so many campuses, including their own. They had not understood how many senior and junior faculty were deeply hostile to Israel and perhaps to Jews, nor did they realize exactly what was being taught in their favorite universities. In classrooms all across the country, students have been learning about the Middle East in ways that are pretty close to the UN resolution that said "Zionism is a form of racism."[55]

All of a sudden, Jewish liberals found that many of their allies on the left were not allies at all and harbored views of Jews, Zionism, and Israel that were appalling. When Jews were murdered in the most horrifying ways, they elicited sympathy for a day or two, if at all—and then the marches and the charges of genocide by Israel began. A Brandeis University survey of college students found that "Jewish students were substantially more concerned about antisemitism coming from the political left than they were about antisemitism from the political right."[56]

The first national poll after the October 7 massacres showed real changes in how American Jews perceived anti-Semitism. A survey done by the Jewish Federations of

North America found that 70 percent of Jews felt less safe. The greatest fears were still among those whose dress in some way marked them as Jews; they were twice as likely to say they worried about their safety "all the time." But now, 72 percent of Jews said anti-Semitism was rising in their local community. In the survey, they responded that it wasn't just that anti-Semites felt freer to express their views, but also that there are simply more people who hold such views.[57]

A Hillel survey of Jewish college students found that 35 percent "say there have been acts of hate or violence on campus against Jews" and 54 percent said they were "scared." What's the effect? Thirty-seven percent "say they have needed to hide their Jewish identity."[58]

Now the question is, how will the American Jewish community react? Will there be serious and lasting pressure on these many colleges to police the anti-Semitism and punish its perpetrators—whether they are students or faculty members? Will there be any effort to change the way courses about Israel and the Middle East are taught, and to protect against one-sidedly hostile accounts of the Jewish state? Will anything be done about recruiting processes that seem to weed out anyone right of center or markedly pro-Israel? Will American Jews become a powerful lobby for ridding colleges of expensive and overstuffed DEI staffs that never lift a finger to protect Jews , tut-tutting about freedom of speech even to support terrorism while they denounce and punish "microaggressions" against favored groups?

More broadly, the question is whether all these displays of anti-Semitism and deep hostility to Israel are truly going to lead to stronger and more lasting solidarity, cohesiveness, and sense of peoplehood in the American Jewish community.

Will the virulence of anti-Israel and anti-Jewish activity on campuses push Jewish students, and their parents, toward defending Israel more strongly? Will it lead them to be more committed Jews and better Zionists? Or will they hide their Jewish identities, as the Hillel poll found in a third of cases?

We don't know yet.

During the Gaza war, it seemed that American Jews were willing to switch channels on their TV. The *New York Times* reported that "Fox News, long a preferred source of news for the right, has lately become an information refuge for some American Jews who believe that the mainstream media has been too hostile to Israel."[59] That won't last, nor is it important. The real question about this new anti-Semitism in the United States is not whether it will completely upend American Jewish life. It won't. It will not lead millions of Jews to become more religiously observant, to change where they live, to stop trying and succeeding to live full American lives.

Instead, I would pose two questions about the way we live now. First, will the displays of anti-Semitism affect the educational choices Jewish parents and their children make? As so many of the most prestigious private high schools and even public schools adopt a hostile attitude toward Jewish particularism and toward Israel, will Jewish parents seek alternatives for their children—and will alternatives exist? The very same question arises at the college level, and we will look at that question again in the final chapter. What choices do Jewish parents and students have?

Second, what is the impact on the students themselves of being confronted with anti-Zionist and anti-Semitic conduct on campus? Do they back away from controversy, or do the assaults on them and their community provoke them into pride and activism? It turns out, unsurprisingly, that how Jewish students cope with and react to anti-Semitism on campus depends a great deal on the kind of Jewish life they led before they got there. Some will become heroes; some will walk away from the challenges. Some will deepen their Jewish and Zionist commitments and identifications; others will try to avoid trouble. Jewish parents should be thinking, teaching, and planning long before their children reach college about which kind of Jewish students they want their own children to be.

Teach Your Children Well

In a book called *The New Zionists*, Professor David Graizbord explains the impact of campus anti-Zionism on several of his college-student interviewees. He concludes that "my subjects' experience with anti-Zionist sentiment in college has, in several cases, had a pivotal, even life-changing impact. Specifically, it has led some of them to become committed, even ardent Zionists."[60] The animus against Israel, the argument that "Israel is fundamentally illegitimate and should cease to exist as the nation-state of the Jewish people," has, Graizbord states, "galvanized" some of them and moved them from being young people "whose wholehearted support of Israel is nonetheless mostly passive and devoid of a deep familiarity with the country (let alone with Jewish history). Anti-Zionist animus has politicized some of my subjects and developed in them an Israel-specific and very conscious form of Jewish pride."[61]

But that is not the impact of university anti-Semitism on all Jewish students. Which ones react this way? Graizbord explains:

> The respondents' perception of their experiences makes clear that campus-based anti-Zionism has become a particular concern for them, as for other students who either already perceive Israel to be part of their Jewish identity, or who feel vaguely supportive of Israel's existence but are relatively indifferent toward it—indifferent, that is, until the anti-Zionist point an accusing finger and associate them with the country. From the perspective of my interviewees, exposure to anti-Zionist sentiment is transformative for reasons having to do with their personal backgrounds. As I have explained, the subjects arrive in college content to be Jewish. They love their Jewish families. Though these students know relatively little about their people's history and culture, they sense, rightly or wrongly, that when anti-Zionists subject them to sanctimony, the aggressors are attacking them as individuals, and attacking their families, for having and treasuring their collective Jewish identity. The subjects then perceive that they must investigate who they are as Jews, and in the process they find their place among the Jewish people, especially in relation to Israel.[62]

It is critical that Graizbord's subjects are already pro-Israel and have a real and positive Jewish identity; the effect of campus anti-Zionism on *them* is to move them from passivity to a much deeper commitment. Similarly, Mark Rotenberg, vice president of university affairs at Hillel International, told Jewish News Syndicate that "a Jewish student's reaction depends on his prior connection to Jewish life. Those without any are 'even more reluctant to stick their necks out,' he said. However, those Jewish students once only marginally involved with Jewish life have become galvanized."[63] If Rotenberg and Graizbord are right, even the most virulent campus anti-Zionism will not have this salutary effect on Jewish students who are hostile or indifferent to Israel, or are indifferent to their own Jewishness. It seems, from this analysis, that the reaction against such attacks on Israel and on Jews can *strengthen* Jewish identity but cannot *create* it out of whole cloth. From some source—and in the final chapters we will discuss what those sources might be—that identity must be created and nurtured.

To me, the key question to ask about American Jews is whether they feel that sense of collective identity or do not—and if not, are there any realistic steps that might lead more American Jews to feel it? Do they understand themselves to be part of the Jewish people? As one group of Jewish scholars put it, "Peoplehood helps to contextualize Israel within the past, present and future. It combines the notion of 'lineage' of Jews, referring to a shared history and narratives throughout the generations, with the notion of 'linkage,' which encompasses the connections among Jews across space and throughout communities in the present. It makes sense of the Jews as an historical entity and an ongoing, extended family."[64] Peoplehood, they suggested, links Jews vertically, through past, present, and future, and horizontally, around the world to all Jewish communities. But is that the way American Jews see themselves?

The issue of Jewish "peoplehood" is worth exploring carefully, and in the end, it may be a better formula for success in much of the American Jewish community than religion—the religion that most American Jews do not practice. If young Jews—even those not practicing the religion in any traditional way—believe themselves part of the Jewish *people*, a "collective" that extends backwards for millennia and forward forever and extends globally to the Jewish state and to all Jewish communities around the world, their own identities as Jews may be deeply and permanently strengthened.

Most American Jews felt a kinship, a shared fate, with Israeli Jews and Jews around the world on October 7, 2023. We were one people. The question is whether that feeling will last or was merely the temporary product of tragedy. Looking at the survey data on American Jews, we can see that a sense of peoplehood isn't a genetic inheritance and can be—is being—sloughed off by hundreds of thousands of American Jews. We need to think about how "peoplehood" is created and how it can be nurtured.

Chapter Two

ARE YOU PART OF THE JEWISH PEOPLE?

Sixty years ago, Philip Roth, newly famous for *Goodbye, Columbus*, assayed the situation of American Jews in *Commentary* magazine.

> One cannot *will* oneself into a community today on the strength of the miseries and triumphs of a community that existed in Babylonia in the 7th century B.C.E. or in Madrid in 1492, or even in Warsaw in the spring of 1943; and the dying away of anti-Semitism in our own country, its gradual ineffectiveness as a threat to our economic and political rights, further disobliges us from identifying ourselves as Jews so as to present a proud and united front to the enemy. And that is a good thing, for it enables a man to *choose* to be a Jew, and not to be turned into one, without his free accession, by a hostile society.[1]

It is no surprise—and it is worth celebrating—that immigrant groups who come to America can and do assimilate and become part of the American people. The inability of immigrant groups to integrate and become accepted by their fellow citizens and the perpetual existence of ethnic ghettoes are phenomena largely absent in the United States. The American model (for immigrants, and always excepting the story of slavery and the case of Black Americans) has generally dissolved or greatly weakened bonds of ethnicity and nationality to other people in the immigrant group and to the 'old country,' while allowing and indeed celebrating adhesion to religious faith communities. Catholics from Germany or Italy, for example, were expected to Americanize by abandoning their previous national loyalties and transferring them to the United States, but it was understood that they would retain their religious loyalties. Catholics and Jews were not pressured to become Protestant—nor were they, of course, pressured to remain Catholics or Jews or anything else.

Bigotry was not eliminated, but it was increasingly made illegal and called immoral. The Holocaust made anti-Semitism far less acceptable to millions of Americans, and the civil rights struggle in the United States fought bigotry and racism, with considerable support from the Jewish community. Jews began moving out of dense Jewish neighborhoods after the Second World War, and this had an enormous sociological and religious impact. As Jonathan Sarna put it, "Outside the protective womb of the urban Jewish subculture, Judaism could no longer be absorbed, like sunshine, from the surrounding atmosphere."[2] Intense feelings of Jewishness or *Yiddishkeit*—bound to diminish as a cultural or ethnic phenomenon as the Yiddish-speaking immigrant generations passed away—weakened. And after the 1960s, intermarriage began to rise because of greater social mixing and lessened intolerance. As Irving Kristol once joked, the problem was that Christians no longer wanted to persecute us, they wanted to marry us. In 1964, the great Jewish sociologist Marshall Sklare noted rising intermarriage figures and called intermarriage "so bitter a dilemma" that "casts into doubt American Jewry's dual ideal of full participation in this society and the preservation of Jewish identity."[3]

In 1990, Seymour Martin Lipset wrote that "to understand American Jewry, it is important to recognize that their experience on this continent differs qualitatively from those of their coreligionists in other countries. Jews won acceptance as fully equal citizens earlier here than elsewhere. They have faced much less discrimination in the United States than in any other Christian nation."[4] But five years later, Lipset and Earl Raab described the impact of that happy situation: "The unique and otherwise benevolent qualities of America which are largely responsible for the loss of Jewish identity have similarly affected most other ethnic and ethnoreligious groups. Thus, America's exceptionalism...may be seen as a double-edged sword, hacking away at disadvantage, and, on the backstroke, cutting away at identity, Jewish or otherwise."[5]

As outside pressures to remain in the community lessened, fidelity to traditional Judaism—which became known as Orthodox Judaism—waned. But this is not a recent or post–Second World War phenomenon: religiosity began to wane as soon as Jews from Europe hit these shores. As Sarna wrote,

> The best evidence of this collapse may be seen in the astonishing number of immigrant Jews who failed to attend synagogue. Numerous surveys between 1900 and 1917 found that the number of "unsynagogued" Jews exceeded the number of "synagogued" ones by a wide margin. "Out of the estimated Jewish population of one million persons, or two hundred thousand families in the United States, four-fifths are 'unchurched,'" the *American Jewish Yearbook* calculated in 1900.[6]

It is true that there were periods when nativism, especially anti-Catholic bigotry, was powerful. For example, the Blaine Amendments in many states prevented any public funds from "following the student" to Catholic parochial schools. And in the early part of the twentieth century, exclusionary laws attempted to stop or to reduce the number of Jews, Catholics, and Asians immigrating to the United States, giving preference to Northern European Protestants. But since the Second World War, such efforts have diminished, leading to an influx in immigration from all over the globe and including large numbers of Hispanics and Asians, as well as 750,000 Soviet Jews. As we have noted, "social" anti-Semitism against Jews certainly persisted in the decades after the War, including in "restricted" hotels, clubs, and neighborhoods, but this was a losing battle for the bigots. It still is. Whatever its impact on religious Jews and Jews who are deeply involved with Israel, the anti-Semitism that exists in the United States today will not change the overwhelming forces that keep American society open to assimilation *by Jews who are indifferent to Jewish identity.*

RELIGIOUS IDENTITY IN AMERICA

The title of Will Herberg's 1955 book *Protestant-Catholic-Jew*[7] summed up the postwar situation. All three religions were given equal, semi-official status as acceptable American religious faiths. The problem for most Jews was that they saw their own Jewish identities as essentially ethnic or "cultural," not religious, and some came to see a universalist political outlook as the essence of their Jewishness. That meant that the way the society saw them, as a religious group, and the way most Jews saw themselves, as a social or ethnic or cultural group, were quite different. David Elazar described the situation similarly in 1993 when he wrote of the "substantial problem" of American Jewry: "how to maintain itself as a people with a civilization of its own now that it has been reduced to the status of a 'religion' or the possessor of an 'ethnic heritage' in the public mind and in the minds of most Jews."[8]

This was partly a reflection of official US government attitudes; the Census Bureau calls Jews a religious group. As David Graizbord wrote in *The New Zionists*, "The US office of the Census has long issued questionnaires that consistently designate Jews as a religious group, never an ethnic one. This despite the fact that large numbers of American Jews do not profess their supposed religion or practice it minimally."[9]

But more importantly, Graizbord notes that "'faith' offered itself as the most socially respectable means to articulate Jews' increasingly inarticulate sense of peoplehood in the United States.... Locating Jewishness within the ken of 'faith' allowed American Jews to acquire a widely respected shelter for their ethnic particularity within a society dominated by committed Christians and marked in some corners by antisemitism."[10] American Jews were increasingly secular but identified with Judaism as the public face of their ethnic identity; this was a kind of symbolic Judaism. The late Jewish sociologist Charles Liebman called this "the public façade for the essentially communal content of Jewish identification."[11] Thus, as Graizbord writes,

> The bottom line is that American Jews who became adults during the Second World War *experienced* their difference predominantly as a matter of ethnicity yet *understood* it and often speak about it in terms of a Jewish "faith."
>
> In more recent times, American Jews have approached this incongruity by referring to the ethnic content of their Jewish identity as "culture"—a vague term that has the advantage of carrying no "tribal(ist)" connotations. Those who feel Jewishly connected yet relatively alienated from traditional religious belief, practice, and authority thus often call themselves "cultural Jews."[12]

"Cultural Jews"—or perhaps we should also use the Pew terminology of "Jews of no religion"? These scholars are all seeking to describe the unique phenomenon of American Jews, living in a unique society in the long history of the diaspora. This has been the most open society in Jewish history, and many Jews have begun to see themselves—to see their identity—in new ways. The religious commitments and practices were the first to weaken, sometimes almost instantly upon landing in a country where the authority of rabbis and parents, and the force of community pressure, were so much weaker or even absent. But America was a society that valued religion, so Jews identified as part of an officially recognized and honored religious community that "fit" so well in twentieth century America—even as they moved away from practicing that religion. Thus, to state it again, religion came to be symbolic, the public face of their community or their ethnic/cultural identification. Herberg's *Protestant-Catholic-Jew* suggested Jews were now an accepted one-third of American religions despite their small numbers, and the phrase "Judeo-Christian" (as in Judeo-Christian values) suggested that Jews composed half of American civilization. Whatever their own religious practices, Jews were gratified at this symbolic acceptance and even glorification of their ancestral religion.

But like the practice of traditional Judaism, Jewish ethnicity faded over time. This was natural as generations passed and American Jews were no longer predominantly immigrants or even the children of immigrants, nor living in ethnic or religious enclaves. The "melting pot" was real for American Jews; the borders between Jews and non-Jews blurred. Intermarriage, whatever else it means, is a personal choice by both spouses to view their own group identities as properly subordinate to their personal preferences. As Steven Cohen and Ari Kelman wrote, "Intermarriage flows from and helps produce a more personalized rather than collective view of being Jewish.... Intermarriage represents and advances more open and fluid group boundaries along with a commensurate drop in Jewish tribalism, collective Jewish identity, and Jewish Peoplehood."[13] Open and fluid group boundaries certainly characterize American society and the Jewish community in it. In many ways, that is a cause for celebration.

American Jews are not at all unique in facing these challenges to religion from this open society. For one thing, the number of Americans who say they adhere to *any* religion is in steady decline. The role of religion in American society in the 2020s is very far from what it was fifty or seventy-five years ago. In 2012, a Pew survey entitled "'Nones' on the Rise" found that "One-fifth of the U.S. public—and a third of adults under 30—are religiously unaffiliated today, the highest percentages ever in Pew Research Center polling."[14] By 2021, the trends had continued: the religiously unaffiliated ("nones") were up from 20 to 29 percent; self-identified Christians had fallen from 78 percent in 2007 to 63 percent in 2021.[15] A 2022 article in *Christianity Today* told the story starkly: "The current trend is inexorable. People are giving up on Christianity. They will continue to do so. And if you're trying to predict the future religious landscape in America, according to Pew, the question is not whether Christianity will decline. It's how fast and how far."[16]

Similarly, what is left of the once-powerful ethnic identity of Swedish or Polish Americans? And what of the Catholic culture that immigrant neighborhoods and parochial schools (as well as anti-Catholic prejudices) once kept strong? Chaim Waxman concluded that Jews are "undergoing a process similar to that which number of researchers have found for American Catholics—namely, a significant decline in their attachment to the church and its doctrines; especially among the young, Catholic identity is increasingly a matter of personal choice entailing rather amorphous 'feelings.'"[17]

Ross Douthat has described the Catholic situation in ways that are strikingly like that of Jews:

> Since the 1960s, American Catholicism's main dilemma has been how to reach a large population of baptized-and-confirmed Catholics who have drifted from the Church, and it has been able to rely on the ethnic and cultural loyalty of many prosperous cradle Catholics who no longer practice the faith consistently but still support Catholic institutions. Now the Church is entering a very different era, in which the heirs of those lapsed or culturally attached Catholics haven't been baptized, haven't been confirmed, haven't been married in the Church, and don't have any real loyalties at all. Many are no longer "lapsed," but non-believers.[18]

Would Pew call them "Catholics of no religion?" Will their children be Catholics in any meaningful sense?

Other scholars wrote of Jews' "civic religion," which I take to mean a mix of synagogue membership and occasional attendance for holidays, support for Israel, support for communal activities such as helping the poor and fighting anti-Semitism, and usually some form of political liberalism. But as the decades passed, the specifically Jewish content of that civic religion diminished along with the number of Jews who felt the need to engage in it. This is America, so Jews are free to leave the community entirely and assimilate.

For some Jews, what might be called "liberalism" came to replace the specifically religious or even the ethnic/cultural aspects of Jewish life. This was not only a Jewish phenomenon: Shadi Hamid wrote cogently about American society and politics, stating "As Christianity's hold, in particular, has weakened, ideological intensity and fragmentation have risen. American faith, it turns out, is as fervent as ever; it's just that what was once *religious* belief has now been channeled into *political* belief."[19]

But as a substitute faith, liberalism or progressivism cannot keep Jews Jewish in the long run. At the end of the twentieth century, Charles Liebman and Bernard Susser explained that while political liberalism does have genuine bases in Judaic concerns about social justice, "it fails as a strategy for Jewish survival because it lacks the resources to justify Jewish cohesion and particularism." It cannot work, they said, because it is "self-undermining." Their thoughts are worth quoting at length:

> As a survival strategy it may, temporarily, provide much needed sustenance for modern Jews who are skeptical, morally earnest, and disoriented, but it cannot sustain Jewishness because, by its very nature, it finds it awkward, if not actually mortifying, to justify communitarian boundaries. If ecumenical humanitarianism, benevolent cosmopolitanism, and enlightened nonsectarianism are what Jewishness purveys, it would be incongruous, even hypocritical, for the purveyors to insist on their own uniqueness and to encourage their separation from others. A

> strategy for Jewish survival that does not provide the resources to vindicate difference, borders, and internal community cohesion (a fortiori, one that celebrates universalism) may possess the noblest of motives and the most commendable of intentions, but it paves the way to Jewish dissolution. A Jewish community claiming liberal humanitarianism as its content will quickly learn that its members are adept at finding the sources of liberalism elsewhere.[20]

This is even true of many forms of Jewish *religious* liberalism, if it is taken to mean that there should be no borders between Jews and non-Jews, that focusing on differences is somehow regressive and even hostile to non-Jews. In fact, there is a built-in contradiction between the openness that such views of religion foster and the cohesive separation that is required for a small minority community like Jews to survive in America. The problem exists for all religions, but it is far more grave for a small minority and for one whose identity is such a mix of ethnicity and "peoplehood" with religion. If there are no boundaries, there will be no future. Jack Wertheimer has referred to the "spirit of religious individualism that challenges all organized religion" because "it encourages every person to make a personal decision about religious involvement. Ascriptive loyalties to the religion of one's family, ethnic group, or community have drastically declined in recent decades...."[21]

The American term "religious *preference*" reflects this because preferences in religion, as in all other things, may shift over time. In their book *American Mainline Religion* (which, needless to say, was not about American Jews), Wade Clark Roof and William McKinney noted that "faith comes to be expressed as an opinion or point of view, something that can be easily modified or even discarded if one so chooses. Put simply, religion becomes even more privatized, more anchored in the personal and subjective sphere, and less bound by custom and social bonds."[22] That leads to shifting among Christian denominations, but that form of privatized and personal religion is fatal to Jewish cohesiveness and continuity.

As Rabbi Ammiel Hirsch of the Stephen Wise Free Synagogue put it,

> Liberal Judaism is uniquely susceptible to a rejection of Jewish peoplehood, either by word or by deed or both, because we straddle the tension between Jewish particularism and Jewish universalism.... This is the real fault line, and we must be honest with ourselves if we want a future for liberal Judaism in North America. The future of Judaism is Jewish peoplehood, and all those who abandon Jewish peoplehood will be as the leaves falling from the tree."[23]

FAITH OR FEAR

In 1997, I wrote a book called *Faith or Fear: How Jews Can Survive in a Christian America*. That book was a response, in many ways, to the news about the American Jewish community that emerged from the 1990 National Jewish Population Study.

The 1990 survey and several others drew "a portrait of a community in decline, facing in fact a demographic disaster."[24] Why? Jews had declined from 3.7 percent of the US population to about 2 percent, and one-third of all Americans of Jewish ancestry no longer reported Judaism as their religion. And then there was intermarriage: by 1990 it had risen to a rate of 52 percent (a shocking figure for that time), and only 28 percent of the children of intermarried couples were being raised as Jews.

In my book, I weighed the factors that keep people Jewish and suggested that several of the most potent influences were losing their power. Jewish ethnicity and culture, once a strong gluc, were weakening as the immigrant generations passed away and American Jews assimilated; anti-Semitism—as a centripetal force keeping Jews in their neighborhoods, communities, and inmarriages—was declining; and the memory of the Holocaust as a motivator for remaining Jewish was disappearing as were its increasingly elderly survivors. The only solution, the only force that would keep American Jews Jewish, I argued, was their religion—Judaism. "The American Jewish community must conceive of itself as a *religious* community, or it will continue on this path to decline. There is only one real 'continuity agenda' for American Jews. Every other effort to transmit Jewishness across the generations has failed. Only Judaism, as a religion, can perform this task," I wrote. "As an ethnic, cultural, or political entity they are doomed....Jewish ethnicity is no proof against American culture, and American Jewry will survive as a religious community or not at all." And again, "the only answer capable of ensuring Jewish continuity in America lies in Judaism."[25]

That conclusion led to a further argument that the community "must shift energy from its efforts to promote a secular society and to ensure that individual Jews can succeed in America, and focus instead on the goal of sustaining Judaism here.... What is required in American Jewry now is a change in the publicly acknowledged goals and standards of the community."[26] That should mean making "the financing of religious education a central community activity" and "it would mean making the link to Israel far less than a matter of financial support and far more one of personal contact and commitment."[27]

Some of those changes have occurred. In a footnote in that 1997 book, I repeated a 1994 suggestion from Israel's then deputy foreign minister Yossi Beilin that the American Jewish community try to pay for a trip to Israel for every American Jewish teenager. In 1999, Birthright was created, and as of 2024, it has sent over 800,000 young Jews to Israel. And in a few communities, experiments have been tried where any Jewish child who seeks a day school education will find scholarship funds available.

All the data we had then and have now demonstrate that the *religion* of Judaism is far easier to pass from generation to generation reliably than the elusive characteristic of "Jewishness." Orthodox and other practicing Jews are far more successful in keeping their children Jewish than nonreligious, nonpracticing Jews. And their children marry Jews: 98 percent of Orthodox Jews who are married say their spouse is Jewish and 2 percent do not, while 42 percent of all married Jews say they have a non-Jewish spouse. And among non-Orthodox Jews married since 2010, the intermarriage rate is 72 percent, making the 52 percent rate that shocked American Jews in the 1990s seem both ancient and low.

There is no question that Jews who practice their religion, and especially those who are Orthodox, have much greater success in achieving "continuity:" their children are far more likely to marry Jews, to have children (the birth rate is twice as high among Orthodox vs. non-Orthodox Jews), to raise Jewish children who marry other Jews in the next generation, and to believe themselves connected to other Jews in the United States, Israel, and around the world. Their attitudes toward the State of Israel are warmer and they visit more often.

But most American Jews are not Orthodox and are not going to be. So, in numerical terms, the question is how *non-religious* Jews, and those who say their religion is Judaism but do not actively practice the religion, can survive in a Christian America—or in a post-Christian America where religion plays a diminishing role in our common culture. The Pew study found that 40 percent of Jews under age thirty and 33 percent of Jews ages thirty to fifty said they were "Jews of no religion." And those who did describe themselves as "Jews by religion" are not necessarily practicing that religion: only 20 percent of Jews say they attend religious services at least once a month. Which is to say that the great majority of American Jews don't practice *any* recognizable version of Judaism, whatever their Jewish cultural or ethnic affinities.

Because Orthodox Jews have more children than non-Orthodox Jews, and because their children are far less likely to drift away from the Jewish community, the share of the community that is Orthodox is growing. As I noted in the first chapter, Pew found that among Jews who are thirty or older, 7 percent identify as Orthodox; but among those ages eighteen to twenty-nine, 17 percent do so.

It's predictable, then, that as the decades pass the share of the American Jewish community that is Orthodox will grow. But even if that is true, for many decades the great majority of American Jews will not only be non-Orthodox, they will also be practicing Judaism not at all or in a checkered pattern that combines occasional religious observance with some ethnic or cultural identification and practices. The question is whether those Jews, and their children and grandchildren, will survive as Jews in an America that is roughly 97 percent non-Jewish, and is still 65 percent Christian (at least nominally).

JUDAISM AND PEOPLEHOOD: A PATH OR A BARRIER?

When Pew asked respondents "How much, if at all, do you feel a sense of belonging to the Jewish people?" it found that 61 percent of Jews by religion said "a great deal" but only 13 percent Jews of no religion felt that way.[28] A similar gap was reported on questions asking about feelings of responsibility for other Jews around the world. It seems that when religious faith falls away, so does the sense of belonging. For obvious reasons, this does not happen in Israel. Why should younger American Jews, Gen X and Gen Y, feel this way? As David Graizbord explained it, those generations "include many persons of Jewish origin who do not even identify as 'Jews' (except perhaps in the most passive and personally insignificant sense of having descended from Jews), reasoning that they cannot do so because they do not observe any Jewish religious rituals."[29]

For those young American Jews, *the Jewish religion became a barrier to entry into identification as* Jews. This is very striking: lacking religious faith, finding their own Jewish ethnicity to be thin, finding (if Susser and Liebman were right) that their desire for social justice can be pursued outside Jewish auspices, these young people found there is simply little or nothing left. In a sense, this is logical: in the United States, Jews were officially defined by religion and grasped at that definition to fit comfortably in this Christian-majority and (in the years of greatest Jewish migration) religiously-oriented society. But the great majority of Jews lived their lives as Jews culturally and ethnically rather than religiously, so when what they called culture and ethnicity faded due to assimilation, if they were not religiously observant Jews, there was little left of Jewish identity.

There was no sense of peoplehood for too many Jews, no sense of belonging to a community that exists "vertically and horizontally" through time and around the globe. Is this an inevitable and irreversible decline? If one assumes that Jewish ethnicity will inevitably grow weaker and that the American treatment of religion as a personal preference will likely grow stronger, is it also inevitable that there will only be two groups in the long run: Orthodox or traditional practicing Jews, and people "of Jewish background" whose Jewish identity weakens steadily over time and generations?

If that is so, why has what *Look Magazine* called "The Vanishing American Jew" not indeed vanished or at least diminished much more in numbers?

History provides a good part of the answer. As we will see in the next chapter on the American Jewish community's relationship with the Zionist movement and Israel, Zionism was, by European standards, weak in the United States both prior to the 1930s and in the 1950s and early 1960s. What brought Jews together in support of Zionism was the Holocaust and then the founding of the State of Israel as the Jewish homeland. But after 1948, the level of Jewish interest in Israel declined; after the Second World War, Jews were busy here in America, escaping Jewish immigrant neighborhoods in the cities and building middle-class lives. What awakened American Jews again was the miraculous Israeli victory in 1967 and the perils it faced in the 1973 war—and the Soviet Jewry movement in the 1970s and 1980s. But that period, those decades when the "vanishing" of American Jews was combatted by heightened pride in and fears for Israel and Soviet Jewry, was transitory: Israel's strength and the disappearance of the Soviet Union reduced the threat to Israeli survival and freed the last great Jewish population that lived behind barbed wire fences.

Official distancing between the United States and Israel in future decades would not be a new phenomenon but a return to the situation that existed from 1948 to the 1970s. The picture is not so different with respect to American Jews: as we will see in the next chapter, support for Zionism and Israel has risen and fallen over the last century. Like the picture of eternally intimate and supportive government-to-government relations, the story of effusive and universal American Jewish support for Zionism and Israel is also misleading. Today's divisions among American Jews about the State of Israel are an old story, not a new development. And those divisions might plausibly grow deeper.

Those divisions may be especially fateful for the future of American Jewry because of the role of Israel in the Jewish identity and loyalty to the Jewish people of secular Jews. The parts of the American Jewish community that are most observant of their religion are growing organically, and there are individuals who find their way back (*ba'al teshuva*, one who returns to the path of traditional Judaism). Moreover, those American Jews who are most religiously observant are also most involved in every aspect of community life: "religious commitment is the strongest predictor of every other form of Jewish engagement."[30] Those whose lives are most wrapped up in Jewish faith and practice are most actively engaged in community activities, educational institutions, and charities, as well as with Israel.

Yet there is no great wave of non-observant Jews back to traditional observance, and the majority of American Jews are largely non-practicing (even if they tell Pew they are "Jews by religion.") What then of the great majority of American Jews who will not make that religious journey, and their children? Will they drift away not only from the practice of Judaism, but from the Jewish people?

The Role of Israel

Here, Israel has a vital potential role to play. More dramatically put, here is one central way in which Israel can help save American Jewry. "Israel's existence," as Zvi Gitelman wrote, "does expand enormously the possibility of a secular

Jewish identity. In fact, it seems to be the only viable expression today of secular Jewishness."[31]

This is precisely what David Graizbord found among the young American Jews he interviewed:

> Being a Zionist for my subjects is also to adopt a model of Jewishness that breaks the mold of religiosity that still largely underwrites American Jewish culture.... The sheer dependence of American Jewishness on "religion" may leave these Jews grasping for some form of nontraditional or neotraditional social experience and conceptual language, one that expresses their *kinship*, their *sense of shared history*, their *collective memory*, and their connection to a geographic *homeland* beyond the purely theological and residually ethnological.... Zionism is one solution to this problem, for Jewish nationalism weaves together into a meaningful path of life the elements of Jewish ethnicity and religion that Western modernity has tended to disentangle.... As a response to perceived cultural drift and cultural loss, then, Israel attachment allows Jewish millennials who are not religious traditionalists to achieve either a semi-secular, or what one may call a neo-traditionalist *rapprochement* with their ancestral nationality.[32]

This formulation does not marginalize or downplay Judaism, the religion of the Jewish people. "Jewishness" is a complex phenomenon because Jewish religion and peoplehood are and have always been so intimately intertwined and mutually reinforcing—but now we have a new and potent element in the mix: the Jewish State. "To an extent unknown in Christianity," Lipset and Raab reminded us, "the Jewish religion centers around the Jews *as a people*. The Covenant is between God and the nation. The references in the prayer book are almost entirely to the people. There is no way for Judaism to exist or continue as a religion without the communal entity."[33]

Judaism the religion, Jewish peoplehood, and a deep engagement with the State of Israel are inseparable components of Jewish vitality today. For one thing, Jews understand their faith not only as an individual relationship with a supernatural deity, but as a collective one: as Jack Wertheimer put it in *The New American Judaism*, "*Those who contend that the ethnic dimension of Jewishness is not only passé but also unnecessary ignore the power of Jewish peoplehood to provide religious meaning*.... With the establishment of the Jewish state, which among other things is home to the largest Jewish community in the world, a connection to Israel, its people and culture, is an essential dimension of Jewish religious life."[34] And Wertheimer quoted a powerful line from Yossi Klein Halevi on the same point: "Because Judaism is a particularist faith intended for a particular people, unlike the universal faiths of Christianity and Islam, strengthening peoplehood is a religious category, a precondition for the fulfillment of Judaism itself."[35] Judaism is not an individual religious preference nor a faith for hermits. As the Reform Jewish theologian Eugene Borowitz wrote, "Jewish peoplehood is an indispensable part of Jewish religious thought and Jewish religious practice. A specifically *Jewish* religious life...means, therefore, life in and with the Jewish people, the Covenant community."[36]

This is the answer to those who may wonder whether my concentration here on identity, community, and peoplehood ignores Judaism—Jewish religious beliefs and practices. The influence of Jewish faith, of the practice of Judaism, on Jewish peoplehood is clear and predictable. Less obvious but critically important is the reverse connection, of the Jewish people to the Jewish religion. As Nathan Glazer wrote nearly sixty years ago, as long as there is a "refusal to become non-Jews," as long as individuals consider themselves part of the Jewish people, "it has the effect of relating American Jews, let them be as ignorant of Judaism as a Hottentot, to a great religious tradition.... It means that the Jewish religious tradition is not just a subject for scholars but is capable now and then of finding expression in life. And even if it finds no expression in one generation or another, the commitment to remain related to it still exists. Dead in one, two, or three generations, it may come to life in the fourth."[37]

The vitality of the Jewish people is a religious value and objective; Judaism does not survive without Jews. It is simply a fact that religion has weakened as the critical element of Jewish cohesion in the United States over the last century; large percentages of people of Jewish ancestry no longer practice Judaism. This should lead us to two conclusions: those who care about the Jewish people should be wondering about other sources of vitality and identity, such as the State of Israel, and those who care about more Jews returning to Judaism should acknowledge that those individuals will come from the reservoir of individuals who consider themselves part of the Jewish people. It is senseless to argue about whether Jews should concentrate on building the religious faith commitments or instead building the sense of Jewish peoplehood and Jewish identity of uncommitted Jews. Judaism is the religion of the Jewish people. Committed Jews will, except for a very few converts, be raised in and emerge from the Jewish people.

For the first time in 2,000 years, Jews find themselves in an exceptional situation: there is now a Jewish state that contains, or will soon contain, a majority of the world's Jews and is the center of world Jewish life. *For Jews who do not practice traditional Judaism, a relationship with the state of Israel can play a unique role in reawakening, building, or maintaining their attachment to the Jewish people* in the way that rabbinic or traditional Judaism did for most Jews over the centuries (aided greatly, of course, by being forced to live as a people apart in Muslim or Christian lands).

There are ways for American Jews to enhance their own—and more importantly their children's—relationships with other Jews and with Israel. I will later describe what I believe are the best ways this can be achieved, but first we should turn to the story of the United States' relations with Israel and of American Jews and their relationships with Zionism and Israel. If American Jews believe their relations with the Jewish state are important to our community, it's important to start with an understanding of what they've been like before this generation. The Jewish people, the Jewish state, the United States, and American Jews: what brought us to where we now are?

Chapter Three

The United States and Israel

Looking backward for roughly a century from Israel's seventy-fifth birthday in 2023 to the Balfour Declaration in 1917, relations among the triangle of United States, the Zionist movement and then the State of Israel, and the American Jewish community can be divided into three periods. The fifty years from 1917 to 1967—from the Balfour Declaration and First World War through the Holocaust, the Second World War, and the establishment of the State of Israel on to the 1967 "Six Day War"—were decades of relatively lower interaction among the three sides of that triangular relationship. Then we entered a sort of golden age from the 1967 war to the early years of the twenty-first century. Americans Jews were proud of Israel (even if they rarely visited), Israel and the United States mostly agreed on major issues, and the United States was the key—and often only—friend Israel had in a world where it faced isolation.

But we now live in a period where all that is changing. Because most leaders of the American Jewish community came of age between the 1960s and 1990s, they came to see the relationships of the "golden age" years as normal. They became used to it and came to think it was natural or even permanent. But it was just a moment—a wonderful moment in many ways—and it was slowly receding even as we enjoyed it. As we think about the future of American Jewry and its relationship with the State of Israel, we should recognize that that future may not be played out against the familiar background of recent decades. After many years of strong bipartisan and evangelical support for Israel in the United States, there is no guarantee that these conditions will remain. This chapter is meant as a reminder that the breadth and levels of bipartisan and interreligious support for Israel in the roughly three decades after the 1967 war were an exception.

In future decades, the relationships American Jews build with Israel will be constructed against a very different backdrop where political support for Israel in the United States is far from a consensus matter. In that sense, the American Jewish community may find itself in a situation more like that of other large diaspora communities—such as those in France, the UK, and Australia—where individual Jews and the community must build their own relationships with Israel even when bilateral official relations are sometimes frosty and when political and social elites are often hostile in their views of the Jewish State.

A century ago, the world Jewish population was perhaps thirteen million, and the center of world Jewish life was Europe—where roughly ten million of those Jews lived. Europe was world Jewry's population center, cultural center, and religious center, where the great rabbis, seminaries, and yeshivas were located. For the Jews living in the Yishuv (the Zionist settlements in Palestine) before the First World War, the governing power was the Ottoman Empire; from 1917, the governing power was Great Britain, which formally held the Palestine mandate after 1922. For Jews then living in Mandatory Palestine, relations with United States were essentially private—with relatives who, like them, had come from Eastern Europe. They were literally cousins. There were very limited relationships in the early years with the United States government, which did not wish to interfere much in Britain's handling of the mandate. Of course, this changed with the Holocaust, the Second World War, and the founding of Israel—but not as fast as our current and selective memory of those decades suggests.

After the Holocaust, the center of world Jewish life moved to the United States—especially to New York, where millions of Jews lived—not to what was then Palestine, where perhaps 500,000 Jews lived in 1945 and 700,000 in 1948. But now Israel has emerged as the center of the Jewish world, displacing Europe and the United States. For the first time in modern history, half of the Jews in the world now live there, and that percentage will grow due to emigration there from the diaspora communities and Israel's high birth rate, while the American Jewish community is not growing by any meaningful definition.

Israel has only started to debate what those changes mean for its relations with the world's second largest Jewish community, in the United States. Israel already sends various forms of support to many small Jewish communities around the world; will this pattern emerge in the United States as well? What responsibilities arise as Israel becomes the world's largest Jewish community? What forms of Israeli help might be possible and useful for an American Jewish community that is, in many ways, in decline? These could theoretically range from a greater stress on aliyah to an effort to teach more American Jews to speak Hebrew. Others have suggested that Israel turn more attention to evangelicals in the United States as a firmer and larger base of support. Israel's relationship to Americans Jews is decreasingly one of taking charity, which was central for decades. Will that situation be reversed—so that Israel subsidizes American Jews? From the 1940s to the end of the century, Israel had a dual dependency on the United States—on its government due to Israeli international isolation and on American Jews. Both of these dependencies seem very likely to weaken in the coming decades.

THE OFFICIAL VIEW OF ZIONISM AND JEWISH STATEHOOD

Everyone knows about the decades of strong US government support for Israel, which was the subject of complaint and assault by the Soviet Union and the Arab states for an equally long time. In truth, however, the period of truly strong and close support is short, not long; it spans perhaps four decades out of the last ten, and the intimacy of the relationship has risen and fallen as American presidents imposed their own views and policies. If the United States and Israel become less intimate and Israel becomes less dependent on the United States, that will be less of a break with the past and more of a return to relations as they existed before 1967.

But let us begin a century ago with the American reaction to the Balfour Declaration, where considerable public and Congressional support for Zionism and Israel met with a cold and stiff official attitude. The Blackstone Memorial of 1891, which called for giving Palestine to the Jews, was endorsed by an exceptional combination of congressmen, the Speaker of the House, financiers (including J. P. Morgan and John D. Rockefeller), Christian pastors, the Chief Justice of the Supreme Court, university presidents, and newspapers (including the *New York Times*). It was presented to President Benjamin Harrison—and received no response whatsoever. The State Department thought it knew better, then and later. For the most part, Zionist efforts were seen in official circles as a complication in international relations, not least with the Ottoman Empire, and as an impossible dream. Selah Merrill, the US Consul in Jerusalem on and off from 1882 to 1907, wrote in 1891 that the authors of the Blackstone petition "appear to be ignorant of two great facts, (1) that Palestine is not ready for the Jews and (2) that the Jews are not ready for Palestine."[1]

The pattern we see here was one repeated over the decades: the State Department, under Secretary Robert Lansing in 1917, was hostile to the Zionist movement, while the White House and Congress were more sympathetic. Supreme Court Justice Louis Brandeis (the first Jew to serve on the Court) used his relationship with President Wilson to elicit backing for the proposed British statement about a homeland for the Jews, and the Balfour Declaration was soon delivered to Lord Rothschild—after the British were assured they would have Wilson's approval. Lansing resented being outmaneuvered this way. He wrote to Wilson: "My judgment is that we should go very slowly in announcing a policy for three reasons. First, we are not at war with Turkey and therefore should avoid any appearance of favoring taking territory from that Empire by force. Second, the

Jews are by no means a unit in the desire to reestablish their race as an independent people; to favor one or the other faction would seem to be unwise. Third, many Christian sects and individuals would undoubtedly resent turning the Holy Land over to the absolute control of the race credited with the death of Christ."[2] But it was too late: Wilson had already told the British they would have his support.

In 1922, Congress spoke: on June 30, a joint resolution (opposed by the State Department and the *New York Times*) was adopted echoing the Balfour Declaration: "The United States of America favors the establishment in Palestine of a national home for the Jewish people, it being clearly understood that nothing shall be done which should prejudice the civil and religious rights of Christian and all other non-Jewish communities in Palestine, and that the holy places and religious buildings and sites in Palestine shall be adequately protected."[3] As with the Blackstone Memorial, it's reasonable to say the Congressional resolution had no impact on official US policy—another pattern that was often repeated later.

American Jews were unable to change the official policy of distance, even of indifference—a policy that reflected Lansing, not Blackstone. And that policy remained fixed for decades, including in the 1930s when Hitler took control of Germany and when the British began to close the doors of Palestine to Jewish refugees. As Walter Russell Mead wrote,

> In 1937 Britain issued the Peel report and sharply limited Jewish migration to Palestine even as Nazi persecution of the Jews was intensifying. The United States put no pressure on Britain to

> change its policy. During the 1930s and 1940s, despite vigorous efforts, American Jews were unable to mobilize America against Hitler, unable to persuade the American public to admit Jewish refugees from Nazi persecution, and unable even to persuade Franklin Roosevelt to bomb the rail tracks leading to Auschwitz. When the Jews needed the United States most, the United States was nowhere to be seen; if there was ever a time for American Jews to demonstrate their mastery of the American political process, from the standpoint of the interests of Jews around the world, that would've been the time to do it.[4]

While Mead's focus in that passage was on the powerlessness of American Jews, the US policy he describes continued decade after decade. And those were the decades when power, globally and over the Middle East, began to shift from London to Washington. Initially, Zionist efforts had focused on London because of the immense power of the British Empire, but during the Second World War that began to change. The Zionist leader David Ben-Gurion visited the United States twice during the war, and his longer trip (December 1941–October 1942) culminated in the critical Biltmore Conference, where the American Zionist mainstream first clearly supported statehood. It took a great effort to convince American Jews to take a stand against British policy in Mandatory Palestine, and the other great Zionist statesman of those decades, Chaim Weizmann, was opposed to doing so because he continued to emphasize that good relations with Britain would be necessary for postwar state-building. Ben-Gurion foresaw Washington rising and London fading, and he wasn't afraid to antagonize the British.

But little ground was gained under Roosevelt, who played a careful—and some would argue duplicitous—game in which protecting the Jews and advancing Zionist objectives held a small place, if any. FDR's attitude toward the Jews is now the subject of considerable debate, spurred initially by David Wyman's 1984 book, *The Abandonment of the Jews*,[5] and more recently by Richard Breitman and Allan Lichtman in *FDR and the Jews* (2013)[6] and Rafael Medoff in *The Jews Should Keep Quiet: Franklin D. Roosevelt, Rabbi Stephen S. Wise, and the Holocaust* (2019).[7] Roosevelt's exchange of letters with the Saudi king, Ibn Saud, just a week before FDR's death in April 1945 is an example. FDR met Ibn Saud in February 1945. On April 5, he gave the king secret assurances, stating that "the attitude of the American Government toward Palestine" was that "that no decision be taken with respect to the basic situation in that country without full consultation with both Arabs and Jews." FDR continued, "I assured you that I would take no action, in my capacity as Chief of the Executive Branch of this Government, which might prove hostile to the Arab people."[8] Would this have led Roosevelt to oppose the Zionist declaration of statehood in 1948 and refuse to grant recognition?

Harry Truman is by contrast (and rightly) a hero to American Jews and in Israel for his historic decision to recognize the Jewish state minutes after its announcement of independence. Yet, a closer look reveals the dominance of the older pattern, wherein the State Department and other came to control US policy. It is simply untrue that Truman finally purged Washington's earlier hostility or indifference to Zionism and then Israel.

Truman himself sought to balance a genuine desire to help the stateless Jews who emerged alive from the Holocaust against a resistance to any action that might draw the United States into conflicts. In August 1945, the new president told a press conference that "the American view of Palestine is, we want to let as many of the Jews into Palestine as it is possible to let into that country. Then the matter will have to be worked out diplomatically with the British and the Arabs, so that if a state can be set up there they may be able to set it up on a peaceful basis. I have no desire to send 500,000 American soldiers there to make peace in Palestine."[9] That same month Truman wrote to British Prime Minister Attlee urging the admission of 100,000 Jewish refugees to Palestine. Truman explained his thinking in his memoirs:

> It was my attitude that America could not stand by while the victims of Hitler's racial madness were denied opportunities to build new lives. Neither, however, did I want to see a political structure imposed on the Near East that would result in conflict. My basic approach was that the long-range fate of Palestine was the kind of problem we had the UN for. For the immediate future, however, some aid was needed for the Jews in Europe to find a place to live in decency.[10]

Truman's approach was, at that point, humanitarian rather than political. Many politicians were supportive of or well ahead of the Executive Branch, at least in rhetoric: Both the Republican and Democratic platforms in 1944 promised to push for unlimited Jewish immigration to Palestine and a national home for the Jews there, and on July 4, 1945, thirty-seven state governors petitioned Truman to allow further movement of Jewish refugees to Palestine.[11] And Truman, both a good politician and one fundamentally sympathetic to the plight of the Jews, moved with them. The White House issued this statement in October 1946 after a conference on Palestine in London:

> I have...maintained my deep interest in the matter and have repeatedly made known and have urged that steps be taken at the earliest possible moment to admit 100,000 Jewish refugees to Palestine....
>
> The Jewish Agency proposed a solution of the Palestine problem by means of the creation of a viable Jewish state in control of its own immigration and economic policies in an adequate area of Palestine instead of in the whole of Palestine. It proposed furthermore the immediate issuance of certificates for 100,000 Jewish immigrants. This proposal received widespread attention in the United States, both in the press and in public forums. From the discussion which has ensued it is my belief that a solution along these lines would command the support of public opinion in the United States. I cannot believe that the gap between the proposals which have been put forward is too

> great to be bridged by men of reason and good will. To such a solution our Government could give its support.[12]

Still, the statement was cautious, and Congress remained more supportive than the administration. In December 1945, a joint resolution had passed with more vigorous language urging "that the United States shall use its good offices with the Mandatory Power to the end that Palestine shall be opened for free entry of Jews into that country to the maximum of its agricultural and economic potentialities, and that there shall be full opportunity for colonization and development, so that they may freely proceed with the upbuilding of Palestine as the Jewish National Home."[13]

But Truman's and Congress's views were opposed in the State and Defense departments and in the intelligence community, which resisted with considerable success. Why? The opposition of Secretary of State Marshall and Secretary of Defense Forrestal was based in the Cold War: their main concern was the Soviet threat, and in their view, supporting Partition and backing Israel or the Jews could exacerbate the challenge to US interests in the Middle East by alienating the Arab states. As Jeffrey Herf concluded, "Harry Truman blunted the anti-Zionist consensus in the State Department and Pentagon but he could not defeat it entirely, based as it was on a broadly shared consensus that establishment of the Jewish state in Palestine was at cross purposes to the Cold War and to American access to Arab oil."[14] "The architects of the policy of the containment of communism," Herf wrote, "believed that policy was incompatible with the establishment of a Jewish state in Palestine."[15]

The result was continuing efforts to stop the Zionists. That included imposing an arms embargo (this during the height of the Arab war to crush the new Jewish state), instructing US diplomats in Europe "to urge governments there to prevent Jewish immigration to Palestine," and even pressing the FBI and Treasury Department to "stop American supporters of Israel from assisting clandestine Jewish immigration" in order to prevent combat-age men from reinforcing Zionist forces.[16] As Herf found, when the earliest form of the Mossad in 1947–1948 worked to bring in immigrants and weapons, "At the behest of the State Department and the Pentagon the United States did what it could to prevent both from a timely arrival. In May 1949 the Israeli Prime Minister, David Ben-Gurion, told Ambassador McDonald that if the Jews had been dependent on the United States for survival in the 1947–8 war they would have been exterminated."[17]

The combat between Marshall, in particular, and Truman over US policy toward Zionism exploded on May 12, 1948, in the Oval Office. From March through May 1948, Truman was supporting partition and a new Jewish state, while the State Department was backing a trusteeship for Palestine. But May 14 was approaching, so on May 12, Truman called a meeting.

The memoirs of Clark Clifford, a key adviser to Truman, are worth quoting at some length here both because they are dramatic and because Marshall's attitude and that of Under Secretary of State Robert Lovett, Marshall's deputy, actually characterized much of US policy even after May 14, 1948. The dramatis personae included Marshall, Truman, Clifford, and Lovett. Clifford wrote:

> At 4 p.m. on Wednesday, May 12, a cloudless, sweltering day, we assembled in the Oval Office. President Truman sat at his desk, his back to the bay window overlooking the lawn, his famous THE BUCK STOPS HERE plaque in front of him on his desk. In the seat to the President's left sat Marshall, austere and grim, and next to Marshall sat his deputy, Robert Lovett.

Lovett said the Jewish Agency was overreaching. Clifford continues:

> Marshall interrupted Lovett: he was strongly opposed, he said, to the behavior of the Jewish Agency. He had met on May 8 with Moshe Shertok, its political representative, and had told him that it was "dangerous to base long-range policy on temporary military success." Moreover, if the Jews got into trouble and "came running to us for help," Marshall said he had told them, "they were clearly on notice that there was no warrant to expect help from the United States."

At Truman's request, Clifford then made the case for recognition. Then Marshall spoke again.

> I had noticed Marshall's face reddening with suppressed anger as I talked. When I finished, he exploded: "Mr. President, I thought this meeting was called to consider an important and complicated problem in foreign policy. I don't even know why Clifford is here. He is

> a domestic adviser, and this is a foreign policy matter." I would never forget President Truman's characteristically simple reply: "Well, General, he's here because I asked him to be here."

Lovett then chimed in, "How do we know what kind of Jewish state will be set up? We have many reports from British and American intelligence agents that the Soviets are sending Jews and communist agents into Palestine from the Black Sea area." Clifford continues:

> "When Lovett concluded, Marshall spoke again. He was still furious. Speaking with barely contained rage and more than a hint of self-righteousness, he made the most remarkable threat I ever heard anyone make directly to a President: "If you follow Clifford's advice and if I were to vote in the election, I would vote against you."[18]

This was indeed a direct and consequential threat to the President, who was up for election just six months later in a race he was very widely expected to lose.

Courageously rebuffing Marshall, Truman took the risk and recognized the new Jewish state—but then backed away from further support for it. And that is the point. Marshall lost the battle on May 12, 1948, but it may be said that he won the war. During Israel's war of independence, the United States provided no practical support, and Israel's request for a $100 million loan (and indeed, even for *de jure* recognition) was delayed until January 1949.

The Official View of the New State of Israel

Jeffrey Herf's conclusion about the critical period surrounding Israeli independence is sharp:

> The American alliance with Israel that emerged in full force only after the Six Day War of 1967 tends to obscure from memory the opposition and distance of the days of Israel's birth. In fact, in 1947 and 1948, despite the support of President Truman, the US government was more of a hindrance than a help to the Yishuv and then to the new state of Israel.[19]

The US supported pressuring Israel to give back the Negev, which it had conquered in the war of independence (Marshall specifically endorsed the proposed Bernadotte Plan put forward by the UN Mediator for Palestine, which called for this), and to accept Arab war refugees. The US opposed Ben-Gurion's decision in December 1949 to make Jerusalem the capital of the new state. American diplomats boycotted meetings at the Ministry of Foreign Affairs in Jerusalem for several years.

The arms embargo was particularly dangerous, and its purpose was clear: "The embargo's stated rationale was to help curb the violence surrounding the Palestine issue, but it was generally recognized as designed specifically to press the Jewish authorities, who were the most handicapped by it, to seek an accommodation with the Arabs by accepting something short of a sovereign state."[20] Despite the conclusions of US military leaders that the embargo might lead to the Jews' defeat, and despite the entry into the war of five Arab states on May 15, 1948, the US did not budge. Fortunately for the Jews, Czechoslovakia was instructed by Stalin to provide arms, and France provided the airplanes.[21]

In the aftermath of Israel's victory in its war of independence, the United States gave it minimal assistance and denied it any high-level diplomatic contact. Recall that as a Zionist leader, David Ben-Gurion visited the United States several times during the Second World War and spent over a year here. But as prime minister of Israel from 1948 to 1963, he visited the United States only three times, always very briefly, and never once visited Washington. He never met with Truman when Truman was in the White House, never met President Eisenhower, and met with President Kennedy only once—in New York City on an unofficial visit. As Walter Russell Mead put it, "In the 1950s and early 1960s, when Israel was a weak regional power, the American attitude toward Israel was distant and cold. Israeli Prime Ministers did not visit the White House; the United States not only did not send Israel military aid but Israel was prevented from buying American weapons. It was only as Israel became a more influential and powerful country in the region that American attitudes shifted. Israel the victim never drew much American support; Israel the victor found America eager to cooperate."[22]

For Eisenhower, the contest with the Soviets in the Middle East was the key concern, and as Steven Spiegel explained, "the Arab-Israeli conflict was viewed as blocking American influence and administration designs to contain the USSR in the area."[23] Israel was simply a problem—especially in the view of the foreign policy establishment.

The most significant thing United States did with respect to Israel in the two decades after May 14, 1948, was what Eisenhower did in the Suez crisis of 1956, forcing Israel, the British, and the French out of Sinai. While Eisenhower later called that the greatest mistake he had made as president, it encapsulated US policy: the problems were Israel and British and French neocolonialism, which interfered with our contest with the Soviets—not the Arab radicalism and nationalism led by Nasser. In 1953, Secretary of State Dulles returned from a Middle East trip and reported that the Israelis were "a millstone around our necks."[24] As one historian put it, "Dwight D. Eisenhower's administration uniformly considered Israel a hindrance to U.S. political and security interests in the Middle East and elsewhere."[25]

The levels and nature of US aid to Israel in the 1950s and 1960s, until the 1967 war, reveal the lack of engagement and support. There was a loan in early 1949, but no foreign aid in 1948 to 1952. The fiscal year 1952 aid legislation included $72 million to help pay Israel's import bill and resettle refugees from displaced persons (DP) camps in Europe and from Arab countries. The amount might have gone higher, but the State Department lobbied to bring it down and the $72 million was a compromise figure.[26] From 1949 through 1965, US aid to Israel averaged about $63 million per year, over 95 percent of which was economic development assistance and food aid. Economic grants and loans steeply declined in the 1960s until after the 1967 war. US military aid to Israel only began in 1962 with a $13 million military loan for Israel to begin buying American arms. That same year, President Kennedy authorized the first American major weapons systems sale to Israel, the MIM-23 Hawk surface-to-air missile.

For the prior fourteen years—the first fourteen of Israel's existence and during the 1948 and 1956 wars—it received no US military assistance and there were no arms sales.

Whatever influence American Jewish leaders had in Jerusalem, they had little in Washington. As Spiegel put it, "Since Israel's existence was not at stake and Middle East issues in the early Eisenhower years usually involved intra-Arab issues rather than Arab-Israeli conflicts, fewer people outside the American government took interest than in the early Truman period." Moreover, Spiegel wrote, "the pro-Israel forces lacked the strength of both earlier and later days. Israeli backers had drifted into other interests after 1948 and later crises had not yet called them."[27] Finally, Jews had little access to Eisenhower. He had few Jewish friends, and he did not need Jewish electoral support. Between the United States government and the State of Israel, there was an arm's length relationship and precious little military aid.

American Jewish supporters of Israel concentrated on economic help for Israel to absorb immigrants and stabilize itself. For centuries, Jewish communities in Palestine had been the object of Jewish charity. For American Jews, Israel remained an object of charity after 1948. This was unsurprising in view of the postwar population balance. In 1948, there were approximately 4.5 million Jews in the United States but only 700,000 in Israel. The attitudes of American Jews will be discussed in more detail later, but while American Jews were charitable, there was no aliyah, and there was not even very much travel. Once the state had been established and could act as a haven for displaced Jews, American Jewish life continued much as it had before, and American diplomatic activity centered on the Arab states.

Though there had been a surge of interest, activity, and help from American Jews and of course from Truman in 1948, that level of activity subsided in the two decades that followed. There were three great centers of Jewish population at that time: the United States, the Soviet empire, and Israel—and the first two had far more Jews than Israel. Connections between Soviet Jews and Israel were prevented by the Soviet government, which had a cold relationship with the Israeli government. Relations between American Jews and Israel were not constrained by the US Government, but they were limited by American Jews' concentration on their lives in the United States, where the goal of the postwar generation was assimilation, not Zionism or aliyah. It is unlikely that American Jews could have changed their government's attitude toward Israel between 1948 and 1967, but it is fair to say that doing so was not a priority.

1967 and After

The US–Israel relationship changed dramatically after the 1967 war, and again after the 1973 war. From 1976–2004, Israel was the largest annual recipient of US official foreign assistance. From 1949 to 1970, the yearly total had generally been well under $100 million. Then in 1971, it rose to over $600 million. In 1974, aid reached $2.6 billion and has stayed above $2 billion since 1980 and above $3 billion most years since 1985—and is most recently closer to $4 billion per year. (The composition has changed because economic aid was eliminated in 1998; today, the aid is entirely military.) Moreover, during the 1973 war, the United States undertook an exceptional airlift of arms to Israel. The United States Air

Force provided 22,000 tons of tanks, artillery, ammunition, and supplies between October 14 and November 14, 1973, so that Israel could survive the coordinated surprise attack by Egypt and Syria—both backed by the USSR. What's more, in the face of a threat from Leonid Brezhnev, the Soviet leader, to send in Soviet troops, President Nixon raised the military alert level for all US forces around the world to DEFCON 3, the highest stage of readiness for peacetime conditions.

Then came the years of peace processing—years when US and Israeli policy largely overlapped in the search for an agreement between Israel and the Palestinians. Think of the Sadat visit to Jerusalem in 1977, the Camp David talks in 1978, the Reagan Plan in 1982, the Madrid Conference in 1991, Camp David again under Clinton, and the so-called "Roadmap" and the Annapolis conference in 2007 under George W. Bush. These were, in bilateral US–Israel terms, the best of times. In the years after the first Camp David Agreement in 1978, the United States maintained a unique diplomatic role due to this support of Israel, brokering the Camp David Accords and helping the Oslo Agreement move from the initial breakthrough to actual agreements between Israel and the Palestine Liberation Organization (PLO). While Arab governments except for Jordan and Egypt did not speak to the Israelis, the United States spoke to all parties, including the Palestinians. The US policy objective became the two-state solution and consecutive administrations—Reagan, Carter, Bush, Clinton, Bush, and Obama—devoted great efforts to achieving it, including involvement of time and capital by presidents, secretaries of state, and special envoys.

The close relationship with the United States contrasted with Israel's diplomatic isolation, making US–Israel relations even more valuable. After the 1967 war, at the Khartoum Conference, the Arab League adopted its "Three Nos" policy: no peace with Israel, no recognition of Israel, no negotiations with Israel.[28] Moreover, the Soviet bloc countries and many African countries broke relations with Israel. Egypt eventually recognized Israel in 1980 and Jordan followed suit in 1994, but no other Arab country followed them for decades. These years saw not only Israel's diplomatic isolation but the most vicious attacks on it, culminating in the infamous 1975 "Zionism is a Form of Racism" resolution sponsored by Arab states and the Soviet Union in the United Nations General Assembly—by a vote of seventy-two to thirty-five, with thirty-two abstentions.[29] Among those voting yes, in addition to the Muslim nations and the Soviet bloc, were Brazil, India, Mexico, and Portugal, while most Latin American countries abstained. Such was Israel's international position, which made its close relations with the United States indispensable.

There is no single way to measure the closeness of the official relationship between Israel and the US (Financial assistance? Arms sales? Diplomatic support in the United Nations?), but one useful guide may be official visits. Remember that Ben-Gurion had no official visit to the White House and came to the United States only three times in all his thirteen years as prime minister. Menachem Begin served as prime minister for six years and made eight official visits as well as five private visits, in two of which he also met the sitting president. Yitzhak Shamir came six times in his six years as prime minister. Yitzhak Rabin served three years as prime minister and visited the United States eight times. Ariel Sharon served five years and visited the US ten times as prime minister. Israel was getting a *lot* of attention.

The Soviet Jewry movement of the 1970s and 1980s was symbolic of the best years of these relationships. US Government policy (at least after 1976) was to push the Soviets to let Jews leave through the Jackson Amendment and other pressures; the United States provided ten billion dollars in loan guarantees so Israel could borrow funds at low rates to find the resources to assimilate this great wave of immigration. This cause linked human rights, pressure on the Soviets, Jewish solidarity, and support for Israel in a way that united the American Jewish community internally and united it with American foreign policy.

Yet this is too one-sided or rosy a picture. There were also intermittent confrontations in those years. President Carter's relations with Prime Minister Begin were famously frosty. Carter's perceived lack of sympathy for the Jewish state led to a significant reduction in Jewish voting support for him when he sought reelection in 1980. President Reagan did not support Begin's destruction of Iraq's nuclear reactor or Israel's 1982 invasion of Lebanon. Those confrontations triggered a suspension of the delivery of F-16 aircraft to Israel and of a major US–Israel strategic pact and arms deals. President George H. W. Bush and Secretary of State James Baker had a stormy relationship with Prime Minister Shamir and withheld loan guarantees meant to aid the resettlement of Soviet Jews over a fight regarding West Bank settlements.

The United States and Israel were closely allied on several key issues through the George W. Bush administration (2001–2009), especially against Iran and Sunni terrorist groups. Bush's "War on Terror" found a close ally in Israel. But in the Obama years, American policy shifted focus away from the Middle East as the War on Terror declined in centrality and as the threats from Russia and China grew. Moreover, the United States continued to place the Israeli–Palestinian dispute at the center of Middle East politics. In 2011, President Obama's National Security Adviser James Jones (a former Commandant of the Marine Corps and Supreme Allied Commander in Europe) said, "I'm of the belief that had God appeared in front of President Obama in 2009 and said if he could do one thing on the face of the planet, and one thing only, to make the world a better place and give people more hope and opportunity for the future, I would venture that it would have something to do with finding the two-state solution to the Middle East."[30]

This was not an idiosyncratic view, as Walter Russell Mead noted: "In effect, the Obama administration saw Israel the way John Foster Dulles and the Arabists saw it.... Like the Arabists, the Obama administration thought that the Israeli alliance made the natural and necessary warm U.S. relationship with other Muslim Middle East countries more difficult if not impossible and carried a heavy cost that the U.S. needed to work to offset."[31]

This view has a long pedigree, as Dennis Ross wrote in his history of US–Israel relations: "a number of interrelated assumptions about Israel and the region...embedded themselves in at least part of the national security apparatus—and frequently informed presidents. From Truman to Obama... three stand out: the need to distance from Israel to gain Arab responsiveness, concern about the high cost of cooperating with the Israelis, and the belief that resolving the Palestinian problem is the key to improving the U.S. position in the region."[32]

THE NEW ISRAEL EMERGES

Perhaps such views are truly matters of only historical interest now. The United States remains Israel's most important friend and ally by very far, its defender in the United Nations, and its key arms supplier, but Israel's position in its region and in the world economy has changed greatly in recent decades. Diplomatically, the absolute isolation of the Khartoum Declaration gave way to two peace treaties and more recently to the Abraham Accords, and it improved relations even with Arab states (such as Saudi Arabia) that have not "normalized" diplomatic and economic relations. June 2021 saw Israel's then foreign minister Yair Lapid inaugurating its new embassy in Abu Dhabi—the first visit ever of an Israeli foreign minister to the UAE and the first Israeli embassy in a Gulf state. To reach the Emirates, he flew through Saudi air space, which is now open to Israeli commercial aviation (and has remained so even during the Gaza war). Between 2020 and 2022, an estimated half million Israelis visited the UAE.

All this is a culmination of Zionist efforts that began at least as early as 1901, when Theodor Herzl met with the Ottoman sultan, Abdul Hamid, to persuade Ottoman, Arab, and British leaders that a Jewish entity in Palestine would be in the interest of the region. In 1896, the Sultan is said to have told a messenger from Herzl that "I cannot sell even a foot of land....I cannot give away any part of it...Only our corpse will be divided.."[33] Those Zionist efforts made progress with the British in 1917 with the Balfour Declaration, but not with the Arab states until far more recently.

In 1919, Ben-Gurion wrote, "Everybody sees a difficulty in the question of relations between Arabs and Jews. But not everybody sees that there is no solution to this question. No solution! There is a gulf, and nothing can fill that gulf. It is possible to resolve the conflict between Jewish and Arab interests only by sophistry. I do not know what Arab will agree that Palestine should belong to the Jews—even if the Jews learn Arabic."[34] But things have changed in a hundred years.

The Abraham Accords represent a conclusion by Arab leaders that in a region whose most powerful countries are now Iran, Turkey, and Israel, the Jews are a better, safer partner than the Persians or Turks—a startling reversal of a century of Middle East politics (perhaps since the Faisal–Weizmann agreement of 1919 and certainly since the negotiations with the Emir Abdullah in the 1930s). They see the Jewish State as powerful—and they find this an attractive trait.

Economically, offshore gas discoveries have turned Israel from a vulnerable energy consumer whose supplies had to be guaranteed by the United States into an exporter engaging in gas deals with Egypt, Jordan, Cyprus, and Greece. Israel is a magnet for venture capital, much of it in the high-tech sector where Israel is a global leader. Israel's per capita income is now at European levels, and it typically receives over twenty billion dollars a year in foreign direct investment. In the decade after it joined the Organisation for Economic Co-operation and Development (OECD) in 2010, Israel cut its unemployment rate in half, raised living standards, and reduced public debt. US military aid, once a third of Israel's defense budget, now constitutes about 16–20 percent. Israel's growing wealth is why US economic aid was ended by mutual agreement. With a GDP of over $500 billion and a GDP per capita of about $50,000 in 2022, Israel is a prosperous nation. As the *New York Times* noted in a 2021 story, "In 1981, American aid was equivalent to almost 10 percent of Israel's economy. In 2020, at nearly $4 billion, it was closer to one percent.[35]

Dependence—and Discord

Yet the Gaza war that began in 2023 demonstrated how dependent Israel remains on the United States. A US veto on December 9, 2023, saved Israel from a UN Security Council resolution demanding an immediate ceasefire; the vote was thirteen-to-one, with only the US on Israel's side. (The Biden administration refused to veto a ceasefire resolution on March 5, 2024, abstaining instead and allowing it to pass.) The steady flow of American shipments of arms and ammunition allowed Israel to continue fighting when its own stocks were depleted. The stationing of American aircraft carrier task forces and destroyers in the Mediterranean and the Gulf were warnings to Hezbollah and Iran about expanding the conflict.

Despite President Biden's powerful support of Israel, there are significant differences between the US and Israeli positions on two issues where Israeli opinion is largely united. The first is negotiating a two-state solution, meaning that over time, Israel would withdraw from the West Bank and a Palestinian state would arise there. While the US government still supports the two-state solution, for most Israelis that objective is now peripheral at best, and for a growing number of Israelis it's neither realistic nor desirable. The war between Israel and Hamas in 2021 persuaded many Israelis that, given the results of the 2004 withdrawal from Gaza, military withdrawal from the West Bank in favor of a Palestinian state is simply too dangerous. That opinion became even more prevalent in Israel after the Hamas attacks of October 2023.

Yet the Biden administration remained fully committed to the two-state solution, and US policy may continue to support it despite the security threat posed to Israel by the creation of an independent and sovereign Palestinian state. The growing weakness and illegitimacy of the Palestinian Authority, its apparent inability to maintain order in the West Bank, the high levels of violence that arise intermittently between settlers and West Bank Palestinians, and settlement expansion in the West Bank could once again create a real gap and significant friction between American and Israeli policy.

Moreover, Israel and the United States sometimes see Iran the same way, but they often do not—as we saw in the Obama years. Israel's opposition to the Joint Comprehensive Plan of Action (JCPOA) in 2015 and to its renewal in 2022 demonstrated that distance can grow as well as diminish: the fundamental gap between Israeli and US government views will reassert itself whenever a US administration seems to place its faith in a similar negotiation with Iran. Israel has no faith in such agreements to protect it from Iranian development of a nuclear weapon, and Israeli leaders right and left have continued to declare that Israel will act to prevent such a weapon from being developed (much less deployed), as Israel did in Iraq and Syria. The official US view is also that deployment of an Iranian nuclear weapon is "unacceptable," but that is an observation, not a policy. The tolerance for Iranian nuclear weapons is much greater in Washington than in Jerusalem. The powerful protest movement that arose in Iran in 2022, combined with Iran's military support for Russia's invasion of Ukraine, froze the nuclear negotiations. Yet the underlying problem remains: unless the Islamic Republic collapses, Iran's rulers seem intent on moving closer and closer to a nuclear weapon. Preventing Iran from acquiring a nuclear bomb may require a military strike, and on that question, Israel and the United States may find themselves holding different views.

Even if real discord does not emerge on those two issues, the Palestinians and the Iran nuclear program, my point in relating the history of US–Israel relations since 1948 is providing a reminder that there is no guarantee relations will always be close. For long periods they were not, and there has been considerable friction from time to time. Comparing Barack Obama's and George H. W. Bush's attitudes toward Israel to those of Bill Clinton and George W. Bush demonstrates the possibility that a future president will seek greater distance between the United States and Israel. And the invaluable diplomatic, military, and economic assistance the United States had provided to Israel during the war in Gaza in 2023 and 2024 shows that US support is still essential to Israel. It is no longer poor or isolated, but it remains vulnerable to the relentless Iranian efforts to weaken and ultimately destroy it.

Prior to the 1967 and 1973 wars, the American Jewish community was not deeply engaged in promoting a very close and special official relationship between the United States and Israel—and the efforts that were made were largely unsuccessful. Since then, the community has done much more and with much greater success—but it has also been pushing on a door that was more and more widely open. The assessment of Israeli military prowess after 1967, and the view that Israel was more of an asset than a liability, developed due to events in the Middle East and not as a result of lobbying by American Jews. Not only American Jews but Americans of all faiths were supportive of Israel, so politicians were not taking risks by joining the chorus. There have been moments of confrontation, such as the sale of AWACS jets to Saudi Arabia in 1981 or the Iran nuclear deal in 2015, but within the context of a close alliance. Thirty percent of American Jews are sixty-five and older, and they may have some memory of the sometimes tenuous relations between the United States and Israel. But that means 70 percent have no such memories, raising the question of how they will react if bilateral relations fray or if US public opinion becomes far less supportive. How close are their ties to Israel, and how strong are their feelings? Already it has become difficult, even dangerous, on many campuses to stand with Israel—to be ostracized and accused of the crime of Zionism. What if one or both parties, or significant wings of those parties, become far more critical of the Jewish state and demand an end to American support?

We are going to find out because those are the trends in public opinion. As the next section will discuss, support for Israel in the United States is declining. What's striking about this phenomenon is that it did not begin against a backdrop of growing international rejection and criticism of Israel that Americans are simply joining; quite the contrary. It developed during years when bilateral relations were good and Israel's international position was improving.

American Jews may find that the last few decades were an "era of good feeling" in which supporting Israel was easy: there was broad bipartisan support in this country, and conflict in the region was rare (Israel has not fought an Arab state since 1973, and the last intifada was a generation ago). But today, attacks on Israel are far more widespread in world capitals and in American cities. In the future, American Jews will need to be more active in asserting their own ties to Israel and assuring that their children have such ties—for two reasons. With backing for Israel declining in parts of American society, Israel—whose dependence on the United States was demonstrated clearly during the Gaza war—needs the American Jewish community to be a strong and reliable base of political support. And at the same time (as I will discuss later), it is impossible to see the American Jewish community thriving and growing if it distances itself from the Jewish state. That state is the center of world Jewish life, and those who try to distance themselves from it and from a sense of Jewish peoplehood, are unlikely to remain Jews for many generations.

THE DECLINE OF SUPPORT FOR ISRAEL IN THE UNITED STATES

While some of its most important neighbors and more distant friends are more positive about Israel, that trend is absent in the United States. Support for Israel in the United States is not as overwhelming as it was in some earlier decades, and it has changed from bipartisan to quite partisan. If one of the two major parties comes to be far more critical of Israeli society and foreign policy, and more broadly, if support for Israel in the United States diminishes, this will eventually be felt in official US policy. There may be a time delay, because the opinion of senior leaders (such as President Biden) was formed decades ago and policy may not be affected until new generations replace them. Greater criticism of Israel among younger Democratic Party leaders and voters is already quite visible. This did not appear to have an impact on the Biden administration, but should these changes continue, they will inevitably affect the outlook of future Democratic administrations and members of Congress.

In Israel's early years, public opinion did not heavily favor her. A Gallup poll in November 1947 asked, "if war breaks out between the Arabs and Jews in Palestine, which side would you sympathize with?" Twenty-four percent said the Jews and 12 percent the Arabs, but 64 percent said neither or no opinion.[36] In July 1948, the National Opinion Research Center (NORC) asked: "in the conflict in Palestine, do you sympathize with the Arabs or the Jews?" Thirty-four percent said the Jews, 12 percent said the Arabs, but again the majority, 54 percent, said both, neither, or "don't know." The same question asked in March 1949 got nearly identical answers. In November 1953, NORC asked "which side do you feel is more to blame in this dispute—Israel or the Arabs/Egypt?" Eleven percent blamed the Arabs more, 9 percent the Israelis, and a whopping 67 percent offered no opinion.[37] That is presumably a measure of how little attention Israel was getting among Americans.

These numbers changed after the 1967 war and Israel's astounding victory. The war began on June 5. A Gallup poll in June 1967 found 56 percent of Americans sympathized more with Israel and only 4 percent with the Arabs. In January 1969, a year and half later, the numbers had not changed much: 50 percent with Israel, 5 percent with the Arabs. Similarly, after the 1973 war Gallup found (in December 1973) Americans sympathizing more with Israel by a margin of 48 to 7 percent. That kind of margin no longer exists, and Gallup found that while support for Israel averaged 4.8 times that for Arabs/Palestinians in the 1970s it was "only" 3.5 times in the period 2000–2020. Gallup's early 2022 poll found Israel at 55 percent and the Arabs/Palestinians at 26 percent, obviously a margin reduced to just over two times.[38]

There is a great irony here. For decades, the Arabist argument against American support for Israel was that defending Israel is a liability to the United States. It's too expensive, Israel is too weak and isolated, and the cost of US support is too high. Today, that argument is hard to sustain; Israel is powerful, and Israel's power is now, in so many ways, an asset for the United States. Those who argued against a close US–Israel relationship on realpolitik grounds would now have to change their views. But now we face a new argument against supporting Israel on different grounds: the case in recent years has been that Israel does not share our values, it's too right-wing, it's oppressive, and it violates the laws of war. We saw all those arguments rolled out during the small 2021 war that Hamas started by attacking Jerusalem and then deployed far more widely during the 2023 Gaza war. Those arguments are already affecting the views of the American Left, and it remains to be seen whether they will come to hold sway more widely in this country. Or perhaps, given the declining margins of support for Israel, they already have.

The most striking feature of poll numbers is not the decline in overall support for Israel; it is the significant partisan shift, and it is visible in poll after poll.

A May 2021 Economist/YouGov poll by Kathy Frankovic found this:

> Although 22% of Democrats regard protecting Israel as a "very important" U.S. goal overall, fully 61% of Republicans do so. In the longstanding conflict between Israel and the Palestinians… three in five Republicans (61%) say their sympathies lie with Israel, while Democrats are more likely to say they sympathize with both sides (35%) than support either Israel (16%) or the Palestinians (23%). Only 5% of Republicans say their sympathies lie more with the Palestinians.[39]

A separate May 2021 poll by Quinnipiac College asked "From what you know about the situation in the Middle East, do your sympathies lie more with Israelis or more with the Palestinians?" The poll found that among Republicans, 74 percent said their sympathy lay with Israelis and only 8 percent with the Palestinians. But among Democrats, 43 percent said Palestinians and only 22 percent with Israelis.[40]

This reflects a change over time, as the *Washington Post* demonstrated with a February 2021 Gallup poll:

> A decade ago, by margins of about 2-to-1, Democrats said their sympathies were more with Israelis than with Palestinian Arabs. Polling in February showed Democrats now closely divided, with 42 percent saying their sympathies were with Israelis and 39 percent citing the Palestinian Arabs. That compares with a 79 percent to 11 percent split in favor of Israelis among Republicans.[41]

In May 2022, the Pew Research Center reported on support for Israel in the United States and once again found a significant partisan gap. The report states that:

> Republicans and those who lean toward the Republican Party express much more positive views of the Israeli people (78% very or somewhat favorable) than of the Palestinian people (37%), and they view the Israeli government far more favorably (66%) than the Palestinian government (18%).
>
> By contrast, Democrats and Democratic-leaning independents hold about equally positive views of the Israeli people and Palestinian people (60% and 64% favorable, respectively) and rate Israel's government on par with the Palestinian government (34% vs. 37%).[42]

In July 2022, Pew found that "In the U.S., views of Israel differ substantially across partisan lines and among age groups. Around seven-in-ten Republicans and independents who lean toward the Republican Party have positive views of Israel, compared with 44% of Democrats and independents who lean toward the Democratic Party."[43]

In March 2022, Gallup summed up its own findings:

> More than three-quarters of Republicans sympathize more with the Israelis (77%) than with the Palestinians (13%)—a 64-percentage-point difference. That gap narrows to 28 points among independents, with 54% siding with the Israelis and 26% the Palestinians. By contrast, Democrats are statistically divided, with 40% favoring the Israelis and 38% the Palestinians.
>
> The current divide among Democrats on the Middle East question is the latest in a decadelong decline in that party group's net sympathy for Israel, from 35 points in 2013 to 2 points today.[44]

A generational analysis in 2022 by Samuel J. Abrams and David Bernstein for the Jewish Institute for Liberal Values found similar declines: "Israel sympathizers out-number [*sic*] Palestinian sympathizers by almost a 2:1 ratio, or 39% to 21%, to be exact." But when they compared "Boomers," ages 58–76, to "Millennials," ages 26–41, the results changed dramatically:

> Among the Boomers, on the who-do-you-favor question, Israel sympathizers outnumber

> Palestinian sympathizers by over 4:1 (52% vs. 12%). But among the Millennials, Israel sympathizers and Palestinian sympathizers are almost equal in number (31% vs 29%). A 40 point pro-Israel margin among the Boomers drops to a two point pro-Israel advantage among the Millennials, amounting to a 38 percentage change in one generation.[45]

Political identity and ideology explain most of the differences, and the result is that "the long-standing widespread support for Israel in the American public is clearly at risk. As we have seen, pro-Israel attitudes are less frequent among younger likely voters than their parents' generation." Thus their prediction: "given the tendency for Democrats, liberals/progressives, and highly woke people to score lower on Israel support, we can readily anticipate further erosion in Israel support in the years to come, as generational succession inevitably unfolds."[46]

Polls taken after the Gaza war of 2023 were similar in showing a large partisan gap.[47] About a month after the Hamas attacks, for example, a Quinnipiac survey found that Republicans approved "the way Israel is responding" by 75 to 14 percent, while Democrats disapproved 49 to 33 percent.[48]

In each poll, the numbers differ but the conclusion is the same: Republicans are significantly more supportive of Israel than Democrats, and Democrats are now equally or more sympathetic to Palestinians. Whether this is good or bad news depends, of course, on one's own views of the Middle East and partisan leanings. But it certainly suggests that unless the current trends can be reversed, the bipartisan support Israel received for a few decades—roughly the 1970s to about 2000—will wilt, and logic suggests that US support will diminish with it.

On the "progressive" left, support for Israel is increasingly under assault; in September 2022, Rep. Rashida Tlaib said "I want you all to know that among progressives, it becomes clear that you cannot claim to hold progressive values, yet back Israel's apartheid government."[49] Tlaib went on to call Israeli attacks on Hamas "genocide."[50] The explosion of support for Hamas in October 2023 divided the left, when demonstrations in favor of Hamas and against Israel's response to the October 7 massacres elicited everything from shock and consternation to near despair among many left-leaning Jews.

Why has support for Israel on the left side of American politics diminished? This phenomenon is not terribly surprising in one sense: for decades, Israeli politics have been moving to the right while the Democratic Party in the United States has been moving more to the left. Israel had Likud prime ministers from 2001 to 2021—until Benjamin Netanyahu was replaced by Naftali Bennett, who led a coalition opposed to Netanyahu even though he came from another right-wing party. By the end of 2022, Netanyahu was back, this time leading a coalition including the most right-wing parties ever to enter an Israeli government. It is commonplace to say that the Second Intifada (2000) deeply undermined the "peace movement" and left-of-center parties in Israel. In the November 2022 Israeli election, Israel's Labor Party, which had governed for decades, was reduced to four seats (out of 120) and its frequent partner on the left, the Meretz Party, was unable to win enough votes even to enter parliament.

The American Jewish community has not had a similar evolution. In the 2022 congressional election, it's estimated that more than 65 percent of American Jews voted for the Democratic Party.[51] And in the 2020 presidential election, the estimate is that 68 percent of Jews supported Biden against Trump.[52]

Rising criticism of Israel on the left is a global phenomenon, especially visible in Europe and Latin America; why should the United States be immune? Walter Russell Mead argued that "Attitudes toward Israel became a kind of marker: the more radical one's politics in general, the more radical one's position against Zionism—and, for that matter, the more critical one was of the United States and capitalism generally."[53]

Mead attributes the strong support that continues, at least among Republicans and white evangelicals, to religion:

> Those who say American policy is pro-Israel because evangelicals are strong have missed at least half of the story. It is less that Israel is strong in American politics because of evangelical support than that the existence of Israel helped evangelical religion become a major force in American life. For hundreds of millions of evangelical and Pentecostal Christians in the United States and beyond, the rise of Israel is seen to prove the truth of salvationist Christianity in the real world.

> The return of the Jews to the Holy Land and the establishment against all odds of a powerful Jewish state in the deserts of Palestine strikes many people as a concrete demonstration of the essential truths of the Christian religion. God exists; he drives history; he performs vast miracles in real time; God's word in the Bible is true."[54]

Mead's conclusion raises at least two questions that should trouble those who wonder if American support for Israel is a permanent policy: do younger evangelicals share their parents' enthusiasm for Israel? And does the religious base of support for Israel reflect an America that is passing or has largely passed, where religion played a far more central role in public and private life and where the Bible was read almost universally (including in public schools)?

The first question is easy to answer: among young evangelicals, support for Israel has diminished. One widely-cited 2021 poll found that support for Israel among evangelicals ages eighteen to twenty-nine had fallen to 33.6 percent, with 24.3 percent more supportive of the Palestinians and 42.2 percent with neither side. This was a drop by half, from 69 percent, only three years earlier.[55] Similarly, a University of Maryland poll in 2018 found "a dramatic drop in young evangelicals' support for Israel since 2015.... While 40% of young evangelicals wanted the U.S. to lean toward Israel in 2015, only 21% said the same in 2018. At the same time, while only 3% of young evangelicals wanted to lean toward the Palestinians in 2015, 18% gave that reply in 2018."[56]

Nor are these polls outliers; the trend seems clear, whatever the explanation.

The larger question about religion in America is far more complex. In Chapter Two, we noted the so-called "rise of the nones," of Americans who report no religious affiliation. Gallup cautiously concluded in 2019 that "Americans as a whole are less likely to say they have a formal religious identity, and less likely to report being frequent church attenders."[57] Pew had similar findings in surveys conducted in 2018 and 2019:

> 65% of American adults describe themselves as Christians when asked about their religion, down 12 percentage points over the past decade. Meanwhile, the religiously unaffiliated share of the population, consisting of people who describe their religious identity as atheist, agnostic or "nothing in particular," now stands at 26%, up from 17% in 2009.... The data shows that the trend toward religious disaffiliation...has continued apace.[58]

So, we see support for Israel diminish in two key bases of past support in the United States: one of the two major US political parties and among evangelicals (or at least younger evangelicals). We also see today many national security officials and experts telling us that we need to shift attention and effort away from the Middle East after decades of war—and of failed peacemaking efforts—to focus on the greater current challenge from China.

The golden age that began after the 1967 war—of bipartisan support for Israel, strong evangelical support for Israel, and deep US commitments to the Middle East—seems to be closing. This would, in many ways, be a return to the decades prior to 1967, when the relationship between the United States and Israel (and before that, the United States and the Zionist movement) was far from close. It would be a return to the condition of public opinion prior to 1967 as well.

Is it possible to imagine an American president in a future decade who is not particularly sympathetic to Israel, perhaps presiding over a Democratic Party whose young leaders share that lack of sympathy, and facing public opinion (including younger evangelicals and some on the far right in the Republican Party) that is also less pro-Israel? Why not? If two of the bastions of support for Israel in the United States are weaker in that support, the constraints on a president who wished to create greater distance between the United States and Israel would be loosened. This could happen regardless of the views of American Jews; with Jews composing 2–3 percent of the US population, future US–Israel relations will not be determined by what the Jewish community thinks—if it thinks any one thing. As Walter Russell Mead has written, "The driving forces behind Americans' fascination with Israel originate outside the American Jewish community."[59] And if the support by American Jews for President Obama during his most difficult confrontations with Israel over Iran and the "peace process" is suggestive, a majority of American Jews might not even stand strongly with the Jewish State.

It is possible to imagine, then, a return to the years when US–Israel relations were not intimate and supportive. The feelings about Israel that President Biden so obviously holds may reflect a generation, and a period of US history, that is followed by presidents whose views are closer to those of President Eisenhower or President Carter—and whose policies reflect this.

If that happens, what will be the relationship between American Jews and Israel? This is less a question about politics than about the role Israel has played and may come to play in the minds, hearts, and futures of American Jews in decades where US–Israel relations may not be close.

Before looking forward, we must look back—as we did regarding US–Israel official relations—at the history of American Jewish attitudes and activities. What was their view of and relationship with the Zionist movement and the *Yishuv* (the Zionist presence in Ottoman Palestine and then the British Palestine Mandate) prior to 1948? What was it from 1948 to 1967? How is it changing now? What role does Israel play in American Jewish life today and, more importantly, what role *should* it play? And those questions must be placed within the broader context that we have just seen: the signs that American support for Israel may diminish over the coming decades. Since 1967, American Jews have lived in the golden age where their relationship with Israel was experienced within the context of their country's very warm embrace of the Jewish State. If that changes, will their own embrace of it strengthen or weaken?

Chapter Four

American Jews, Zionism, and Israel

In 1917, the United Kingdom issued the Balfour Declaration, committing Britain to support a Jewish homeland in Palestine. At that time, the world Jewish population was perhaps thirteen million, and the heart of world Jewish life was Europe, where around ten million of those Jews lived. Europe was world Jewry's population center, cultural center, and religious center. Three million Jews lived in the United States, half of them in New York.

For Jews in the United States, settlement of Palestine was a distant though important charity project. Many immigrant households had the Jewish National Fund's little blue metal boxes, or *pushkes*, in their kitchens—a place to put a spare penny to help the poor Jews of Palestine. But it was not the only project to help poor or threatened Jews. In 1905, German Jewish leaders in New York founded the American Jewish Committee, not coincidentally two years after the Kishinev pogrom. The condition of Jews in Eastern Europe and Russia was a great concern. The early meetings of Jewish leaders with presidents—in 1903 with Teddy Roosevelt, then with Taft when he succeeded Roosevelt—concerned Russian Jewry, not Palestine.

What was the attitude of the American Jewish community toward Zionism, toward the creation of a Jewish state? In his history of American Zionism, Melvin Urofsky recounted that "when Charleston Jews dedicated the first Reform temple in America in 1841, Rabbi Gustav Poznanski had proudly proclaimed: 'this country is our Palestine, this city our Jerusalem, this house of God our Temple.'"[1] This remained the Reform movement's attitude for many decades. "In 1898," Jonathan Sarna wrote, "a resolution of the Union of American Hebrew Congregations spelled out the Reform anti-Zionist position in detail: 'We are unalterably opposed to political Zionism. The Jews are not a nation, but a religious community. Zion was a precious possession of the past.... As such it is a holy memory, but it is not our hope of the future. America is our Zion."[2] The Basel Program adopted by the First Zionist Congress in 1897, which called for Jewish settlement in Palestine, was rejected by the Reform movement in the US; Rabbi Kaufmann Kohler, later the head of Hebrew Union College, called Zionism "a blasphemy and lie upon the lips of every American Jew."[3] American attendance at that Zionist Congress "foreshadowed how difficult it was going to be to get American Jews on board," Daniel Gordis wrote; "despite the fact that there were some 937,000 Jews in America, of the approximately 200 delegates to the Congress, only four came from the United States."[4] One observer noted that "in contrast to European Jewry, which was heavily influenced by the early Zionist movement, American Jews at the end of the nineteenth century viewed Zionism as a marginal issue."[5] Here and in Europe, many Orthodox rabbis rejected the Zionist movement as well: the return to Zion would come when God determined and should not be forced by secular Jews for political reasons.

The elites, not the masses, were hostile to Zionism as a threat to the position of American Jewry: the *pushkes* were in the kitchens of tenements, not on Fifth Avenue. For the most part, the German Jewish elite that led the great Jewish organizations in those years before the Holocaust and the Second World War were anti-Zionist. Louis Marshall and Jacob Schiff, founders of the American Jewish Committee, were staunchly anti-Zionist; Schiff said Zionism creates "a separateness which is fatal."[6] There were important exceptions, the most prominent of whom was Louis Brandeis, and sometimes elite families split over this question: while FDR's Treasury Secretary Henry Morgenthau Jr. was a Zionist, his father Henry Morgenthau Sr.—the financier who was ambassador to the Ottoman Empire during the First World War—was a fervent anti-Zionist. In June 1921, a *New York Times* article entitled "Zionism a Fallacy, says Morgenthau" quoted him blaming Zionism for fomenting Arab animosity against the Jews and calling Zionism "the most stupendous fallacy in history," "wrong in principle and impossible of realization," and concluding that "Zionism is a surrender, not a solution.... [I]t is a betrayal...which, if it were to succeed, would cost the Jews of America most that they have gained of liberty, equality and fraternity."[7] Morgenthau was not unsympathetic to the plight of the Jews living in Palestine, and in 1914 had organized other Jewish leaders in the US to provide $50,000 for their relief. But this was philanthropy, not Zionism.

To a large extent, the Zionist movement in the United States was part of a broader desire to help poor and persecuted Jews around the world. American Jews often saw Palestine as a potential home for homeless Jews—but unlike those unfortunate people, American Jews were not homeless. (There is a famous incident when an American Jew made just this argument to Theodor Herzl, who replied "All Jews have homes, and yet they are all homeless."[8]) European Jews needed a refuge; American Jews had found theirs and had found political freedom and legal equality. Thus their support for the poor Jews of Palestine was often a form of charity, a view that infuriated European Zionist leaders. Max Nordau, who cofounded the Zionist Organization with Herzl, "had no patience for what he called 'the social work Zionism of the Americans helping their poor European cousins.'"[9] Chaim Weizmann, president of the British Zionist Federation after 1917 and of the World Zionist Organization after 1920, well understood that "the American Jews were by no means as deeply permeated with the Zionist ideal as the Europeans." Nevertheless, he wished to relocate the Zionist movement's central agencies to the United States, where he sought material help at the minimum.[10]

ZION AS REFUGE

After the First World War, attitudes toward Zionism among American Jews began to change—in part because America as a refuge was no longer available. New immigration restrictions imposed in 1924 ended the waves of migration that had brought 2 million Jews to America between 1880 and the 1920s. While anti-Semitism rose in Europe, the "Golden

Door" was closed and other means of escape were obviously needed. In the United States, a synthesis was formed, largely by Brandeis, that rejected the elite negation of Zionism and reinterpreted it as compatible with American patriotism. "The highest Jewish ideals are essentially American in every important particular," he said in 1915. "It is Democracy that Zionism represents. It is Social Justice which Zionism represents, and every bit of that is the American ideals of the twentieth century." He summed it all up in the famous dictum, "To be good Americans, we must be better Jews, and to be better Jews, we must become Zionists."[11]

The emphasis, Urofsky wrote, was on the kind of "social work Zionism" that Nordau had scorned. This was not about leaving America to move to Palestine. Instead, it was the "concrete task" of raising funds for and giving political support to "practical work in the rebuilding of Palestine."[12] The religious and spiritual aspects of Zionism were downplayed, and a problem was created that would only be understood decades later when Israel became more powerful and prosperous. If American Jews' support for Zionism was based on the need to create a refuge for persecuted Jews and to sustain that refuge economically, what role would American Jews play when those needs evaporated in the twenty-first century? If Zion did not need American Jews' charity, what was to be the relationship between American and Israeli Jews?

These problems seemed to be far in the future in the 1920s and 1930s. What was increasingly clear was the imminent threat to European Jews and the growing role that American Jewry would have to play. Urofsky summarized the situation in *American Zionism*:

> Most importantly, within the Jewish community organized anti-Zionism had practically disappeared. After the failure of the Évian conference, even previously hostile or neutral groups like B'nai Brith and the American Jewish Committee endorsed Zionist demands for open immigration to Palestine and supported the building of the Yishuv. If nothing else, Adolf Hitler had convinced American Jewry that a national home in Palestine was an absolute necessity. Even Reform leaders changed their minds.... When Great Britain, in whom the Zionists had put so much trust, reneged on its promises and then closed the door to further immigration at the precise moment when Hitler's refugees needed a homeland most, American Zionists realized that only a country controlled by the Jews themselves would meet the needs not only of Zionism but of Judaism itself. It is doubtful whether a strong Zionist nationalism could have appealed to American Jewry before Hitler; but with the Holocaust, an independent Jewish state became the sine qua non of the Zionist movement."[13]

The divisions among American Jews began to collapse in the face of Nazi brutality and the inability to find any country willing to accept Jews fleeing for their lives. The July 1938 Évian Conference was called by Franklin D. Roosevelt and was attended by thirty-two countries, but delegates did not reach any practical conclusions about helping desperate Jews in Germany and Austria escape Hitler's grasp. The Munich Agreement with Hitler came in September 1938, allowing him to seize the Sudetenland, and Kristallnacht followed that November. And the British, assigned the Palestine Mandate in 1919, issued the 1939 White Paper that closed Palestine as a significant Jewish refuge: Jewish immigration was limited to 75,000 people over five years, and Jews would permanently remain a minority there. The Jews of Europe had nowhere to go; they found no country to take them in. The need to create one became very clear even to American Jews who had resisted that conclusion.

The 1942 Biltmore Conference of American Jewish leaders, held in New York City, marked the change from half-hearted support for Zionist goals to focus on a state rather than an amorphous "homeland." The 586 American Jewish delegates (and 67 foreign leaders including Weizmann and Ben-Gurion) left behind the factionalism and caution that had marked American Jews' attitudes toward Zionism: "Before Biltmore, American Zionists saw Palestine as a refuge; after Biltmore they fought for a state."[14]

The exact language of the Biltmore Declaration called for "the fulfillment of the original purpose of the Balfour Declaration and the Mandate which recognizing the historical connection of the Jewish people with Palestine was to afford them the opportunity, as stated by President Wilson, to found there a Jewish Commonwealth." Citing Nazi persecution and "Jewish homelessness," the Conference demanded "that the gates of Palestine be opened; that the Jewish Agency be vested with control of immigration into Palestine and with the necessary authority for upbuilding the country, including the development of its unoccupied and uncultivated lands; and that Palestine be established as a Jewish Commonwealth." Moreover, the Declaration called for "a Jewish military force fighting under its own flag."[15]

By 1942, then, it can be said that the American Jewish community was Zionist—if being a Zionist is defined as calling for a Jewish state in Palestine. Yet even the terrible challenges of rescuing fellow Jews from the Holocaust, helping survivors and displaced persons, or working to establish the State of Israel did not overcome divisions along personal, denominational, and political lines. The viciously anti-Semitic Breckinridge Long, who as a State Department official did more than any other individual to prevent the arrival of Jewish refugees in the United States, wrote in his diary in 1944 that "the Jewish organizations are all divided amidst controversies.... there is no cohesion nor any sympathetic collaboration [but] ... rather rivalry, jealousy, and antagonism."[16] Anita Shapira noted in her biography of Ben-Gurion that coming to America in October 1940, he "found a public with strong Jewish identification and definite Zionist instincts, but confused and disorganized, with a leadership embroiled in petty quarrels over honors and positions."[17] In a letter to Mrs. Tamar De Sola Poole, president of Hadassah, Ben-Gurion himself complained that "I shall not deny the distressing feeling which American Jewry has awakened in me. Even in Zionist circles I didn't find an adequate awareness of the seriousness of this desperate and tragic hour in the history of Israel. Does the fate of millions of their kin in Europe concern Jewry in America less than the fate of England affects the people of America? I fear that American Zionists have not yet fully grasped the tremendous and weighty responsibility which history has imposed upon them in the present fateful hour."[18]

When the war ended, the American Jewish community pressed the United States government to demand that Britain let Jewish refugees and displaced persons emigrate to Palestine. As we've seen, the Truman administration declared that it favored opening the doors of Palestine to allow in 100,000 Jewish refugees, and Gallup polls showed that was a popular position. But the effort largely failed; whatever pressure was put on Britain was not strong enough to work. And the alternative of allowing Jewish refugees to come to the United States was unpopular both inside the government and among the public at large.

Once the Jewish state was established in May 1948, the debate among American Jews over whether or how to support it was still not over, at least among some Jewish elites. Financial support for Israel, through mechanisms like Israel bond sales, did rise steadily. In 1951, Ben-Gurion created the Israel Bonds program. By 1957, it had raised $250 million in bond sales from American Jews—which equaled 35 percent of Israel's special development budget and roughly matched the aid from the US government. But concerns about the dual loyalty charge, Israeli "interference" in the "internal affairs" of diaspora communities, and efforts to promote aliyah to Israel led to a remarkable exchange in 1949 and 1950 between Ben-Gurion and Jacob Blaustein, the American Jewish Committee's president.

Charles Liebman's account of the episode states that a 1949 Blaustein letter to Ben-Gurion "intimated that if Israel contemplated a campaign for immigration to Israel from the U.S., the AJC would have to reconsider its support for

Israel." In a meeting with Israel's ambassador to the United States, Blaustein said the AJC would stand against "the propagation of Jewish nationalism in the U.S." A letter to Ben-Gurion from the AJC's previous president demanded that he issue a statement "categorically disclaiming any intention on the part of the State of Israel to interfere with the life of American Jewry."[19]

These pressures ultimately elicited a 1950 statement by Ben Gurion:

> The Jews of the United States, as a community and as individuals, have only one political attachment and that is to the United States of America. They owe no political allegiance to Israel.... The State of Israel represents and speaks only on behalf of its own citizens and in no way presumes to represent or speak in the name of Jews who are citizens of any other country. We, the people of Israel, have no desire and no intention to interfere in any way with the internal affairs of Jewish communities abroad.[20]

As we will see later, in 2022, Israel adopted a new "Basic Law" entitled "Israel as the Nation-State of the Jewish People" that directly contradicts that last sentence. Ben-Gurion also pulled back from encouraging aliyah to Israel, calling it entirely a matter of free discretion and personal choice rather than an obligation for Jews or a central feature of modern Jewish history.[21] As Liebman concludes, "this 'exchange of views' can be understood only as a response to the pressure brought to bear by a segment of Diaspora Jewry."[22]

Why did Ben-Gurion make these concessions? He understood both the important financial support that American Jews could send to Israel and their potential role in affecting American opinion and government action. As we have seen, he had spent long parts of the war years in the United States: three and a half months in 1940 and then ten months from December 1941 to October 1942. He had foreseen the changing nature of world politics after the war. As Michael Bar-Zohar wrote in his biography of Ben-Gurion, "Ben-Gurion believed the focal point of power and leadership in the free world would soon shift from London to Washington, and America would emerge as the leading power in the post-war world."[23] In the 1950s, the United States had clearly assumed this role and Ben Gurion carefully reacted to it.

But his and Weizmann's concerns about the attitudes of American Jews were equally borne out in those years: American Zionism was a thin version of the support the movement had had in Europe.

AMERICAN JEWS AND THEIR ZIONISM

It would be attractive to describe a crescendo of American Jewish concern starting in the 1930s with the rise of Hitler and the deadly actions against Jews in Europe, then continuing in support for the establishment, preservation, and success of the State of Israel—but that is inaccurate. The levels of support that existed for some years after 1967 have been read back into American Jewish history inaccurately. Daniel Gordis described the reality: often when being handed a cherished bar mitzvah or wedding photo by an American Jewish family, he wrote,

> I turn the photo over. More times than I can count, a handwritten caption on the back has read: "wedding of —, June 1944." Or "Bar Mitzvah of —, May 1943." Across the Atlantic, at the very moment those photographs were taken, European Jewry was being exterminated.... The horrifying difference between the placid lives depicted in the photographs and what was transpiring in Europe at the very same moment is a stark reminder of how differently history has played out for Jews in the United States and elsewhere.[24]

American Zionism consisted more of Brandeis's "practical work," meaning financial support rather than passionate political work or aliyah—despite the Holocaust and the establishment of the State of Israel. Nathan Glazer described this straightforwardly:

> The two greatest events in modern Jewish history, the murder of 6 million Jews by Hitler and the creation of a Jewish state in Palestine, had had remarkably slight effects on the inner life of American Jewry up until the mid-fifties.... When Israel was established, there was much to talk about what this would mean for American Jewry.... What happened after the state was established was that the major Zionist political organization, the Zionist Organization of

> America, rapidly declined. The establishment of Israel meant little for American Judaism specifically."[25]

This will strike many American Jews as startling or even implausible, but other historians confirm it: Jonathan Sarna wrote that "Israel remained largely peripheral to American Judaism in the 1950s. A survey of Jewish education in the United States at the end of that decade found to its surprise that only forty-eight out of over 1000 teachers 'reported teaching Israel as a subject of study.'"[26] Pledges to United Jewish Appeal for assistance to Israel dropped each year after 1948, and "from 1949 to 1967 there was certainly a substantial depreciation in the image of Israel as perceived by the leadership—and probably also by rank-and-file members—in the Jewish communities and their federations."[27]

This is an accurate and deeply striking portrait of American Jews' collective attitude until the late 1960s and the 1970s. Three things then changed the way American Jews saw their own situation and that of the Jewish state: the 1967 and 1973 wars, growing attention to the Holocaust, and the Soviet Jewry movement.

The Awakening

So much has been written about the "awakening" of American Jewry by Israel's near-miraculous victory in 1967 and its days of isolation and deep peril in 1973 that we need not dwell too long on the phenomenon. The impact of the Six-Day War in 1967 was "completely unanticipated and unpredictable," and one concrete way of measuring this is through dollars: donations to United Jewish Appeal quadrupled and Israel's ambassador commented that rather than fundraising, Israel suddenly "had an administrative problem how to handle the flow of money."[28] The same happened during the Yom Kippur War of 1973: UJA donations reached the highest level they ever obtained between 1940 and 1980.[29] Israel bond sales in the 1960s were approaching the $100 million mark annually, but in 1974, the year after the Yom Kippur War, they exceeded $400 million.

Dov Waxman described the Six-Day War as "a quasi-religious experience for many Jews," after which "ardent support for Israel came to dominate American Jewish public life" by providing a "common cause and rallying cry."[30] As I noted in the introduction, Arthur Hertzberg wrote in *Commentary* that "the mood of the American Jewish community underwent an abrupt, radical, and possibly permanent change...far more intense and widespread than anyone could have foreseen."[31] While Hertzberg was wrong about the permanence of the change, observers are unanimous in remarking on the transformation of American Jewish attitudes towards Israel in that period.

In these same years, gradually but very steadily, attention to the Holocaust returned as a central feature of American Jewish life. Public interest in and knowledge about the Holocaust grew slowly in the decades after the Shoah ended in 1945. Single events captured public attention: the diary of Anne Frank was published in English in 1952 as a book and became a Broadway play in 1955; Leon Uris's novel *Exodus* was published in 1958 and became a film in 1960, the same year Elie Wiesel's memoir *Night* was published; the Eichmann trial was in 1961. Still, there were no Holocaust museums in the United States nor were there high school and college curricula offering (and twenty-three states requiring[32]) education about the Holocaust.

"That began to change in the late 1960s, some say around the time of the 1967 Six-Day War between Israel and its Arab neighbors," recalled Dan Freedman, but "the year 1978 was pivotal." NBC's miniseries *Holocaust* attracted 120 million viewers and "introduced the genocide and the word 'Holocaust' to a wide swath of Americans." That was the year when President Carter established the Commission on the Holocaust and asked Elie Wiesel to chair it, the first official step toward the construction of the Holocaust Museum in Washington. Freedman reports that Holocaust education was introduced into public schools for the first time in 1972.[33]

In the same period, the plight of Soviet Jewry became a nearly universal cause in the American Jewish community, and anyone driving past a synagogue in the 1970s and 1980s would likely have seen a "Free Soviet Jewry" sign outside it. Elie Wiesel's book about Soviet Jews, *The Jews of Silence*, was published in 1966; by 1970, there were thirty-two local groups formed under the Union of Councils for Soviet Jews; the first World Conference on Soviet Jewry was held in 1971, the same year the National Conference on Soviet Jewry was founded. In 1972, Senator Henry M. Jackson introduced what became known as the Jackson-Vanik Amendment, linking trade benefits for the USSR to freedom of emigration and securing enthusiastic and widespread Jewish support. After a struggle with the Nixon administration, that amendment became law in 1975; the heroic "refusenik" then known as Anatoly Shcharansky was arrested in 1977. Ten years later, in

December 1987, a freedom for Soviet Jewry rally mobilized 250,000 people to demonstrate in Washington. The names of individual "refuseniks" like Shcharansky, Ida Nudel, and Yuli Edelstein became widely known among American Jews.

These phenomena—the impact of Israel's wars, new attention being paid to the Holocaust, and the Soviet Jewry movement—were linked. The rising attention to the Holocaust itself; Israel's isolation in 1967 and the days of fear in 1973 that it would be defeated and overrun, leading to another mass slaughter of Jews; and the desire of American Jews to save Soviet Jews as they had failed to save European Jews in the 1930s and 1940s combined to produce greater activism in the American Jewish community on behalf of all those causes. As Yossi Klein Halevi said of the passage of the Jackson Amendment, "For American Jews, it was a stunning example of their capacity to influence international politics on behalf of their people—a powerful reversal of the failures of the Holocaust." Klein Halevi explained that "saving Soviet Jewry meant retrieving not only the last great Jewry of Eastern Europe but also the lost honor of American Jewry," explaining that his attraction as a teenager to the Student Struggle for Soviet Jewry arose because "The group's slogans, which focused on our determination not to repeat the Holocaust-era sin of silence, spoke precisely to my need: 'This Time We Won't Be Silent'; 'I Am My Brother's Keeper.'"[34] Klein Halevi was very far from unique in holding these views about the Soviet Jewry movement as a "reversal of the failures of the Holocaust."

The story of American Jews, Zionism, and Israel is not, then, one of great, unchanging, and unanimous enthusiasm. Zionism was a divisive issue, especially among Jewish elites, until the need for a Jewish refuge, the Holocaust, and the establishment of the State of Israel raised the level of support in the late 1930s and the 1940s. And then it dropped off again. Nathan Glazer's remarkable comment that I noted a few pages back is worth repeating: "The two greatest events in modern Jewish history, the murder of 6 million Jews by Hitler and the creation of a Jewish state in Palestine, had had remarkably slight effects on the inner life of American Jewry up until the mid-fifties." In fact, when Glazer wrote his classic work *American Judaism* in 1957, he did not even mention "the Holocaust." For post-war American Jews, the two decades after the war were a time of assimilation into American life by a generation born in the United States and moving from city to suburb. In fact, Glazer may have been wrong to say "up until the mid-fifties;" up until the mid-sixties is more accurate.

And then the community was awakened by the risk of war and annihilation faced by Israel, and by the plight of Soviet Jews. And simultaneously, the subject of the Holocaust began its steady rise in levels of attention. There is an obvious link: the two largest communities of Jews outside the United States were under threat, and American Jews saw the threat and worked to protect them. American Jews had failed to protect fellow Jews in Europe or gain them refuge in Palestine or in the United States in the 1930s. Now there was a determination to celebrate heroism and prevent disaster. An observer might have thought the worry about American Jewish assimilation, or about distancing from Israel, was quite far-fetched.

But that observer would have been wrong. For one thing, the number of Holocaust survivors declined year by year. The explosion in the numbers of Holocaust memorials and classes about the Shoah risked turning a unique event in world history into a routinized, academic study with monuments and classes that increasingly failed to grip the emotions. In 2024 I counted eighty-three Holocaust markers, museums, centers, and the like in the United States. Universities now offer certificates and degrees in all sorts of Holocaust studies—about music, history, literature, psychology, genocide, and many other variations.

It is still the case (according to the Pew 2020 survey) that more American Jews say "remembering the Holocaust" is essential to being Jewish, 76 percent, than say that about *anything* else—from leading an ethical life (72 percent), to caring about Israel (45 percent), to observing Jewish law (15 percent), or being part of a Jewish community (33 percent).[35] But "remembering the Holocaust" is, I would suggest, a phrase that has little meaning. The need to "remember the Holocaust" has been fully institutionalized not only in American Jewish life but in American public life more generally. Nearly half the states require teaching about it in public schools. But "remembering the Holocaust" appears to have no impact on the lives of American Jews, and the rise in attention to the Holocaust in the last few decades has coincided with all the negative trends about Jewish life, continuity, community solidarity, and support for Israel. With the passage of time and generations, fewer and fewer American Jews have any memory of the Holocaust or any contact with survivors. Some predicted that increased attention to the Holocaust would produce nothing positive for American Jews, even as that attention first began to grow. As the philosopher Michael Wyschogrod put it in 1971, "There is no salvation to be extracted from the Holocaust, no faltering Judaism can be revived by it, no new reason for the continuation of the Jewish people can be found in it."[36]

As to the enthusiasm occasioned by the struggle for Soviet Jewry, the collapse of the USSR and the freeing of its Jewish population more than thirty years ago ended that movement. It is now largely forgotten, and unlike the very widespread study of the Holocaust, there are virtually no college courses or monuments that remind us now of the Soviet Jewry movement—or of the success of American Jews in supporting it. In 1965, Elie Wiesel traveled to the Soviet Union and published *The Jews of Silence* in 1966, a report and call to action that greatly helped the Soviet Jewry movement capture the minds and hearts of American Jews. Today, that entire movement is wrapped in silence, almost unknown to American Jews born since the 1990s.

DECLINING ATTACHMENT TO ISRAEL

The previous pages have shown, I believe, that the existence of a united American Jewish community strong in its support of Israel is a myth, or (more kindly described) an extrapolation backward and forward of the extraordinary situation that existed for a while after the 1967 and 1973 wars. The American Jewish community was never as committed to Zionism and to Israel as other diaspora communities, as Zionist leaders like Weizmann and Ben-Gurion well understood. One cannot point to a single moment when the "practical work" of American Zionism was completed, but as Israel slowly reached European levels of prosperity and became a regional military power, the level of American Jewish interest waned (except among the Orthodox).

This is, of course, a generalization, but an accurate one—and one way to judge is the simple matter of visits. The National Jewish Population Survey of 2000 found that just over one-third of American Jews had ever visited Israel even once.[37] Of that roughly 35 percent, it's reasonable to estimate 10 percent were Orthodox because the Orthodox community constitutes about 10 percent of American Jewry. That allows us to estimate that in 2000, about 65 percent of American Jews and 75 percent of non-Orthodox American Jews were not sufficiently interested in the Jewish state to set foot there even once. This was not the case for French or British Jews, nor for Australian and Canadian Jews; by some estimates, 70–80 percent of those communities had visited Israel.

Today, according to the Pew survey, and even with more than half a million young American Jews having visited Israel through Birthright, only 45 percent of Jewish adults have visited Israel even once. And among the 27 percent of American Jews whom Pew calls "Jews of no religion," 78 percent have never visited Israel.[38] Pew does not ask whether they have ever left the United States, or whether they have ever been to London or Paris, but I would wager a great deal of money that that 78 percent figure represents lack of interest rather than an aversion to foreign travel.

The travel numbers should remind us again, as we look at the levels of American Jewish support for Zionism, that moderate support was more typical historically than deep engagement. At the elite levels, there was often distancing and criticism; among the broader Jewish population, there was stronger support but less active engagement than was visible in other Diaspora communities. Levels of aliyah were very low. If there were no longer rejections of Zionism as alien to Americans because America was the *goldene medina* or promised land, American Jews did not often have one foot in their home country and one in Israel, as French Jews have so often had in recent decades. It is interesting to imagine why: in Europe, was it the history of Nazism and the importance of Israel as a potential refuge? The small size of Jewish communities relative to fast-growing Muslim populations? Whatever the explanation, the moments when the American Jewish community shared the levels of emotional attachment to the Jewish state found widely in the Diaspora were rare and atypical.

And those levels of attachment are declining. The Pew report is clear, especially about younger American Jews:

> Young U.S. Jews are less emotionally attached to Israel than older ones. As of 2020, half of Jewish adults under age 30 describe themselves as very or somewhat emotionally attached to Israel (48%), compared with two-thirds of Jews ages 65 and older.
>
> In addition, among Jews ages 50 and older, 51% say that caring about Israel is essential to what being Jewish means to them, and an additional 37% say it is important but not essential; just 10% say that caring about Israel is not important to them. By contrast, among Jewish adults under 30, one-third say that caring about Israel is

> essential (35%), and one-quarter (27%) say it's *not* important to what being Jewish means to them.[39]

These are significant declines by age group, but they will surprise no one minimally familiar with discourse in the American Jewish community. Criticism of Israel is now widespread, though it varies from that of committed supporters who oppose one policy or another to outright rejection of Zionism and of the Jewish state entirely. Many Reform and Conservative rabbis and congregants, for example, are offended by the rejection of non-Orthodox Judaism by Israeli rabbinic authorities and by their influence over government policies. J Street calls itself "pro-Israel, pro-peace" but has engaged in systematic criticisms of Israeli government policy, including with respect to central security issues. Further left, organizations such as the Jewish Voice for Peace (JVP) support BDS: boycotts of Israel, divestment in companies that do business there, and sanctions against the Jewish state. JVP claims sixty chapters in the United States.

A signal moment displaying the change in opinion in parts of the American Jewish community came in 2021, when nearly ninety rabbinical students from several non-Orthodox seminaries accused Israel of apartheid and "violent suppression of human rights."[40] Their statement was published in May 2021 while Hamas was engaged in a series of rocket attacks on Israel; the letter did not mention Hamas nor did it express concern about the safety of Israeli civilians who were under attack. And all of that happened *before* Israel's 2022 election and the victory of the most right-wing coalition ever to enter office.

Before the 2023 Gaza war, Israel had become a divisive issue in many communities and congregations. Pew's 2020 survey includes a three-page digression discussing that phenomenon, and stating:

> Speaking about Israel from synagogue pulpits is harder now than it used to be, because American congregations are less unified on the subject....
>
> Many of the [two dozen rabbis interviewed by Pew] said their synagogues include more critics of the Israeli government than they did in the past. Asked how they approach the topic in sermons, several rabbis said they choose their words carefully and try not to unintentionally or unnecessarily alienate people in their congregations, which they know contain both staunch supporters and persistent critics of the Israeli government.[41]

This isn't a novel or recent phenomenon: for example, in 2011, an official of the national Jewish Council on Public Affairs noted that "One of the concerns we have—and we hear this over and over again from rabbis and community leaders—people are afraid to discuss Israel."[42]

The brutality of the Hamas attacks shocked most American Jews, who supported Israel's right to defend itself and to try to destroy Hamas. The pro-Hamas activities of some Jewish groups on the far left marked their own isolation from the rest of the community. It became obvious to most American Jews that organizations like JVP were anti-Zionist and anti-Israel. But soon enough, there were many voices suggesting that the war had to end and that the Israeli military activity in Gaza was "excessive" or "disproportionate."

How long will the rise in concern about Israel last? Will the shock of October 7, 2023, lead to significant and lasting changes in the American Jewish community? I believe that in 2024 and beyond we will see the same phenomena we saw after 1948 and after 1973: the wave of support for Israel is genuine, but it crests and the support—and interest and attachment—will then decline again. Without the kinds of actions I'll describe in the next chapter, the longer-term patterns will reassert themselves because they reflect deep, longer-term changes in Israel and in the American Jewish community.

What explains the distancing from Israel, particularly among younger generations of Jews?

To begin with, Israel's own situation has changed greatly—and with that change, many American Jews have come to see it in a different light. Back in 2007, Steven M. Cohen and Ari Kelman put it this way when they tried to explain the distancing from Israel:

> Those born after 1974 draw upon memories and impressions less likely to cast Israel in a positive, let alone heroic light. The First Lebanon War in 1982, the First Intifada, the Second Intifada and the Second Lebanon War are all perceived as far more morally and politically complex than the wars Israel fought between 1948 and 1974, casting Israel in a more troubling light.

> In addition, in the 1950s Israel was widely admired as a plucky, progressive and largely successful social experiment. In the 1970s, it earned favor for withstanding multiple onslaughts from implacable enemies. In contrast, Israel's position over the more recent years has come under steady criticism from a variety of quarters, with the inevitable impact upon American Jews.[43]

This may be seen as a return to the mean (and only moderate) levels of American Jewish support for Zionism and for Israel from the levels to which they rose during the 1930s and 1940s, and then again after the 1967 and 1973 wars. But what of politics? Are American Jews, and especially younger American Jews, distancing themselves from Israel now because of the policies of its right-wing governments—especially the settlements and "the occupation?"

This is logical; most American Jews are left of center while Israel has become a right-of-center country. There's no great mystery here: as Cohen and Kelman put it, "the political left seems more critical of Israel than the political right, and with so many Jews (still) situated on the left, it stands to reason that Jews generally and Jews on the left in particular should feel less connected to Israel."[44]

In its early decades, Israel was ruled by the Labor Party, and American Jews voting for the Democratic Party experienced no cognitive or political dissonance in their support for Israel and its successive governments. The Jews of Israel and of the United States often shared not only East

European origins but a heritage of European socialism. As Naomi Cohen wrote,

> Justifying Jewish nationalism to Americans, Zionists projected their American liberal values onto their ideal Jewish state.... After 1948 the image of Israel as a microcosm of America or the extension of American liberal values took on a pragmatic dimension. Zionists took pride in portraying the Jewish state as the bastion of democracy in the Middle East....
>
> Envisioning Israel as an ideological extension of American liberalism was an obvious reinforcement of both American and American Jewish commitment to the Jewish state.[45]

Cohen then added a logical caveat: that basis for backing Israel "had its weakness too. In the first place, were Israel to deviate from the accepted canons of liberalism, it ran the risk of alienating American Jewish support."

And that is what happened. In 1977, a political upheaval in Israel brought Menachem Begin to power. In the nearly fifty years since, left-of-center prime ministers have been in office for fewer than ten—creating a gap between the politics of American Jews and that of Israelis. And in these years, Israeli politics has been increasingly controversial among American Jewry. Cohen, recalling the decades of accusations of dual loyalty that long faced American Jews, wrote that there is "another and more troublesome threat of dual loyalties: Jewish loyalty to liberalism versus Jewish loyalty to Israel."[46] Jerold Auerbach has hit the same theme:

> For a decade after that momentous week in June [1967], American Jews basked in the glow of their new identification. Israel, for so long a source of American Jewish uneasiness or indifference, suddenly became a tangible symbol of Jewish pride and power, even the new religion of American Jews.
>
> Yet what is remarkable in retrospect is the brevity of the attachment....
>
> The latent quandary of American Jews was rooted in their resolute identification of Judaism with liberalism....
>
> By 1948, for American Jews, liberalism and Judaism were ideologically indistinguishable.[47]

The "latent quandary" that Auerbach mentioned then appeared, and the risks that Cohen raised became reality, when Israel was led for decades by Menachem Begin, Yitzhak Shamir, Ariel Sharon, Ehud Olmert, and Benjamin Netanyahu, and especially when those men quarreled with Democratic presidents. Israeli politics was changing, in good part in reaction to Palestinian terrorism in the intifadas. The terrorism and the Palestinian refusal under Arafat and Abbas to negotiate seriously for peace fatally undermined the "peace camp" and the entire Left in Israel. Those events did not have a similar impact on American Jews. There were few or no changes in voting patterns, nor in the levels of support for policies calling for creation of a Palestinian state.

This is likely to happen again now, in the years after the barbaric attacks of October 7, 2023. As usual, there is greater solidarity and an acceptance that Israeli must defend itself at first, but those thoughts and emotions do not last. The impact of that attack was much deeper in Israel than in the United States. While the US government immediately began to call for negotiations over a two-state solution, Israelis moved to the "right" in thinking that creation of a Palestinian state was now impossible to risk. Two months after the attack, Israel's president, Isaac Herzog, a former leader of the Labor Party, raised his voice:

> Joining the ranks of Israeli officials pushing back against US rhetoric regarding the establishment of a Palestinian state, President Isaac Herzog called on Thursday for the postponement of talks of a two-state solution when the country's pain from Hamas's October 7 onslaught is still fresh.
>
> "What I want to urge is against just saying 'two-state solution'. Why? Because there is an emotional chapter here that must be dealt with. My nation is bereaving. My nation is in trauma," Herzog said in an interview with The Associated Press.
>
> "In order to get back to the idea of dividing the land, of negotiating peace or talking to the Palestinians, etc., one has to deal first and foremost with the emotional trauma that we are going through and the need and demand for a full sense of security for all people," he said.[48]

Will American Jews, and especially younger Jews, fully embrace the Israeli view or that of the United States government? History suggests that the familiar patterns will reassert themselves, with distance growing again between Americans who want to see "peace" in the Middle East and Israelis who take a much tougher stance about what real peace would require. October 7 may lead Americans to strengthen their commitment to seek an end to violence and a "solution" to the Israeli–Palestinian conflict through negotiations over a Palestinian state. For most Israelis, with the lives of their children on the line, that will look like an experiment that is simply too dangerous.

The gap between American Jewish and Israeli perceptions of reality may reflect much more than unhappiness with Israeli election results or even the reaction to October 7. It may reflect the very different life experiences and history of each group. Daniel Gordis has argued that "The United States and Israel were created for entirely different purposes, and as a result, they are fundamentally different experiments in how to enable humans to flourish."[49]

Many American Jews wince at Israel's constant use of force and dislike the need to defend it week after week. They denounce restrictions on non-Orthodox worship that most Israeli Jews find to be second-tier issues at most. They cannot support restrictions on Palestinian movement in the West Bank and into Israel that critics of Israel call apartheid. They regret the divisions on the left that the issue of Israel often creates and the criticism from places they have long admired—the *New York Times*, Human Rights Watch, and Amnesty International, for example. They do not live with the threats to their safety and lives like Israelis. It is an obvious principle to American Jews that all people should be treated alike, while most Israelis would find it simple madness to apply that principle to Israelis and Palestinians. Americans on the left increasingly see the conflict with the Palestinians as a human rights issue, Gordis noted, while "for Israelis, even Israelis on the political left, it is first and foremost about security and survival." That is even truer now than when Gordis wrote it in 2019. He concluded that "The world's two largest Jewish communities are therefore divided by radically different instincts about universalism versus particularism as well as by their opposing attitudes toward Jews' involvement in the messiness of history."[50]

Some of that "messiness" is the result of two millennia without a state of their own. In Israel, Jews have been forced to make decisions that American Jews have been able to escape not only by living in America but by being a very small minority within it. In Israel, the Jewish army, the Jewish secret police, and the Jewish spy agency have faced (and with the Iranian nuclear program, still face) violent efforts to eliminate the Jewish state—and every day, they engage in activities American Jews need not undertake themselves as American citizens and may instead comfortably protest. As Yossi Shain put it, "the hope that a state, which must always operate under *raison d'état*, might successfully operate by universal and non-territorial principles was doomed to failure—especially in the jungle that is the Middle East."[51] Robert Kagan famously once wrote that "on major strategic and international questions today, Americans are from Mars and Europeans are from Venus."[52] Whether after Russia's war on Ukraine this aphorism remains accurate today with regard to Europe may be unclear, but it often seems that American Jews are from Venus while Israelis are from Mars—not least when dealing with the issue of Palestinian nationalism and the "peace process."

A useful example of the gap between American Jews and Israelis is the Iran nuclear negotiations conducted by the Biden administration in 2021 and 2022. A 2022 poll found that 68 percent of American Jews supported reentering the nuclear agreement, the JCPOA, and 40 percent of them did so "strongly."[53] Only among the Orthodox and among Jewish Republicans did support fall to a minority. Yet in Israel, there was a left-to-right consensus against the JCPOA, led by the then-Prime Minister Yair Lapid. Like his predecessor Netanyahu in 2015, Lapid argued strongly against the agreement—and as in 2015, so in 2022: American Jews paid no attention. Meanwhile, a clear majority of Israeli Jews not only opposed the JCPOA but favored a strike on Iran to stop its nuclear program.[54] No doubt American Jews, mostly Democrats, were in part supporting the views of the presidents for whom they had voted, Obama and Biden, against Republican critics of the JCPOA. But the indifference to Israeli views on this issue, which a clear majority of Israeli Jews view as existential, is very striking whatever its explanation—as is the gap between Israeli and American Jews on the "peace process."

DISTANCING FROM JEWISH LIFE

For some American Jews, left–right politics may well underlie their distancing from an Israel that has had a right-of-center majority for decades. This is a simple and obvious explanation that no doubt works in some cases, but it's unpersuasive as a broad explanation. The distancing goes beyond politics and reflects what I would call a lack of sympathy and of imagination: too many American Jews are unable or unwilling to empathize with Israelis caught in a different reality. This is quite different from saying that left-of-center American Jews are simply offended and alienated by right-of-center Israeli government policies. In their study, Cohen and Kelman found that

> political identity, for the general population, has little bearing upon feelings of warmth toward or alienation from Israel. Whatever conclusion one may draw from the actions of political elites, or the writing of intellectual figures, left-of-center political identity (seeing oneself as liberal and a Democrat) in the general population exerts seemingly little influence on the level of attachment to Israel.[55]

Cohen and Kelman found that distancing from Israel is not grounded in left–right politics: "Contrary to widely held beliefs, left-liberal political identity is *not* primarily responsible for driving down the Israel attachment scores among the non-Orthodox.... The results point to no clear impact of political leanings on Israel attachment, contrary to the widely held view that left-liberal ideology is especially incompatible with warmth toward Israel."[56]

If not grounded in political differences, where does the lack of empathy with Israel's challenges come from? Why should any Jew not line up instinctively with other Jews facing murderous attacks—facing the desires of Iran and terrorist groups like Hezbollah and Hamas to destroy the society in which those Jews live? Why is the immediate and the lasting reaction not strong solidarity? Why do more American Jews under thirty today turn away or hotly criticize Israel more frequently, when those who were thirty years old ten to twenty, or thirty to forty, years ago did not do so?

As we've seen, a partial explanation is time: the experience of the 1967 and 1973 wars and of the intifadas (the first starting in 1987 and the second in 2001) is a powerful memory for older Jews, but not for those born in 1990s or 2000s. But like left-of-center politics, the passage of time is not a full explanation for the lack of solidarity and empathy.

Here we must turn to another source of the distancing, particularly among younger generations of Jews: some of the apparent effects of intermarriage. Jack Wertheimer noted the numbers: "intermarriage is strongly related to attachment to Israel: 26% of Jews very attached to Israel are intermarried versus more than twice as many (66%) among Jews who claim no attachment to Israel."[57] In a study of the San Francisco Bay area in 2018, Steven M. Cohen found that individuals raised by one (rather than two) Jewish parents were almost three times as likely to say they were not at all attached to Israel.[58]

We noted previously Cohen and Kelman's analysis that "intermarriage flows from and helps produce a more personalized rather than collective view of being Jewish.... Intermarriage represents and advances more open and fluid group boundaries along with a commensurate drop in Jewish tribalism, collective Jewish identity, and Jewish Peoplehood."[59]

It is not politics, then, that best explains the distancing from Israel among younger American Jews (though no doubt it plays a role); nor is it intermarriage per se. *Distancing from Israel instead reflects a more fundamental distancing from the American Jewish community and all aspects of Jewish life.*

As Jack Wertheimer put it, "Simply stated, American Jews who have the most distant or tenuous connection to Israel also are the least involved in *all* aspects of Jewish life. No matter how you cut it, those Jews who are more attached to Israel are also more engaged with being Jewish."[60] David L. Graizbord echoed this sentiment in his book about young American Jews: "Israel attachment is strongest where affiliation to Jewish community is strongest."[61] Non-Orthodox Jews who say they are not at all attached to Israel are far less likely, for example, to have attended a seder, to belong to a synagogue, or to donate to any Jewish charities. And as Wertheimer pointed out, the Pew 2020 survey found that 85 percent of American Jews who said they were very attached to Israel also felt "a great deal of belonging to the Jewish people" while only 11 percent of those not at all attached to Israel felt that way. And 73 percent of those who felt being Jewish was very important to them also felt very attached to Israel, while only 13 percent of those who do not feel attached to Israel felt that way. When it comes to helping fellow Jews in need around the world, 53 percent of those very attached to Israel feel "a great deal of responsibility," while only 8 percent of those not attached to Israel feel that way.[62]

So what we are seeing is, as Wertheimer sums it up, that "those who feel least connected to Israel *in the aggregate* also do not identify strongly with Jewish collective needs."

The problem here isn't how Israel behaves in the West Bank, and as Wertheimer puts it, "there is no reason to assume that major changes in Israeli policies toward the Palestinians will in themselves rekindle what once was a near universal American Jewish love affair with Israel." *Feelings about Israel are the effect, not the cause, of the individual's relationship to the Jewish community*—or as Wertheimer says, "Distance from Israel, then, is a symptom of indifference to the Jewish present and future."[63]

In *The Israeli Century*, Yossi Shain wonders whether "liberal American Jewry" and today's Israel can "coexist peacefully" and asks "If these two factions are drifting apart, is it due to Israel's behavior or the reality of Jewish life in America?"[64] The answer is the latter: the problem is not that a striking proportion of American Jews don't like Israel's policies in the West Bank or even that they don't feel very attached to Israel because that in itself is effect not cause. *The underlying problem is that a striking proportion of American Jews have very weak feelings about being part of the Jewish people in any way at all.*

In *The New Zionists*, David L. Graizbord interviewed thirty-five young American Jews who identified as Zionist or pro-Israel. His goal was to understand their views: How did they reach the understandings they had, and what exactly did they think? These young people had complex and sometimes inconsistent views, but Israel was at the heart of their Jewish identity—in fact, a central part and a key building block. Graizbord argued in the book that "the American Judaism to which they are the latest adult heirs has not fully satisfied their Jewish ethnic attachments and their concomitant search for a natural, unapologetic Jewish identity that does not hinge on religious practice and on universalist politics alone. Israel, by contrast, provides an attractive alternative for achieving such an identity."[65]

One could never write a line like that about Israelis, who have not only religion but also nationality retaining their membership in the Jewish people. But Graizbord argues that young American Jews today often lack both the religious commitments of previous generations of American Jews as well as the ethnic community and commitment that earlier American Jews experienced. As he wrote,

> many of these individuals do not feel Jewish not because of their lack of religious faith per se, but because unlike their grandparents and great-grandparents they did not grow up in predominantly Jewish environments anchored in Jewish collectivity, memory, languages, laws, and customs—that is, environments where social experience ratified a strong feeling of belonging to the Jewish people irrespective of theological (un)belief, spiritual and ritual practice, and political stances.[66]

The gap in their relationship with Jewish peoplehood is filled by Israel:

> Their strong attachment to Israel is an attempt to grapple with and stitch together the two core elements [religious observance and ethnicity] of the now-undone ethnoreligious package of Jewish civilization in a way that is personally

> meaningful yet transcends the purely personal by linking it firmly to the national.[67]

As I've argued, for most American Jews, their Jewish identity came from their "culture" or "ethnicity" while America officially classified them by religion. But that ethnicity has largely faded and the great majority of American Jews do not practice the Jewish religion. Is there an alternative basis for Jewish identity? "Zionism is one solution to this problem," David Graizbord found. He concluded that "Being a Zionist for my subjects is also to adopt a model of Jewishness that breaks the mold of religiosity that still largely underwrites American Jewish culture."[68]

These feelings do not emerge out of whole cloth, and Graizbord warns that they require some base in a familial or community feeling of solidarity with other Jews. In the next chapter, we will discuss how that feeling might be built more strongly in the United States.

The new relationship between American Jews and Israel is truly symbiotic, with each capable of strengthening the other at many levels. The role of American Jews in financial support for Israel is diminished but not ended, given the strains on its economy resulting from rising military expenditures. And American Jewish political support for Israel remains an important factor in both political parties. But the balance is shifting. Natan Sharansky and Gil Troy proposed a full year in Israel for American teens, using the success of Birthright as a jumping off point:

> As American Jews reimagine Israel's role in their children's lives, Israel will have to do some

> reimagining of its own. Israel's leaders initially hesitated to finance Birthright. Many wondered: Why should Israeli taxpayers bring "rich" Americans to Israel? Ultimately, subsidizing Birthright became the first phase of a massive paradigm shift in the relationship between Israel and the Diaspora. As American Jews continued contributing to Israel, Israel gave them something back: a material shift in the ways that young people understood their relationship to Israel and to their Jewish identity.[69]

The point is fundamental. It is impossible to imagine a healthy, thriving, growing American Jewish community that is distant from Israel—any more than one can imagine a Jewish community in Australia or France or Mexico being vibrant while distant from the Jewish state. And the statistics already show this: involvement with Israel, emotionally and physically (through actions such as visits there), is part of Jewish identity in America. Those with the weakest Jewish identity, with the weakest sense of peoplehood and of connection to and concern about the community's wellbeing and its future, have the weakest ties to Israel. For that great majority of American Jews who are not religiously observant, and for whom the beliefs and practices of Judaism is not at the center of their lives, to be distant from Israel, to have no concern about or involvement with the Jewish state, is to be distant from the Jewish people—whether in Israel, around the world, or here at home. As Brandeis put it a century ago, "To be good Americans, we must be better Jews, and to be better Jews, we must become Zionists."

Rabbi Ammiel Hirsch of the (Reform) Stephen Wise Free Synagogue was blunt when I interviewed him in 2022:

> Israel now plays and will increasingly play a dominant role in setting the agenda for world Jewry. It's why we can't distance from Israel. Not because of Israel; Israel will do fine unless you envision some catastrophic scenario. Israel is getting stronger. We can't marginalize from Israel for our own sake because we will then marginalize from the world Jewish experience. And it will make it even more difficult to create and sustain Jewish continuity.[70]

The State of Israel has become the center of world Jewish life. It is a vibrant society growing faster than any diaspora Jewish community; as Shmuel Rosner has noted, "gone are the days of demographic apprehension" or concern about *yordim* who leave for Palo Alto or for Europe. The birth rate alone is another source of Israeli strength, especially when compared to that of American Jews.[71]

Rabbi Elliot Cosgrove of the (Conservative) Park Avenue Synagogue told his congregation in early 2022 that "None of us chose to live in this miraculous era of a sovereign Jewish state, when—after thousands of years of exile—Jews have the right to national self-determination, but we do. For me that means that to be Jewish today is to be actively engaged with Israel."[72]

Rabbi Cosgrove is right; the data show that active engagement with Israel is part of Jewish identity—for those Jews to whom Jewish identity and Jewish peoplehood matter.

It is here that we may return to Pew's measures of the Jewish population and its JBRs and JNRs. What we see in those Jews who are disengaged from Israel and from Judaism is that they are drifting away from this collective known as the Jewish people. Living in a country that is 97 or 98 percent non-Jewish, in an open society where assimilation out of any meaningful sense of Jewish identity is easily possible, and at a time when as we have seen 72 percent of non-Orthodox Jews married in the previous decade, instilling in the next generation a sense of peoplehood is difficult. For that great majority of American Jews who do not practice Judaism in any meaningful way, it requires significant efforts on their part, on the part of the Jewish community as a whole, and on the part of the State of Israel.

What efforts will work? What helps build Jewish identity, continuity, peoplehood?

Chapter Five

WHAT IS TO BE DONE?

Nearly forty years ago, Calvin Goldscheider posed the question the American Jewish community faces today: "The secularization of Judaism and Jews has long been observed in America. The critical question is whether alternative sources of group cohesion have emerged as religious centrality has declined."[1] What are the alternative sources?

Actually, we know what works.

And it is more important than ever to focus our efforts on what works because American Jews may no longer have the luxury of living in a country where there is no significant anti-Semitism and where the official ties with Israel are strong and unbreakable.

The intimate alliance of the United States and Israel has been a sometime thing, as the previous chapters have shown. During Israel's three-quarters of a century of existence, there was no close relationship for the first two decades. Since then, there have been years when long and deep arguments about policy—the fundamental issues of establishment of a Palestinian state and more recently policy toward Iran and its nuclear program—marked bilateral relations and created significant distance. But even in those years, US military aid was very large and the United States—with some significant exceptions—defended Israel in international organizations. Those pro-Israel policies reflected public opinion, and especially two of the strongest bases of support for Israel in decades past, the Democratic Party and the evangelical movement.

But today statistics show that younger Democrats and younger evangelicals simply lack the enthusiasm for Israel of their parents' and grandparents' generations. With support clearly fraying in both those places, it cannot simply be assumed that the closeness of the US–Israel relationship is permanent. It will need defending, especially by a very active and committed American Jewish community whose ties to Israel are close and that is committed to Zionism and a close bond between the United States and the Jewish State. Will that commitment exist, and will it be strong enough to fend off both old and new critics?

As we've seen, triumphalism about the vitality and growth of the American Jewish community is misplaced. By any meaningful definition, the number of Americans who consider themselves part of the Jewish people, whose identity can be measured not by answering polls but in the way they live their lives and raise their children, is not growing. Here, the role of Israel can be critical in engaging young Jews and reminding them (or sometimes showing them for the first time) that they are part of the Jewish people. Israel can be central in cementing their Jewish identity and strengthening the core of the American Jewish community.

What works to achieve those goals?

KEY INSTITUTIONS AND IMMERSIVE ENVIRONMENTS

There are concrete steps that can be taken by parents, by the organized Jewish community, and by the State of Israel to strengthen those "alternative sources of group cohesion"—to deepen the sense of Jewish identity and group cohesion of young American Jews and strengthen their ties to the Jewish people and to the Jewish state. Those steps divide into three ways of creating an immersive Jewish environment: *Jewish education, Jewish camping, and time in Israel.*

This triad does not include synagogues—whose vital role in American Jewish life can certainly suggest that my focus on Israel, education, and camping should be widened. Rabbi Ammiel Hirsch had his own triad:

> I think there are three main Jewish institutions in America that are responsible for the bulk of Jewish continuity, not counting the Orthodox. They are Jewish schools, summer camps, and synagogues. But because of the all-embracing nature of the synagogue, the cradle-to-grave dimension of it, because small numbers go to Jewish day schools, and because of the limited amount of time that most spend in camp, the synagogue is the center of Jewish life and continuity.... In my view, the synagogue is the central institution of American Jewish life. There's no replacement for the synagogue in terms of institutions that are able to create and sustain Jewish identity over a lifetime.[2]

When Jack Wertheimer asked "How to Save American Jews" in *Commentary* magazine in 1996, he provided his own broad answer:

> The key institutions requiring support are synagogues, day schools, summer camps, youth groups, campus programs, and religious and cultural institutions of higher learning—that is to say, institutions which emphasize Jewish particularism and foster strong identification with the group. These settings for natural and intense social interaction also teach the lesson that there is a distinctive Jewish worldview, and that being Jewish means, to some degree, being different.[3]

Wertheimer was particularly concerned about efforts to reach out to the unaffiliated in ways that could weaken the institutions more affiliated Jews need to be able live Jewish lives—weaken the core, that is, to attract the periphery. And as he noted then, "religious commitment is the strongest predictor of every other form of Jewish engagement."[4]

Quite so—but what of the large majority of American Jews who are raised without that religious commitment? For them, Goldscheider's "alternative sources" are key. I have no doubt about the central role of religious Jews who are faithful to traditional Judaism, nor about that of the synagogue. My argument is different: for the very large majority of American Jews who are neither Orthodox nor religiously committed Conservative or Reform Jews, synagogue life is minimal or absent, especially after their children's *b'nei mitzvah*. And with many valuable exceptions, synagogue-based supplemental education ("Hebrew school") is failing to cement the bonds of peoplehood and Jewish identity for Jewish youth. To me, it seems that active participation in synagogue life is far more likely to be the *effect*, rather than the *cause*, of Jewish identity for non-Orthodox Jews in America.

So, let's focus here on what Wertheimer called the "settings for natural and intense social interaction" among young Jews: building Jewish identities for those whose personal and family religious commitment did not (or did not sufficiently) do so. And let's divide those "settings" into two parts: those in America and those in Israel.

A. JEWISH EDUCATION

Jewish Education in America

In the 1950s and early 1960s, like my non-Orthodox Jewish neighbors, I attended what was called "Hebrew school." This meant classes two or three times a week (in the late afternoon and on Sunday morning) at the synagogue to which my family belonged. This was standard for American Jews who did not attend Jewish day schools, which is to say the great majority of Jewish children—except those getting no Jewish education at all. But those who attended "Hebrew school" got almost no Jewish education as well. Despite the name, Hebrew was not taught in any systematic fashion, nor was anything else. This form of supplemental education for Jewish children failed then and has largely continued failing, yet it remains in place.

Nor has there been any great success in expanding day school education much beyond the Orthodox, or in any widespread program teaching Hebrew.

Mark Charendoff, president of the Maimonides Fund, has described the situation best.

> Today, Jews in America are at the top of the list of religious groups regarding educational attainment.
>
> So how is it that the freest, wealthiest, and, secularly, the most educated Jewish community in history is also, my many measures, the most Jewishly illiterate?
>
> We have all but given up on teaching Hebrew, making American Jew is a historical anomaly—a Jewish community without a distinct language. Jewish day schools, though often excellent, have failed to significantly increase their market share outside the Orthodox community, which represented just 9% of American Jews in 2020. Congregational schools are in desperate need of reengineering: The current generation of parents has no way to explain to their children why they're sending them there—other than a dispiriting, "If I had to go, you have to go."...
>
> Why do we lack the will and imagination to make high-quality Jewish day-school education universal and affordable? Is there any scenario in which the American Jewish community

> continues to thrive, to be a hub of cultural creativity, without a grounding in what this people is all about?[5]

Charendoff's view is not idiosyncratic and few would argue fundamentally with his points. There are efforts around the country to remedy these problems, and *if* there are not a thousand points of light, there are scores of them.

Supplementary school after B'nei Mitzvah

A good and hopeful example is Kehillah High (KH), a program in Houston. Every community is different, and I do not discuss KH because it is adaptable to every Jewish community no matter how small or great its size. Danielle Alexander, who started KH and has led it for a decade, explained the idea to me. KH is a supplemental Jewish education program for students in grades eight to twelve, which is to say for post–b'nei mitzvah kids. They meet on Wednesday nights for two hours, rotating the location among the synagogues who participate in the program. As Alexander said:

> There aren't as many programs like the KH still around the country as they were a few years ago. It takes a lot for synagogues to say we are going to forgo our post–b'nei mitzvah programming and combine and work better together. It's hard because synagogues are doing whatever they can to maintain membership of those families post–b'nei mitzvah. There is a reason [the desire to have children bar or bat mitzvahed] why from kindergarten through seventh grade they have

> to be a member of the synagogue, but what is the motivation after their kids have a bar or bat mitzvah? So I have a really strong relationship with the synagogues that founded KH. It is a program of two Conservative and one Reform synagogues. We rotate every trimester to one of the founding congregations as our host space. It is their post–b'nei mitzvah program in the greater Houston area, and it's also open to any other family, affiliated with a synagogue or not, that wants to join. KH allows you to say to a Jewish friend, 'come join me on Wednesday nights and continue your Jewish learning.' It doesn't matter how you identify, what denomination you are, if you belong somewhere, if you don't belong somewhere, but we can all come and learn and be part of the same community.[6]

KH works in part because it is based on cooperation with synagogues and with other Jewish organizations, such as the B'nai B'rith Youth Organization (BBYO) and the Jewish Community Center. As a simple example, they coordinate calendars so that one organization's events do not conflict with another's. The program consists of dinner, a grade-specific class, and then electives. The electives are "really interest based," said Alexander, "anything that both our students and our teachers are interested in and can dream up, working in partnership with all different organizations in our community." In addition, there are trips at winter break and special Shabbat activities—plus a three-week trip to Israel every other year for the oldest grades. Alexander adds that "the program itself is highly subsidized and we will offer scholarships to any family who needs it."[7]

The basic ideas here are simple enough: synagogue supplemental education is failing students, and broader cooperation among synagogues and other Jewish organizations will work better. "Better" in this context means programming that is better taught and of greater interest to the children, and can gather together children from a wider segment of the community than any one synagogue can achieve. It can group together children whose families belong to participating synagogues and whose families belong to none. And those evenings, Shabbats, trips, and visits to Israel (whose three weeks are twice as long as Birthright visits) can help create a sense of community.

If this all seems logical, it is—yet as Alexander noted, there may be fewer such efforts now than a few years ago. Houston is unique, but every Jewish community is unique. In much smaller Jewish communities (than Houston's estimated 50,000 Jews), this kind of cooperation is even more important to gather enough children together (KH gathers on the order of 160) to make electives and travel practical. In much larger communities, one can envision such programs being established by synagogues in a particular neighborhood or suburb. To make a Hebrew school the exclusive property of each synagogue is (though there are of course wonderful exceptions), as it has been for decades, a formula for failure. Not only is the quality of education often mediocre, but the use of resources is foolish. It is simply not possible that hundreds of Reform and Conservative synagogues will all, each separately, be able to develop and financially sustain first-rate programming with first-rate educators.

What's remarkable to me is how long that failing model has nevertheless survived.

Teaching Hebrew

I noted that Hebrew schools did not teach much Hebrew. As Charendoff said, "We have all but given up on teaching Hebrew, making American Jews a historical anomaly—a Jewish community without a distinct language."[8] Daniel Gordis has argued that this linguistic gap has larger implications: "Given the centrality of Hebrew to the Zionists' sense of accomplishment, the abandonment of Hebrew in the United States was bound to create a rift, a sense of otherness. And on a much more utilitarian level, American Jews' decision not to learn Hebrew means that they have access to a very thin slice of Israeli culture."[9]

Some knowledge of Hebrew is essential for Jews for religious purposes as well as for deepening their understanding of and relationship with Israel. When I spoke with him in 2022, John Ruskay reminded me that earlier in his career he had been principal of the Hebrew School at the Society for the Advancement of Judaism (SAJ) in New York City. That school welcomes children from kindergarten through eighth grade—in other words, until their bar or bat mitzvah. Ruskay explained: "I would say my best job was principal of a Hebrew school.... And you know why? Because forty years later, kids would come up and say, 'you changed my life'.... We came to the view that the essential skill for participating in Jewish life is actually being able to read Hebrew."[10] To read the prayer book and the Passover Haggadah requires Hebrew reading skills—even without understanding all the words—and Ruskay said that took only six to eight weeks. "At the Hebrew school, we said reading is obligatory. That's a skill you need to participate in Jewish life." And that is the beginning, of course: then comes understanding the language and being able to speak it.

Hebrew can be taught in supplementary schools, though the intensity needed is usually absent—a point we will return to in a moment. But it can also be taught in summer camp and immersion programs. A 2021 analysis by Alex Pomson and Vardit Ringvald for Rosov Consulting looked at summer programs teaching children Hebrew at Conservative movement day camps and found encouraging results. A seven-year study of twelve day camp Hebrew immersion programs called Kayitz Kef ("Summer of fun") found real results. The Hebrew immersion campers "exhibit significantly greater gains in their ability to communicate in Hebrew and their parents perceive them to feel more positively about the language."[11] And quite unsurprisingly, learning Hebrew opens new doors to Israel. The parents of children in the Hebrew immersion program "perceive their child to be connected to Israel and Israelis, to be communicating in Hebrew, and to feel positive about the language" much more than parents whose children at the camps did not participate.

> These differences are consistent across an extensive set of measures: the range of meanings their children attribute to Israel; the character traits their children ascribe to Israelis; their child's interest in Israel and Israelis; and the strength of their emotional connection to the country. In all of these respects, Hebrew

> immersion campers' attitudes are perceived to be significantly more positive than those of the other campers. (This is even more striking considering that the other Ramah campers' levels of positive responses across all these measures are already extremely high.)[12]

Because most American Jewish children do not attend Jewish day schools and do not learn much Hebrew in their synagogues' supplemental or Hebrew schools, there's a good argument for taking the teaching of Hebrew out of those schools entirely, as Saul Rosenberg proposed in 2022.[13] Noting that except for those in day schools, Jewish students did not learn Hebrew "accurately, let alone fluently," he asked why. The reasons are logical: many Hebrew schools do not even try; there's no real commitment to teaching Hebrew. And Hebrew school meets only once or twice a week and skips the summer. "But language learning needs *little and often*. Otherwise, students forget part of what they learn from one week to the next. They forget much of the rest over the long summer." And there's little accountability (grades, homework, etc.) and little outside reinforcement. "The children live in a culture in which secular studies matter, but Jewish culture and observance" matter much less.[14]

Rosenberg's proposal is to "Take Hebrew reading out of the Hebrew-school curriculum once and for all." Synagogue Hebrew schools would "focus elsewhere in the universe of Jewish and Israeli culture" and instead synagogues could

> contract with experienced reading tutors and add an hour of one-on-one tutoring to the

> first semester of Hebrew school, during which children will learn to read Hebrew with what I call 'slow fluency.' It's a commitment, but only for the first semester, when the children are not yet overburdened with extracurriculars. If parents are told their children may otherwise never learn to read, many will bite.[15]

But Rosenberg says that this new reading skill won't last when the lessons stop.

> If it is to last, Hebrew schools must get students to continue practicing Hebrew all the way to their bar and bat mitzvah at least. *That* is the challenge: getting students to the point where they read Hebrew fluently enough that they develop a kind of muscle memory, always available to them. Perhaps that level of fluency will keep some engaged. For the others, it will be there for them whenever they step into a synagogue or if they come back to Judaism after a long gap.[16]

Why isn't that being done? Rosenberg suggests that learning a language is disciplined rote learning and there's a bias against that sort of pedagogy, partly for fear of making students unhappy—especially when there are so many other things the student can happily do in those hours.

There are of course many other possible approaches: college and high school courses, online courses, and Hebrew language charter schools are three examples. The organization called Hebrew Public runs five (publicly funded) Hebrew language charter schools with 3,800 students and assists six other affiliated schools. But at the college level, enrollment in Hebrew language courses has been dropping for over a decade.[17]

From two critical perspectives, that of reading and understanding Jewish religious texts and that of engaging more deeply with Israel, Hebrew is central. The failure of American (non-Orthodox) Jews to learn Hebrew is now a long tradition, dating at least to the passing of immigrant generations who often learned it in Europe. Attendance at day schools is one solution, but not one that will work for most Jewish children. Rosenberg's suggestion is that Hebrew schools actually try to teach reading Hebrew year after year (or hire people who will), long enough for it to stick even if learning stops at age thirteen, especially considering the quality of much other Hebrew school education. There would be lifelong benefits for the child and a better launching point if and when that individual—in adolescence, college, or later in life—decides to try to master the language.

In the Pew 2013 survey, even though about half of American Jews say they know the Hebrew alphabet, only 13 percent "say they understand most or all of the words when they read Hebrew."[18] If one subtracts Israeli immigrants to the United States and many Orthodox Jews from that number, among the non-Orthodox, knowledge of Hebrew is at a very low level. There are today so many ways of teaching foreign languages at all age levels that Hebrew illiteracy is a striking attribute of American Jews. And as with other such problems (as we will see in a moment) what is required is a broad commitment by American Jews—and American Jewish leaders and organizations—to make learning Hebrew a priority rather than a not-very-important luxury. The Jewish people have a language, one that unites Jews from every place on earth and is spoken in the only Jewish state. Illiteracy in that language is a profound illness for the wealthy and educated American Jewish community.

Day schools

Jewish day schools provide far greater knowledge of Hebrew and of Judaism, and they offer a greater sense of belonging to a community and a people than any form of supplemental schooling can possibly achieve. Jack Wertheimer and Alex Pomson, in their 2022 book *Inside Jewish Day Schools*, made the case for their importance:

> Day schools possess the special potential to nurture young people with the ability to contribute to Jewish culture; they cultivate Jewish cultural virtuosos. Compared with every other educational institution to which Jewish children have access, Jewish day schools are unusual in the amount of time they have at their disposal and, crucially, the extent to which that time forms part of a rhythmic cycle.[19]

Pomson and Wertheimer emphasize day schools' "powerful community-building dimension.... [It is] a community based on shared values where there is a powerful and palpable sense of being part of the Jewish collective." And that community can, in nondenominational community schools, build a community that also crosses denominational lines: the nine schools they studied in depth "provide some evidence that day schools may temper some of the widespread polarization in the contemporary American Jewish community. Dozens of community day schools with a strong pluralistic orientation work to avoid privileging one understanding of Judaism over another. They nurture a culture of mutual appreciation and respect."[20]

Moreover, day schools are "hubs for extensive social and interpersonal networks [whose] thickening of social relationships is an important contribution to the Jewish lives of young people in their communities."[21] But day schools must offer still more: "without promising an education that comes close to matching or exceeding the academic quality of local independent and public schools, it is hard to see how the schools would attract interest beyond the youngest grades."[22]

As the Strategic Plan of the Samis Foundation in Seattle put it:

> Research continues to support Jewish day school education as integral for preserving and incubating Jewish life. Day schools are the most intensive and immersive educational experience given the sheer number of hours students spend in school, and likewise, the deepest and most worthwhile investment in Jewish continuity. A day school education provides Jewish children a foundation for their Judaism, giving them crucial knowledge about their culture and religion. Students learn Jewish values, interact with other Jewish children, strengthen their Jewish identity and connections to Israel, all while receiving an excellent secular education.[23]

There are many models of day schools, but the best way to understand them is a division into ultra-Orthodox or Haredi schools and yeshivas; Modern Orthodox schools; and non-denominational or community schools and those linked to the Reform or Conservative movements.

The great obstacles to increasing the percentage of young Jews who get a full day school education are cost and perhaps what might be called ideology. By the latter I mean a collection of parental concerns: that the Jewish education will crowd out secular education, especially in STEM and STEAM subjects; that their child will be "ghettoized" and somehow less prepared to thrive in the wider society he or she will soon meet in universities and the world of work; that the child will lose out in the struggle for worldly success and at least partial assimilation into American society. It can be argued that the "ghettoization" issues, which are really about the ability to assimilate into and succeed in American society, are of far less importance nowadays than they were to previous generations of American Jews who were immigrants or the children (perhaps even the grandchildren) of immigrants. The challenge for Jewish parents today is not whether their children can assimilate successfully but whether they will assimilate so far that they will lose their Jewish identity entirely. Nevertheless, questions of school quality and whether Jewish schools adequately handle nonreligious curricula certainly remain.

There are many ways to approach all these ideological and financial issues. In Miami, for example, with its burgeoning Jewish population, the new Jewish Leadership Academy (JLA) accepted its first students in the 2023–2024 school year as an avowedly elite modern Orthodox day school that says, "the JLA student body will consist of young Jewish men and women from diverse religious and socio-economic backgrounds who demonstrate exceptional academic ability."[24]

Why is such a school needed? Rabbi Gil Perl, the founding head of school at JLA, explained that

> the need here in Miami was for a school that really could address the needs of higher-achieving kids. The quality of Jewish education post fifth grade was not up to the standards even of what you can find in New York. And so you just have this exodus of kids, particularly after the fifth grade, into the elite private schools down here. And those schools, they're just filled with Jewish kids.[25]

JLA is not a yeshiva, but it is certainly not pluralistic; it is Orthodox and accepts only students viewed as Jewish in accordance with Jewish law. JLA's beautiful campus and dedication to secular as well as Jewish learning is meant to attract families that insist on both and do not want to see less attention paid to the secular curriculum. They may not be Orthodox Jews or belong to Orthodox synagogues themselves, but they may see Orthodoxy as a more authentic version of Judaism or want their children to get an Orthodox education as well as excellent secular schooling. Rabbi Perl noted that "we are welcoming of every family irrespective of their observance." He described the plans to me this way:

> We're not a yeshiva. We're only teaching two periods of Judaic studies a day. We are supplementing it, though, with a month in Israel. We

> are spending the first month of school, eighth grade through twelfth grade, in Israel every year.... The families that we're looking for are not interested in a half day of Judaic studies and honestly, we couldn't give them the same secular experience that they would be getting in these other schools if we were taking up more of the day of Judaics.... I think many of these families want their kids to be pro-Israel, to be in an environment where they know other Jewish kids.... They want them to get into a good college. They want them to get a great education to succeed in life. And I don't think they've been convinced by our day schools yet that that is a possibility for them.[26]

But some of the political and ideological developments in good public schools and elite private schools have pushed Jewish parents to think again about Jewish day schools, to escape "woke" approaches and assignments that sometimes edge into anti-Israel or anti-Semitic positions. Jewish day schools, like many other non-public schools, were far more likely to be open during the COVID pandemic, when so many public school systems were closed. And because of their size and approach, they can also try offer a less bureaucratic handling of the student body, suggesting to parents that they care about the child's emotional development and happiness as well as his or her Jewish identity.

JLA is one approach to day school education: reach for the top, the very best students. Such an approach requires a large enough Jewish community to make this feasible—

to have a population of Jewish students who meet those requirements. That's true of Miami today (or so the organizers of JLA believe), and presumably of cities like New York, Los Angeles, and perhaps Boston or Chicago. But it cannot be a model that replaces community Jewish schools in smaller communities, nor will that model attract all families—for example, those who might want all their children in the same school regardless of their intellectual gifts or might believe that JLA's elitism is a mistake rather than an attraction.

Moreover, unaffiliated community schools, by definition, will not be strictly Orthodox, itself an attraction for some parents. There will be many Jewish parents who might consider a Jewish day school but are not Orthodox and do not want to send their children to a strictly Orthodox school. The Leffell School in Westchester County, New York, is an example: as Rabbi Harry Pell, Associate Head of School, told me, "the school does not have a formal affiliation. We define ourselves as a halachically pluralistic school." An estimated one-third of students come from Orthodox homes, and two-thirds from Conservative movement–affiliated families. Classes are only one part of the education, as Rabbi Pell explained:

> We have a very active program of Shabbatonim and trips and informal education. If you took away that ingredient, you might lose a lot of that special sauce. We are really going to give you the best of both worlds, and we're going to enable you to live in multiple worlds simultaneously. And that is something that most other schools

> cannot do. You're going to live fully and authentically as a Jew and fully and authentically as a modern citizen of the United States. We are always shooting for that exact equilibrium point, which is exhausting, but I actually think it really makes a difference in terms of the education.[27]

Finding that "equilibrium point" is, for all but Hasidic schools, a key objective because parents want their children to live, as Rabbi Pell said, in multiple worlds.

DAY SCHOOL FINANCING

But in communities small and large, all those issues are not even reached if the costs are prohibitive. For families with several children, tuition fees can simply be unaffordable. In *Inside Jewish Day Schools*, Wertheimer and Pomson state that the immense problem facing day schools of whatever quality is money: "An increasing proportion of parents are not able to afford the full cost of this product" and local Federations are paying five percent of their budgets—at most.[28]

In Seattle, an experiment is under way through the generosity of the Samis Foundation, which has provided $80 million to local day schools over the last twenty-five years. To quote from its 2021–2025 strategic plan:

> At its inception, Samis trustees identified Jewish day school education in Washington State as the top priority of the Samis Foundation.... Today, day school philanthropy remains the largest funding area of the Foundation and Samis is dedicated to ensuring that local day schools are

> bastions of academic excellence, providing the highest quality Jewish and secular education.
>
> Research continues to support Jewish day school education as integral for preserving and incubating Jewish life....
>
> Over the course of the last few decades the national and local landscape of day school education has shifted dramatically. The greater Seattle area, much like other communities throughout the country, has suffered a decline in day school vitality, sustainability, and affordability. Local day school enrollment reached a peak in 2003, but over the past eight years in particular, enrollment declined by 40%.[29]

It's a tough market:

> As one of the "most educated cities" in the country, Seattle boasts an incredibly competitive marketplace for private and public education. One in five students attends an independent private school and many independent schools have a high percentage of Jewish students. Public schools have the critical mass, government mandates, and financial resources to meet diverse students' needs and provide an exceptional education. In addition, the increasingly prohibitive cost of living in Seattle and shifting Jewish generational attitudes away from organized Jewish life and

> day school education, have further compounded the challenges faced by local Jewish day schools.[30]

Samis provides more than one-third of local day school operating budgets, and its funding creates an experiment: Would enrollment rise if tuition declined? The key target is not wealthier families who can pay, nor the poorest, for whom assistance has long been available. Samis instead has developed a day school affordability initiative to reach the large number of Jewish families who fall within what is (for these purposes) considered middle income, though it is far above the average family income in the United States. Samis CEO Connie Kanter described the Initiative: it "provides financial relief for families whose income is too high to qualify for traditional scholarships but for whom day school tuition is still a real barrier given the many competing priorities they face. The program ensures that for families who earn less than $350,000, tuition will not exceed $15,000 a year per child or 15 percent of their Adjusted Gross Income (AGI), whichever is lower."[31]

Did the Initiative expand outreach? The returns were not in when Kanter and I spoke. "We do believe," Kanter told me, "that the availability of the financial help expanded the kinds of families who use Jewish day schools and Jewish summer camps. Is it outreach, or does it alleviate the burden on families? I think there's a little bit of both."[32]

Kanter noted several barriers to recruiting for day school by comparing it to camping, which Samis also supports generously: Jewish camping "doesn't have a free alternative at all, number one. And number two, it's not as scary for people.... So I think camps have a much lower barrier to entry.

Samis funds about one-fourth of all the camp scholarships in Washington for Washington state kids. But for day schools, the financial help is more important than ever because it's such a substantial price tag and they have this formidable competition in the form of public school." Moreover, as she noted, "families feel a tremendous stigma applying for any kind of financial aid."[33]

As with any other project to lower the cost of Jewish activities such as camping, travel to Israel, or day school education, that outreach question is key. In Houston, one approach was launched in 2022: a program to provide scholarships for families who do not yet have a child in Jewish preschool. "Preschool was viewed as an entry point not only for Jewish students, but for families. To me, it's not just the investment in getting the kids into early childhood programs, but it's really ensuring that families have that connection and connect point. So there has been a priority placed on early childhood education," said Kari Saratovsky, CEO of the Jewish Federation of Greater Houston until 2021.[34]

Similarly, when I asked Kanter what she would do if a new donor gave her hundreds of millions of dollars, she replied "Early childhood. We'd probably go pretty deep, because we want on-ramps."[35] Obviously early childhood is one; there are others, such as the completion of primary school in sixth grade. A corollary notion is called "penetration pricing," lowering the price for a child's first year of Jewish schooling (or camping) in the hope that the experience will be successful enough to hook the parents and the children. More and more attention is rightly being dedicated to these issues of cost and affordability. As I researched this book, John Ruskay, former head of UJA-Federation of Greater New York, was leading a study for the Jewish People Policy Institute in Jerusalem, consulting with federations, foundations, donors, and senior professionals in several communities, to address the day school affordability issue. The study looked at two main strategies being tried in various communities: lowering tuition across the board and capping tuition as a percentage of family income.

The experience of Toronto and the community day school there called Tanenbaum Community Hebrew Academy of Toronto (TanenbaumCHAT) is worth examining, which I did in conversation with Daniel Held, Executive Director of the Centre for Jewish Education of the UJA Federation of Greater Toronto. What Held has done as thoughtfully as anyone in the field is to combine a deep dedication to Jewish values and education with some very straight talk about finance. Toronto found that in the decade from 2007 to 2016, tuition rose by 51 percent—and enrollment unsurprisingly dropped. Moreover, the trend lines looked likely to extend forward—continuing tuition hikes and enrollment drops. Retention rates from eighth grade students in Jewish day schools into TanenbaumCHAT, once 72 percent, had fallen to 55 percent and were forecast to drop further.

So Toronto's UJA Federation led a drive to raise funds, lower tuition and cap it as a percentage of family income (with "simple, easy-to-access, predictable" tuition relief), create an "affordability fund," and help the schools strengthen their educational quality and manage their resources better. And enrollments began to rise. Not automatically—a skilled marketing campaign was also employed.

What has Toronto learned? In a paper entitled "Experiments in Affordability Programs: Major Findings," Held wrote:

> Jewish day schools are special, but they aren't unicorns. Indeed, enrollment is driven by the same market forces that impact all consumer decisions. Perceived value is weighted against price. In short, affordability and enrollment are intrinsically linked....
>
> In 2017 we launched the TanenbaumCHAT Affordability Initiative at our community high school. The program was a universal tuition drop, reducing fees by nearly a third. To date, grade 9 enrollment has doubled, from 175 to 350 students. In 2021, we launched the Generations Trust Scholarships, an endowed tuition cap program for nine elementary schools, and have seen kindergarten enrollment increase by 14%.[36]

What works in "effective pricing models?" First, a "long line of sight," meaning predictable tuitions over the years the child will be in day school. "When a family decides to enroll their child in kindergarten, they are looking not just at the coming one or two years but right through to middle school and later. Similarly, when families enroll a child in ninth grade, they are making a decision for all of high school. In considering the cost of Jewish day school education, families need to know that they are going to be able to afford tuition for as long as they choose to send their children to day school."[37] That means "penetration pricing" that reduces costs for only the first year is not going to succeed, and it means financial help must be reliably available for the years to come.

Second, Held wrote, is "The unique psychology of middle-income families.... In the rest of their lives, they are considered affluent. These families typically qualify for a mortgage; pay their shul dues, make a gift to their Federation's annual campaign, and are likely in the top five to ten percent of earners. And yet, because of the cost of tuition, they must put out their hand to ask for help, often for the first time."[38] That means the scholarship system must be easy to access and to use.

Third, "Day school operates on a demand curve." Higher tuition means fewer students, and "scholarship programs that meaningfully reduce the out-of-pocket expense for families will encourage greater enrollment."[39] Elasticity of demand varies by family, and perceived value also matters.

Held tells the story best face to face, as he did when we spoke (via Zoom). Consumption of day schools is in some ways like consumption of any product, he said: cost is weighed against income and against the value of the product. In the Orthodox community, demand is inelastic; just about every child attends a Jewish day school; Orthodox families will sacrifice on the size or location of their home, on vacations, on most other family expenditures, to assure a good Jewish education for the children. But among the non-Orthodox, there is a lot of elasticity. Moreover, for the non-Orthodox, there is a readily available free alternative: public schools. But, says Held, "I believe we can turn the tide." It's true that every Jewish community is different, and outcomes in Canada will differ from those in the United

States and other Diaspora nations, but "Canada is not a unicorn. The demand curve exists for all countries."[40]

The key factors are largely the same in all countries: cost, quality, and perceived value matter everywhere. Experimentation in Toronto has suggested, for example, that lowering tuition carries a risk: placing the tuition at the full cost of educating the child shows the parents how valuable the product is. Then, add the easy-to-access scholarships that can be obtained without any perceived affront to the dignity of the family. And if penetration pricing is used to reach out to new families, show the pathway for all the remaining school years, not only the first one. A long-term affordability plan is essential.

Messaging is also critical, and Toronto has found through polls of parents that raising the level of Jewish knowledge is a key factor but not the only one. For families on the fence, that may not be the argument that wins. The overall wellness of the child, the attention of the school to his or her safety and health, and the open door to parent involvement may be more important factors for many families.

Toronto's TanenbaumCHAT is one experiment well worth studying, but all over the Jewish world, the challenge of attracting more students to Jewish schools is being addressed. Prizmah, the Center for Jewish Day Schools, works with schools across the country to enhance their quality; the Samis Foundation concentrates on what works in and around Seattle; Federations often support local schools. There are many more organizations involved in thinking and experimenting.

PUBLIC FINANCING FOR JEWISH DAY SCHOOLS

The challenge of financing Jewish education is common to every such effort, and here the United States has been an outlier. In most of the other large Diaspora communities, there has long been more public financial help—and a larger proportion of Jewish children attend Jewish schools. The figures change from year to year, but perhaps a third do so in Toronto. Financing varies by province in Canada and is higher in Quebec than in Ontario, and the percentage of Jewish children attending Jewish schools there is also higher. No doubt many ingredients affect those numbers, but it is hard to argue that the final cost of tuition to families is not a contributing factor.

There are many approaches to public or state funding. In Quebec, "Jewish day schools receive a per student allocation that amounts to 60 per cent of the funding that public schools get for their students."[41] In Ontario, there is no direct funding for Jewish day schools but there is a federal tax credit for religious instruction. Tuition paid for religious instruction is treated as a charitable gift. Schools, each year, do a calculation on how much of tuition is for Jewish studies vs. how much for general studies, and the amount for Jewish studies ranges from 40 to 100 percent. Thus, for example, if half of tuition is held to be for Jewish studies and tuition is $20,000, the deduction would be $10,000.

Quite the opposite approach exists in the UK, where the government helps fund secular studies directly if Jewish schools meet certain educational and curricular prerequisites. In the UK, as of 2019 "seven out of every 10 Jews from four to 18 now attend a Jewish day school."[42] In Australia, both the national and state governments provide direct funding to Jewish (and other independent) schools, and the national government supplies 43 percent of total nongovernment school income.[43] In some cases, schools with students from lower socioeconomic groups can receive three-fourths or even more of their funding from public sources. Most Australian Jews live in the states of New South Wales and Victoria; in the latter, roughly 60 percent of Jewish children attend a Jewish school—though as in the UK, even with some state funding, Jewish schools face financial hurdles that keep tuitions high and threaten to reduce enrollments.[44] In New South Wales (where Sydney is located), about 40 percent of Jewish children attend a Jewish school, though the percentages are falling due to high tuitions.[45]

In the United States, public funding for what may be called independent, nonpublic, or non-state schools has been deeply controversial for well over a century. The Blaine Amendments adopted in dozens of state constitutions in the nineteenth century were an expression of anti-Catholic bigotry meant to ensure that no funds would go to Catholic schools. The strict separationist approach—not one dime for anything but government-run schools—was long the position of the American Jewish community, most fervently expressed by the American Jewish Congress. As one scholar at Hebrew Union College noted in 2022, "For decades, the Jewish public policy establishment held to a firmly articulated legal position of church-state separation."[46]

But that is changing. In Supreme Court cases involving support for nonpublic schools, Jewish groups now vary in their approaches; the Orthodox Union, for example, has long supported allowing the funding to follow the child. As a news story in 2012 put it:

> As day school tuition costs are rising, a growing number of Jewish organizations are rethinking their opposition to public support for religious schools. Jewish federations are increasing efforts to obtain state money for things like technology and textbooks, while some Jewish groups are supporting state programs that give tax credits for donations to private schools.[47]

In 2012, the Jewish Federation of Greater New Orleans endorsed vouchers for private schools, the first federation in the United States to do so. In 2015, UJA Federation of New York joined the Orthodox Union and Agudath Israel in supporting a tax credit plan for private schools in New York State.[48]

Slowly, exceptions have become widely accepted; grants from the federal government to support security measures at Jewish day schools, synagogues, and other Jewish institutions are the best example. "Thirty-one states have at least one program that provides public financial help to enable children to attend private schools," and that includes religious schools.[49] The "wall of separation" has been breached; as the Jewish Education Project wrote about New York State, "Non-Public schools in New York State, including Jewish day schools, benefit from an array of state funded reimbursement and aid programs" in addition to various federal funding programs.[50] In the 2022–2023 school year, $58 million was available in New York State to help nonpublic schools pay the salaries of qualified STEM teachers.[51] Government funds are available to reimburse schools for administering state exams, taking attendance, textbooks, school buses, health services, therapy and counseling for students with special needs, teacher training, and many more "exceptions" to the general rule that "government funding" will only go to public schools. Jewish schools energetically seek such funding, and the Jewish community's leadership is slowly moving away from the separationism of the previous century.

What of charter schools, which exist in almost all states and educate 7 percent of all public school students—may they have any religious characteristics? Not until now. But the controversy over the Blaine Amendments comes to mind when reading the December 2022 opinion of Oklahoma's Attorney General and Solicitor General holding that the state's laws prohibiting religious charter schools are unconstitutional. The Supreme Court has held that discrimination against religious schools violates the Constitution; if a state subsidizes private education, it may not exclude religious education from those benefits. Oklahoma law barred charter schools from being religiously affiliated; the opinion stated that "it seems obvious that a state cannot exclude those merely 'affiliated with' a religious or sectarian institution from a state created program in which private entities are otherwise generally allowed to participate if they are qualified.... And that is exactly what this provision does."[52]

In Florida, various programs providing support for Jewish (and other independent) education have surely been a factor in growing enrollments in Jewish schools. At the Brauser Maimonides Academy in Fort Lauderdale, for example, 28 percent of students in 2021 were receiving state scholarship funds, and the head of the Jewish Academy in Fort Lauderdale said Florida's income-based scholarships cut tuition nearly in half. Between 2018 and 2021, the number of Jewish schools in Florida rose from 50 to 64 and enrollment increased by more than 17 percent.[53]

Other states are following the same path, as the *Wall Street Journal* noted in an early 2023 editorial entitled "The School Choice Drive Accelerates." Utah had recently decided to adopt "education savings accounts" of $8,000 per pupil, as had Iowa at the $7,500 level, and legislatures in South Carolina, Nebraska, New Hampshire, Texas, and Virginia, and Oklahoma were "in some stage" of considering similar action.[54]

There are many ways to help finance day school education, beginning with tuition paid by parents (and grandparents) and by philanthropy. But it's obvious that for all Jewish communities, here and elsewhere in the Diaspora, the high cost of quality Jewish education is a challenge that is increasingly difficult to meet. Parents, and the Jewish community as a whole, are paying for state-run schools through their taxes and then paying again to educate their own children in Jewish day schools. The American Jewish community is slowly shifting toward support for various ways parents can reclaim some of the money they pay for state schools—through scholarships, vouchers, and a thousand "special" programs that cover narrow categories of expense. Individual schools, families and communities, and individual states, will experiment with the best approaches. What is critical is that, if Jewish continuity is the objective, the Jewish community realizes that day schools are an essential ingredient. It is worth quoting again the lines from the Samis Foundation noted above in explaining its own support for day schools in Seattle:

> Research continues to support Jewish day school education as integral for preserving and incubating Jewish life. Day schools are the most intensive and immersive educational experience given the sheer number of hours students spend in school, and likewise, the deepest and most worthwhile investment in Jewish continuity.[55]

Jewish education must become a central objective of the American Jewish community, and day school education must be seen not as a special pleading of Orthodox Jews but as a common goal for the entire community. It is an essential ingredient in Jewish continuity in America. No realistic amount of charitable dollars will cover the costs of day schools, so the Jewish community should be fighting for, not fighting against, taxpayer funding to follow the child. We can see in other Diaspora communities that such funding is associated with higher percentages of Jewish youth attending Jewish schools. And there is a further reason for supporting this outcome, even for Jews who have no intention to send their own children to them: just as many non-religious Jews support Jewish camps, Chabad, synagogues, JCCs, or other organizations that sustain Jewish life in America, they should be open to helping Jewish day schools because those schools are critical to helping the American Jewish community survive and thrive.

New schools to replace the famous and prestigious but failing ones

In the last few years, and explosively after October 7 and the Gaza war, Jewish parents have understood and acknowledged the failures of many of the schools they have relied on. These are often the most prestigious and best-regarded private schools and colleges, but all of a sudden, Jewish parents began to fear for their children's safety—physically and intellectually. There was violence on some campuses, and on many more, young Jews feared being identified as Jews and as pro-Israel. The outpouring of venom against Israel from faculty members and administrators on so many campuses made parents wonder what their children were being taught about Israel and about being Jews.

As I've mentioned before, the infamous appearance of the presidents of Harvard, Penn, and MIT at a congressional hearing in December 2023 was the final proof many Americans—Christian as well as Jewish—needed to understand the depth of the problem. All three presidents could not say a simple "No" when asked if promoting genocide against Jews would be acceptable discourse on their campuses.[56]

These concerns have led some parents and should lead many more to reevaluate the schools they have long regarded as the "best" and seek new options. At the Tikvah Fund, we began to plan and then to create a new school—a Jewish day school called Emet Classical Academy that opened in September 2025. This is only one of many such new efforts at the elementary and secondary level. In Texas, an entirely new university is being created—the University of Austin, welcoming students for the first time for the 2024–2025 academic year, is "dedicated to the preservation and transmission of humanity's rich intellectual, scientific, artistic, and cultural inheritance," which certainly includes the Jewish heritage.[57] At the University of Florida, its new president Ben Sasse has created a new multidisciplinary academic unit within the university. The Hamilton Center's "core mission is to help students develop the knowledge, habits of thought, analytical skills, and character to be citizens and leaders in a free society." It is a classical education, aiming to "educate students in the core texts and great debates of Western civilization and in the principles, ideals and institutions of the American political order." And its public programming "will highlight the value of debate and disagreement based on a core commitment to the search for truth and will resist the current push to 'deplatform,' 'cancel,' or professionally destroy those with whom we may disagree."[58]

Jewish communities and Jewish parents have more options now than in the past, and they have the ability to create more each year. They and their children have more options than they perhaps realized, once they free themselves from the belief that they must seek out the prestige schools that have a legacy but perhaps no longer the reality of greatness. Many of those institutions are abandoning the values that made them great and are today simply not hospitable to Jewish students who value their Jewishness, wish to strengthen their Jewish identity, and care deeply about Israel. Jewish education, or more sharply put the education of young Jews, is becoming an area of ferment and growth. It is impossible to say if that will continue because it all depends on whether American Jews have finally understood the mistakes of our past reliance on someone else's definition of how young people should be educated. Jews who care about their identity and their community will need to choose carefully, avoiding some famous institutions, placing education above prestige, creating new elementary and secondary schools and even colleges, and finding the places where their sons and daughters can grow into proud Americans and proud Jews.

B. JEWISH CAMPING

Jewish Camping in America: Education and Immersion

In comparison with Jewish schooling (and engagement with Israel), it may seem that camping is out of place—peripheral or minor in the grand scheme of things. That view would be wrong. I was reminded of this repeatedly during the many interviews I conducted when writing this book.

When I spoke with Rabbi Dan Fink of Congregation Ahavath Beth Israel in Boise, Idaho, he reminded me that the entire state has only about 2,000 Jews—though the numbers are uncertain and the affiliation rate is low. The only Jewish institutions are his congregation and a Chabad house; there is no Jewish Federation, no Jewish Community Center, and no Jewish day school. How is it possible, in such a small community, to give Jewish children any kind of robust or encompassing Jewish experience? Rabbi Fink was crystal clear about Jewish camping:

> Why is camp so important? I think camp is the most important Jewish experience for most of my kids.... This is the one time I have the experience

> to get our kids into a Jewish environment. There's nothing for me that has that kind of impact that camp has, precisely because they live in such an overwhelmingly non-Jewish environment. For me, that experience of living in a Jewish environment is really critical.[59]

In this case, what is true of Boise is also true of New York, Los Angeles, and other centers of Jewish population. The days when all Jews lived in dense Jewish environments are, for the non-Orthodox, over. But summer camp creates an immersive environment. In my conversation for this book with John Ruskay, who led the UJA-Federation of Greater New York for twenty-two years, he reminisced about his own experience: "I am a huge believer in Jewish summer camps. Somehow, I ended up going to a Jewish summer camp and it changed my life. It's there that I experienced Shabbat. It touched my heart and soul. I didn't know I had a heart and soul. It was all about the head, but it just touched me and moved me." Camp was, he said, "an inspired community."[60]

The late Rabbi David Ellenson, who led the Reform movement's Hebrew Union College from 2001 to 2013, was emphatic:

> If you want your grandchildren and great-grandchildren to be Jewish, send them to a summer camp. My impression is that camping has a larger impact longitudinally than any other single factor. There's something about a month or two every summer in a total Jewish environment that creates greater long-term commitment.

> And the other part that I'd add here is that it doesn't only promote endogamous marriage, but if someone does intermarry, they are much more likely to have their partner convert to Judaism or commit to raising their children Jewishly if they have strong Jewish commitments.[61]

When I spoke with the long-time (1983–2018) head of the Cleveland Jewish Federation, Steve Hoffman, I asked what he would say to a billionaire philanthropist who asked how to spend his money to build Jewish identity and solidarity. Hoffman replied:

> I would start first with Jewish camps. We have two challenges, among many, with our kids, and one is basically a dismantled supplemental Jewish education in our synagogues. It's very thin. And the second is affective identification. And that sometimes is more important than the knowledge. Because if you at least feel good about being Jewish, maybe later on you'll figure out what it means. Jewish camping provides this informal education and good affective reinforcement about wanting to be Jewish. And you have Jewish friends, at least in the summertime."[62]

Camp works

These personal reflections are supported by research. "Camp Works: The Long-Term Impact of Jewish Overnight Camp" found that "the childhood camp experience has a significant impact—in some respects a highly substantial impact—on adult Jewish practices and commitment."[63]

The impact is felt in several ways, one of which is motivating campers into leadership positions later in life. "Camp Works" found that camp is an "incubator for developing Jewish leadership." It cited studies "into the shaping of Jewish career choices [that] show that one of the reasons most frequently cited by Jewish communal professionals to explain their career path is the childhood camp experience." And it noted an AVI CHAI Foundation finding that "71% of young American Jewish leaders attended Jewish overnight camp."[64]

Jewish camps also affected young people's relationship with Israel. For one thing, the Jewish Agency for Israel (JAFI) sends more than 1,200 young Israelis to the United States in the Summer *Shlichim* (Messenger) program, to work as staff members at Jewish camps. As the Foundation for Jewish Camp's *Greenbook* noted in a study of Jewish camping, "The program offers camps a one-on-one opportunity to engage with Israel. JAFI *shlichim* become an integral part of their assigned camp's staff and work together with local counselors. Through their personal and professional interactions, they educate campers and staff about Israel and help to build strong, personal relations with Israel for campers and fellow staff members alike."[65]

"Camp Works" found that "The likelihood of feeling 'very emotionally attached to Israel' increases by a remarkable 55%."[66] The study found:

> The item on which camp has the greatest impact, strong emotional attachment to Israel (being not merely attached, but "*very*" attached), requires a pronounced sense of membership in a Jewish collective distinct from the American mainstream. This kind of commitment requires an abstract feeling of solidarity with a worldwide community beyond one's immediate experience.[67]

It's obvious, then, that camp affects the child's entire outlook on Jewish identity—on being part of the Jewish people. "Camp Works" spells it out:

> The impact of camp—with few exceptions—is most profound on those Jewish identity markers that are least common among today's non-Orthodox Jewish adults....
>
> Of the four items appearing in the high-impact cluster, three—attachment to Israel, attend synagogue monthly or more, and donate to Jewish federations—provide clear evidence that camp develops a sense of belonging to a larger Jewish community.[68]

As David Graizbord analyzed it in *The New Zionists*, "Jewish overnight camp recreates the framework of Jewish *ethnic* community that has been mostly lost in the United States, and whose most extensive realization is the Jewish community of the State of Israel." One of Graizbord's interviewees explained how it works:

> It's not a specific program [that works], *it's the framework*. You know, at camp you're living with the same people every day for four to eight weeks; you have...positive Jewish role models who are 18 to...24 years old; and you're doing everything together in this general Jewish framework that [does not exist for you] anywhere else in your life in North America. And from the moment you wake up to the moment you go to sleep, *everything is Jewish*. Where else in the world can you have that same experience from the moment you wake up until you go to sleep, and everything is Jewish? Israel.... You can build a positive Jewish identity [that is not religiously Orthodox] and strengthen it in two places: In Jewish summer camp, or in Israel.[69]

The *Greenbook* concludes that "Jewish camp works—not only as a source of fun for participants, and of inspiration and pride for parents, but also as an especially powerful engine of Jewish identity and commitment in its participants and staff alike. And its effect is long lasting, especially for the college-age counselors on the brink of leadership roles on campus or in their home communities."[70]

These conclusions should, upon reflection, be unsurprising. Camp creates a fully Jewish environment, and within it creates social networks among young Jews. The same phenomenon can be achieved for non-Orthodox youth in various ways, including Jewish day schools (which they are unlikely to attend) and travel in Israel. It is probably the case that the environment—the camp, summer travel group, or school class—is more important than the exact content of the programming. Prior to the Second World War, most American Jews lived within Jewish social networks, and though Orthodox Jews may do so now, non-Orthodox Jews rarely do. So, they must be built quite intentionally.

Jewish day schools can be one critical node, but camps have some real advantages. For now, day schools do not attract large numbers of non-Orthodox children, while camps do. Camps are far cheaper than day schools. Camps require far less of an ideological commitment than Jewish schooling, which non-Orthodox parents may view as removing their children from American society and culture in ways they did not themselves do and may not favor. As *Greenbook* noted, "For whatever reason, American Jews—in numbers that are proportionately greater than other groups—seem to be drawn to summer camp. Jewish camps thus hold the potential to reach large numbers of children who are unlikely to participate in other Jewish educational or identity-building programs, such as Jewish day schools."[71] And while day schools compete with the completely free alternative of public schooling, camps do not: parents who want to provide some summer activity for their children will end up spending money to do so. So why not camp? And why not a Jewish camp?

Given the reach of Jewish camps, the number of children who attend for the first time each year, and the data the Federation of Jewish Camps and others have found, it's obvious that the experience of Jewish camping has a real impact on children who attend.

Camps can provide what Jeremy Fingerman, head of the Foundation for Jewish Camp (FJC), called "joyous

Judaism."[72] Nowadays, the Foundation has a membership of roughly 150 overnight and 170 day camps, which accommodate about 150,000 campers and counselors every summer. (These numbers will vary from over time and declined during COVID. They may also undercount some Chabad or ultra-Orthodox camps.) *Greenbook* estimates 80,000 campers and 11,000 staff of overnight or residential camps. This is a significant part of the cohort. If as *Greenbook* estimates there are between 500,000 and 700,000 Jewish children in the relevant age groups, the 80,000 would constitute 13 percent in any given summer, but "FJC estimates that the overall percentage of Jewish children who have ever attended Jewish camp over their camp-eligible years is likely to be 30-35%."[73] A rough calculation based on the Pew 2020 survey would suggest that there are about one million children under the age of eighteen growing up in homes with at least one Jewish parent who identifies as Jewish by religion. If the relevant ages for camp are four to seventeen, that might mean about 750,000 children in that cohort. And if 150,000 children attend Jewish overnight camps and day camps, roughly half each, that would mean that about ten percent of the cohort attend day camps and ten percent overnight camps.

These are probably low numbers because they do not catch ultra-Orthodox children attending camps that are not part of FJC, and do not catch children going on organized Jewish travel to Israel or elsewhere. There are many such trips: "Such programs include NCSY's Give West, an Orthodox girls' travel program in the Western U.S.; BBYO's domestic Stand Up and Trek programs, which include numerous offerings throughout North America; and USY on Wheels, the Conservative movement's domestic teen travel program."[74] The percentage of the relevant cohort of Jewish children engaged in some immersive summer activity, camping or travel, is far from trivial—but far from what it might be.

Questions about Jewish camping

The research on Jewish camping cannot answer all the questions we may have about its impact—and how that impact is achieved. The scholars gathered in the Collaborative for Applied Studies in Jewish Education (CASJE) worked with the Foundation for Jewish Camp to try for better understanding. In "Jewish Experiential Education at Camp," they concluded that "Many agree that there is a certain 'magic' at Jewish summer camps. Identifying what contributes to this magic is a complicated task." Here's the problem:

> More than 20,000 children attend Jewish camp for the first time each year, and more than 300 traditional and specialty overnight camps exist in the United States; all seek to instill Jewish values and culture in young people through time-honored camp activities. Though we have seen that children with quality Jewish camp experiences are more likely as adults to value their Jewish identity, engage in their communities, and support Jewish causes, we are not certain about the causes and sources of these outcomes.[75]

Some questions are obvious though the answers are not: How many summers must a camper attend camp for there to be a real impact? Only one? Several? How many weeks of sleepaway camp are needed per summer? Only two, the usual minimum? Or the full summer of six or eight weeks? The *Greenbook* asked key questions: "We do not know, for example, how much exposure to Jewish camp a child needs to attain the benefits to Jewish identity that Jewish camp can provide. The existing research that found strong outcomes from Jewish camp was based largely on a seven- or eight-week camp session. From an educational perspective, is there any such thing as an 'optimal' session length? How many summers? How much is enough to make an impact?"[76]

There are other questions too: What can be done during the other months of the year to maintain or even heighten the impact of camp? How much "Judaism" must be programmed, for example in forms of Shabbat observance, or is that not critical to the impact of Jewish camping? Do for-profit and non-profit camps differ on any or all these counts and on their overall impact?

And there is the question of outreach: Are camps in a sense preaching to the converted, because campers and their families are already deeply attached to their Jewish identities? When I discussed this with Dr. Richard Joel, president of Hillel and then of Yeshiva University, it was his question: "Camping is exactly right. But what's the percentage of Jewish kids who go to Jewish camp? I think Jewish camp is a great maintainer. But what's the outreach that camps can do? In other words, how does it get the uninvolved to go?"[77] As Rabbi Ethan Linden, former director of Camp Ramah in the Berkshires, put it:

> There is a mission piece that we are missing here. That is, I am taking families of kids that are already pretty highly affiliated and, in some ways, keeping them in the fold. We are not taking kids who have light affiliation or interest or activity and moving them toward more. What we are really doing is, I would say, strengthening a community that is already highly affiliated and active.[78]

Camp Ramah, in its locations all around the country, is affiliated with the Conservative movement, and Linden's comment may not apply equally to camps affiliated with the Reform movement or to community camps run by Jewish Community Centers or other community-wide bodies. Still, the "mission piece" is an important challenge as Jewish camps try to increase attendance.

Why are the camping numbers not higher? Cost is a central issue. Rabbi Fink of Boise told me, "Cost is the biggest obstacle I faced in getting kids to camp. Jewish camp is not cheap." Steve Hoffman of the Cleveland Federation commented, "If we could get the cost down, I think we could double the enrollments."

The "One Happy Camper" program backed by the FJC and funded both at the national and local level provides $1,000 for the camper's first summer. The program is need-blind, and usually requires two to four weeks at camp. The hope is that the parents and the child will get hooked—will love the experience and want to repeat it. Other programs provide more money, and given all the data on the impact of camp, much more should be done. Right now, dividing family incomes into quartiles, fewer than 10 percent of campers come from the lowest while the bulk of campers come from the middle quartiles. In the top quartile, even more expensive activities such as family or "teen tour" international travel are viable and frequent options. Financial help could expand the very low percentage of less affluent Jewish children who can attend overnight camps, and expand the percentage of those in the second and third quartiles who do so—or perhaps expand the amount of time they can spend in camp or the number of years they can attend.

Like Jewish schooling or visits to Israel, Jewish camping works to help create a lasting sense of Jewish identity and is associated with a far more active Jewish life when the camper grows up. Given the lower barriers to entry than with day schools, both financially and ideologically, Jewish camping is a target-rich environment for philanthropy and for the organized Jewish community. Camping *works*, creating an immersive Jewish community from dawn to lights out—a community that is unique outside of Israel for non-Orthodox campers. Like Birthright, it is an opportunity before us and limited today simply by the shortage of funds—primarily funds to allow children from families that are not wealthy to attend, but also funds to ensure that Jewish families are aware of the opportunity and the impact and invited (yes, and lured) into trying it out. The impact on the American Jewish community could be lasting.

C. THE ROLE OF ISRAEL

Birthright and travel to Israel

There are countless opportunities for the American Jewish community to engage with Israel, in travel or study. The Jewish National Fund's Dream Israel Teen Travel Initiative gives up to $7,500 for a high school semester there. BBYO, NCSY (part of Orthodox Union), the Reform movement, and Young Judea have many varied programs with $3,000 travel vouchers, and there is hardly a Jewish community that does not sponsor some trip. Birthright has proved that even a short organized visit can matter.

Above all, the Birthright program demonstrates that even brief exposure to Israel can have an exceptional and lasting effect on participants. By now, over 800,000 young Jews from around the world (almost all of them ages eighteen to twenty-six) have gone on ten-day trips to Israel, and the years of experience have provided reliable data about the impact. RootOne sponsors somewhat longer (three to six week) visits in coordination with various organizations such as the Conservative and Reform movement youth groups and BBYO. Funded by the Marcus Foundation, it sends thousands of young American Jews who are not in Orthodox day schools to Israel each summer. RootOne's goal, in its own words, "is to maximize the number of North American Jewish teens who experience Israel first-hand, and to maximize the impact that these experiences have on each teen."[79]

But Birthright has the best data. What does it show? Leonard Saxe of the Cohen Center at Brandeis, who has been studying Birthright for two decades, and his collaborators reached some key findings about Birthright's first decade: "Birthright participants are much more likely to have a Jewish spouse or partner compared to similar nonparticipants," and "Birthright's impact on choice of spouse is evident among those with one Jewish parent as well as among those with two Jewish parents."[80] Birthright's impact is both direct and indirect: participants are far more likely to marry Jews (nearly 40 percent more likely), and inmarriage is associated with more engagement with Jewish life. But those participants who did not marry Jews feel the impact of Birthright as well. Saxe and his coauthors said it this way:

- ☆ Because Birthright participants are more likely to be partnered with other Jews, they are more likely than similar nonparticipants to raise their oldest child Jewish, to have *brit milah* for their oldest son, to be connected to Israel, to be synagogue members, to volunteer for Jewish or Israeli causes, to participate in events sponsored by Jewish organizations, to have Jewish friends, to celebrate Shabbat, to attend Jewish religious services, and to celebrate Jewish holidays. These effects represent Birthright's *indirect* impact.
- ☆ Birthright has an additional, *direct* impact on partnered participants, even on those who have non-Jewish partners, in some of these domains. Birthright participants who are partnered with non-Jews are more likely to feel connected to Israel, to have Jewish friends, to attend Jewish religious services, and to celebrate Rosh Hashanah and Passover.

These findings provide strong evidence of Birthright's impact. Few other educational interventions (in the Jewish world or otherwise) demonstrate similar evidence of long-term effects.[81]

As to Israel, Birthright participants were twice as likely as nonparticipants to feel "very much" connected to Israel. And comparing those who only went to Israel on a Birthright trip to those who had never been to Israel, nearly three times as many felt "very much" connected to Israel.[82]

When Saxe and colleagues studied the Pew 2020 data, they found that participants in Birthright were far more likely to be "somewhat" or "very" attached to Israel (63 percent of participants vs. 34 percent of non-participants), far more likely to feel "a lot" in common with Israeli Jews (71 percent of participants vs. 45 percent of non-participants), and far more likely to have a Jewish spouse (39 percent of participants vs. 15 percent of non-participants).[83]

Birthright is not a magic bullet and some of the "first decade" data can be seen as disappointing. Years later, 35 percent of participants say they feel "a little" or "not at all" connected to Israel, and among participants whose Birthright trip was ten to eighteen years ago, only a third (34 percent) had returned to Israel at least once—a lower number than might have been predicted.[84] Saxe and his coauthors noted that "there are other areas of Jewish life where participation in a 10-day Birthright trip does not seem to have a demonstrable impact," such as "enrolling children in any form of formal Jewish education (including preschool) or in Jewish day camp."[85] "Nevertheless," they rightly add, "the fact that key differences between participants and nonparticipants persist 20 years later is itself surprising."[86]

Indeed it is, for all of this is measuring the impact of *ten days* in Israel—not a three or six week trip in the summer, not a semester, not a gap year, not a junior year of college in Israel. Their impact will be far greater.

Gap Year In Israel

While most Jewish students will not go to day schools even if the financial burden is somewhat alleviated, gap year programs might be attractive to a larger percentage of Jewish families and youth. This is the year between high school and college, and the advantages and attractions are obvious: a break from studies, a change of scene, and adventures abroad may appeal to students, while they, their parents, and their eventual universities know full well that an additional year such as this will produce a more mature young person and student.

Some of these benefits would accrue no matter where the student went. But a gap year in Israel can be an extraordinary opportunity for American Jewish youth, the Jewish community, and for Israel as well. The attractiveness and benefits will depend on how well the gap year programs are organized. To take some obvious examples, the program should not be entirely academic and should include travel in Israel, shabbat activities, opportunities to meet young Israelis, and holiday celebrations such as Passover seders. Group activities are critical to group morale and can easily be organized according to what city the students are coming from, what universities they will be attending, and what organizations they've been involved with at home. Building on these affinities will be critical in maintaining group contacts after they return to the United States.

Natan Sharansky and Gil Troy have made the case for a new gap year program for American Jewish youth:

> It's time to give generations of young Jews a year away from the illiberal liberalism that characterizes too many campuses today, a year of being wholly embraced by Jewish civilization, a year of leaving America behind so that they might understand it better and even help it mend.
>
> Think Birthright Israel—only even more ambitious....
>
> Our effort will succeed only if American Jews recognize en masse that a gap year is, in fact, a not-to-be-missed opportunity that better prepares their children for college emotionally, intellectually, ideologically, even socially....
>
> We need a raft of new, redrawn, and scaled-up programs that model the kind of classically liberal approach to critical thinking that universities once fostered. The programs will build students' skills in these essential areas, while also strengthening their connections to Jewish civilization and to other young Jews and Israelis.[87]

Sharansky and Troy also mention another critical point: college credit. At least partial credit will alleviate the possible view of students or parents that the year is "lost," and may in many cases also reduce college costs, even shortening the number of years or semesters the college requires. In a reaction to Sharansky and Troy, the CEO of Young Judea Global, Adina Frydman, wrote:

> Another solution is to work with universities to more universally accept the credits earned from gap year programs. Even the accredited programs are not accepted by all universities. In Young Judaea's Year Course, you can finish your gap year and begin university with up to 26 college credits, essentially entering as a second semester sophomore! This mitigates the challenge of the cost of an additional year of university and, in the best case, might even save you a semester."[88]

A gap year in Israel is now normal for Orthodox students, but much will be needed to make it so for the non-Orthodox. As Frydman wrote, "To move toward a universal gap year, there needs to be a radical expansion of the non-Orthodox gap year marketplace. Diverse programs that cater to the diversity of participants out there."[89] Today, the Marcus Foundation's RootOne programs encourage summer programs in Israel by providing partial funding of $3,000 to Jewish youngsters across the nation. Participants in such programs are a logical marketing target for gap year programs, and as Frydman states, "Creating a pipeline from a summer teen Israel experience to a gap year in Israel will deepen and extend the impact of the initial travel experience across various markers of Jewish identity and connection to Israel."[90]

And then there is the issue of finance; no significant expansion of gap year participation will be possible without funding. Experiments have begun: in Atlanta, the Zalik Foundation began its Atlanta Gap Year Fellowship to give vouchers for $10,000 to $15,000 to students to help fund a gap year program. Usually, that cuts family expenditures in half. The goal was to reach Jewish teens and families who are not already on track to do a gap year in Israel, which mostly means non-Orthodox youth who are not in yeshivas. Unsurprisingly, the number of students choosing a gap year in Israel grew. The program does not provide the gap year activities, and instead links with about a dozen organizations that do so. Students can, for example, choose to learn Hebrew intensively, take courses at Hebrew University, study in a yeshiva, study high-tech coding, or do community service projects. The scale is small: twenty-eight young Atlantans in 2022. But the model is an excellent one. Such a subsidy for 10,000 American Jewish high school graduates would cost an annual $100 million. As Birthright has demonstrated, such a sum is not beyond the financial capability of the American Jewish community. And some of the necessary financing might come from the State of Israel.

Birthright itself states that

> Birthright Israel is founded on three values that are central in the Jewish world: Unity, Community and Mutual Responsibility. The project itself is therefore a gift of the Jewish people to its younger members, given with no strings attached as a pledge by the State of Israel, worldwide Jewish communities and nearly 40,000 annual donors

> all putting partisan and theological differences aside to ensure the vibrant future of world Jewry and the State of Israel.[91]

That is a slightly edited history of Birthright: it began as a gift less "of the Jewish people" than of a handful of immensely generous American philanthropists. What remains to be seen in the next decade is whether, as those individuals step back or pass from the scene, other individual donors, Jewish communities as a whole, and the State of Israel will step forward—keeping Birthright whole and financing it as a "gift of the Jewish people to its younger members."

Israeli Politics

It is reasonable to ask (after Israel's deeply divisive "judicial reform" crisis of early 2023) whether Israel's political divisions, its turn to the right in recent decades, and the victory in its 2022 elections of its most right-wing coalition ever, mean that exposure to Israel will not henceforth have these positive effects. I would argue exactly the contrary. Living in the United States, reading the harsh criticisms of Israel and its conservative governments in the *New York Times*, hearing the denunciations of Israel on the campuses where so many young Jews live at any given time, their diet of information will be mostly, if not uniformly, negative—and political. How is it possible to bring young American Jews beyond politics and whatever may be the government of Israel in any single year, to engage with the people and the society?

That sort of engagement is very difficult to achieve without visiting—and the more time spent there, the better the effect is likely to be. This conclusion should not be surprising; most of what American Jews see and hear about Israel is about Israeli politics, but while visiting Israel themselves, American Jews will not be sitting down with politicians or watching Knesset harangues. It may be that the only effective way to bring American Jews beyond political debates and toward understanding and support of the Jewish state is precisely by their physical presence and their engagement with the nation and its people.

The State of Israel's Role

Remember Natan Sharansky's views of how Israel can help American Jews, which I quoted in Chapter Four? Discussing their gap year proposal, Sharansky and Troy wrote that "as American Jews reimagine Israel's role in their children's lives, Israel will have to do some reimagining of its own." "Subsidizing Birthright," they argued, became the first phase of a massive paradigm shift in the relationship between Israel and the Diaspora. "As American Jews continued contributing to Israel, Israel gave them something back: a material shift in the ways that young people understood their relationship to Israel and to their Jewish identity."[92]

The interest of the State of Israel in achieving this is obvious, and contributing to the sums required should not be prohibitive for a country whose annual government budget is roughly $200 billion. Obviously Diaspora communities will defray much of the expense, so the real point is ideological not financial: rather than relying on Birthright, the State of Israel should adopt an active policy of seeking to assure that large percentages of young American Jews visit there and spend as long a period of time there as is possible—not only Birthright's ten days but a summer, a high school semester, a gap year, a college year abroad, or even four years at an Israeli university. Just as Birthright has become something of a rite of passage for young American Jews, and far longer time in Israel is the norm for Orthodox Jews, Israel should seek to make longer stays the norm for a greater and greater percentage of Diaspora—and especially American—youth. According to the Institute of International Education, in 2023 there were 2,444 US students at institutions of higher education in Israel, and while that was more students than any other sending country, it's still a low number.[93] Israel is seeking to double the overall number of foreign students, and Israeli universities have their own efforts under way to increase their own numbers (with help from government funding).[94]

But these efforts are not large enough; Sharansky and Troy are right to call for programs that bring young American Jews to Israel en masse for longer than Birthright's effective ten days. And they are right to call for diversity: the goal is not to get American Jews into one program, but to expand the number that participate in the hundreds of programs that exist and that already cater to every portion of the community: Orthodox, Conservative, Reform, nonreligious, teenagers, college students, and so on. Time in Israel is a rite of passage today only for Orthodox youth, and that must change.

The "role of the State of Israel" means two things, and the lesser meaning is the activity and spending of the government of Israel to attract and finance the presence of young American Jews. Much more important is the role we have discussed earlier in this book: the ability to provide to young Jews with a far more powerful sense of identity, of membership in the Jewish collective, that only an immersive experience seems to achieve. Moreover, even immersive experiences like summer camp and day school will not provide the understanding of and attachment to the Jewish state that time spent there will provide. Such experiences, and the way the family raises its children, will lay the foundation of Jewish identity on which a deep and long-lasting connection to Israel can be built.

Changing Roles of Israel and Diaspora

After centuries in which Jewish communities in what is now Israel, including the Jewish state in its formative decades, were objects of generosity and assistance by the Diaspora, today Israel is the source of assistance and strength. This has been far clearer to Jewish communities outside the United States, which often have tighter ties to Israel. Those communities are smaller and less prosperous than the American Jewish community, and less influential politically in part because their numbers are so much smaller. It has long been far more common for Australian or Mexican Jews to visit Israel and study there, for example, than American Jews.

The changing roles of Israel and the Diaspora—who is the giver of aid and who the recipient—have now been ensconced in Israel's Basic Law. In 2018, what was commonly known as the "nation-state law" was adopted and included this language in a section called the "Connection to the Jewish People":

(a) The state shall strive to ensure the welfare of members of the Jewish people in trouble or in captivity due to the fact of their Jewishness or due to their citizenship.

(b) The state shall act within the Diaspora to strengthen the affinity between the state and members of the Jewish People.

(c) The state shall act to preserve the cultural, historical and religious heritage of the Jewish people among Jews of the Diaspora.[95]

This is broad language; what does "act within the Diaspora" or "act...among Jews of the Diaspora" mean? Is Israel "implicitly asserting interpretive sovereignty over essential issues of Jewish identity worldwide"?[96] It is certainly "a paradigm shift from the request in the Declaration of Independence asking diaspora Jews to assist the newly born State of Israel."[97] There, the founders of the new state said, "We appeal to the Jewish people throughout the Diaspora to rally round the Jews of Eretz-Israel in the tasks of immigration and upbuilding and to stand by them in the great struggle for the realization of the age-old dream—the redemption of Israel."[98]

That Israel should try to free captives or should try to help Jews in communities under great pressure (in Ukraine, for example) is not controversial. That it must assist American Jews is a newer concept. Yet as long ago as 1994, this notion of Israel being strong enough to take some responsibility for all Diaspora Jews was being expressed officially. On a visit to the United States, then deputy foreign minister Yossi Beilin said, "We do not need your money. We do not need charity anymore. Your own communities need it more than we do."[99] It was during this trip that Beilin proposed a program that pays for a trip to Israel for every American teenager, which was brought into existence with Birthright five years later. Far more recently, Israel's then minister of Diaspora affairs Nachman Shai visited Florida in 2021 when an apartment building with numerous Jewish residents collapsed in Miami. Here is a part of his interview with *Jewish Insider*:

> "There's a message here that I believe should be delivered, that when you're in trouble, we are there to help," Shai told *Jewish Insider* in an interview on Sunday night. "When we are in trouble, you are coming to help us. I remember that every single opportunity that is needed any assistance, any help from the United States with any administration—by the way, Republican, Democrats, in general—you're always there for us."...
>
> "I was told that they raised the question, 'Will Israel come to help us?' I don't think Italians will ask this question when it comes to Italy, and I don't think Irish will," Shai said. "But when it comes to Jews, they look at Israel as a source of hope, power."
>
> In the past, Israel had relied on the assistance of Jewish communities around the world during times of crisis. "That world has changed," said

> Shai. Now, Israel is "relatively safe, and much less dependent on world Jewry. So it's now time for us to give, not only to get."[100]

It's clear that the levels of American Jewish support for Israel that reflected its poverty, underdevelopment, and international isolation as well as the threats of its annihilation have eroded substantially. They may rise and fall as the perception of threats to Israel do. After the 1973 war and in the decades of increasing Israeli prosperity as the "Start-Up Nation," the perception that Israel was under threat diminished substantially. But now, after the 2023 Gaza war and with the realization that Iran and its proxies really do intend to destroy the Jewish state, the perception of danger has grown. Shai's evaluation of Israel as "relatively safe" seems overly optimistic. Still, Israel is not at war with any Arab state and its economy and population have grown fast. It is the center of world Jewish life. It is entirely appropriate that Israel help not only small Diaspora communities at immediate risk but also the largest Diaspora community. Given the continuing need for diplomatic and military support from the United States, the condition of the American Jewish community and the level of its engagement with Israel is a matter of great national interest for Israel—even a matter of national security.

D. BEST BETS

The cost of visiting and spending weeks, semesters, or a full academic year in Israel, of Jewish camping, and of Jewish education is a significant barrier to entry for many American

Jewish families. As Daniel Held has shown in Toronto, demand among non-Orthodox Jews is elastic and will respond to changes in cost—and in perceived quality and value. The genius of Birthright, of course, was to eliminate almost all barriers to entry for a visit to Israel. This will be much more difficult due to the cost of full-time schooling and even camping.

But they are, in my view, the best bets we can make today because each in its own way creates a sense of identity, community, and peoplehood. *Each creates an immersive experience for the young, non-Orthodox American Jew to live as a Jew among Jews—something that he or she may very well never have done before.* And the impact, according to the (imperfect, to be sure) data we have, can be lasting and life changing.

In Jewish communities in Europe and among Jewish immigrants to the United States, this kind of immersive experience was the way life was lived even for those without religious faith and who eschewed religious practice. But in the last seventy-five years, as Jewish ethnic neighborhoods disappeared, only the Orthodox still live this kind of densely Jewish life in America. To provide such an experience to young non-Orthodox American Jews seems to me the single most likely path to generating or regenerating their sense of belonging to a community, a people, that extends globally in space and forward and backward through time.

Jews, Judaism, and Israel

Why be so concerned if the Jewish community becomes smaller, less vibrant, and less engaged with Israel, so long as a core remains committed and strong?

When it comes to that core itself, larger numbers of Jews of all sorts provide a sort of protective cocoon. Sheer size permits the existence of Jewish institutions—homes for the aged, religious and cultural institutions, institutions or programs of higher learning, and defense agencies, for example—that certainly benefit the most engaged Jews, of whom a high proportion are religiously observant.

And sheer size will matter when it comes to American politics: it's obvious that Israel will be better off if there are five or ten million American Jews rather than two or three million. Walter Russell Mead has argued that American Christian support for Israel has, in the long run, been more consequential than American Jewish support, and one should not exaggerate the role the Jewish community played. But times are changing: in those past decades, the United States was a far more religious, and a far more Christian, society than it is now, and evangelical support for Israel was rising rather than (among younger evangelicals) declining. In the coming decades, if evangelical support softens, American Jews will become an increasingly important component of the support base for Israel.

Political support for Israel is not guaranteed in the coming decades. It is quite possible to see Israel becoming far less a point of bipartisan agreement, especially if younger generations of Democrats pull away from it and younger evangelicals lose their parents' and grandparents' enthusiasm for the Jewish State.

The conclusion should be clear: American Jews are needed as a firm base of support for Israel among the American public, and for that to happen, support for Israel must be maintained and enlarged in the American Jewish community. This will be almost automatic among Orthodox and other traditional practicing Jews, but not among the far larger percentages of American Jews who do not practice the religion—whether they call themselves Jews by religion or Jews of no religion. As we've seen, the data show more and more people with Jewish parents, one Jewish parent, or what Pew called a "Jewish background," dissociating themselves from the Jewish community or collective—from the sense of Jewish peoplehood and accordingly from engagement with Israel.

The strengthening of support for Israel and of a sense of Jewish peoplehood among American Jews are two sides of the same coin, and the role of Israel is critical for both. The American Jewish community, like all Diaspora communities, will not thrive outside of a deep engagement with the first Jewish state for 2,000 years. To imagine that it can, as a sort of rival for influence in the Jewish world and as an alternative model Jewish community that can survive and strengthen without embracing Israel, is folly. Israel is the center of world Jewish life and increasingly of the world's Jewish population.

Today, engagement with Israel is neither an act of charity nor "merely" an act of solidarity with endangered Jews. Today, engagement with Israel is the most vital building block of future Jewish identity for non-observant Jews throughout the Diaspora—and (to borrow a word from Daniel Held) the American Jewish community is not a unicorn. Like Australian or French, Canadian or British, Brazilian or Mexican Jews, our community must also realize that Israel is the center of Jewish life. Coming to know, embrace, and love Israel is central to religious Jews as a matter of faith—but it is as important *or more so* for those who lack that faith and seek another building block for their Jewish identity. Jewish peoplehood survived for two thousand years without a Jewish state, but it will not survive today outside of a relationship with that state. That engagement with Israel is both a way to build the sense of Jewish identity among younger Jewish generations, and a critical base for sustaining the relationship between the United States and Israel.

I have tried to show here that what is sometimes called the 'deep and unbreakable bond between American Jews and Israel,' itself a piece of the similarly 'deep and unbreakable bond between the United States and Israel,' are inaccurate descriptions of the past—and perhaps of the future. American Jews were sometime Zionists whose commitment to Israel has risen and fallen over time. That commitment has rarely compared to the ties felt—and lived—by Jews in other Diaspora countries. If the American Jewish community's ties to Israel are to be maintained and strengthened in the next generation, this will be because American Jews *intentionally* build them. And the key to that is *physical*: to go there and spend time there, to travel and study there, to live there for weeks, months, semesters, years.

For the American Jewish community, that benefit is clear: nothing seems to be more powerful not only in creating a lasting connection to the Jewish state but in awakening a sense of peoplehood among average, non-Orthodox American Jews. And for Israel, facing declining support among younger Democrats and younger evangelicals in the opinion polls, building a stronger base of knowledgeable and active supporters among young American Jews is an important goal. That is why I have argued that Israel should take a more active role in the programs that bring American Jews to Israel for travel and study.

However much Israel may need American Jews in future political and policy struggles, American Jewry needs Israel as a source and sustainer of Jewish peoplehood. The gradual erosion of ethnic group identity in America is a broad phenomenon, so I think many Americans—Jewish and non-Jewish—can be forgiven for failing to see this as a tragedy we must work hard to avoid. Among Jews, the Pew survey found, only 45 percent of "Jews by religion" said it was "very important" to them that their grandchildren be Jews; and of "Jews of no religion," only 4 percent did so.[101] It seems that the number of American Jews who care about that collective identity is diminishing.

You can't persuade people who simply don't care that they should do so. Instead, my goal is to persuade those *who do care* that the community is not growing stronger and that there are practical steps that can and must be taken to reverse some of the negative trends. There are no mysteries here. We have a very good idea of what should be done. The question is whether American Jews can take a hard look at ourselves, our community, and our philanthropy, and make the changes that are needed.

Conclusion

Visiting Israel several times since the October 7 massacres and the Gaza war, I've found a changed country. The terrible divisions among Israelis in the months before the war were pushed aside by the urgency of saving their country. Political struggles will surely return because the divisions are deep, but the lesson has been learned: Israelis cannot afford to see each other as enemies while their real enemies prepare to strike the Jewish state.

For American Jews, there were also lessons. Many "allies" abandoned the Jews as soon as the conflict began. Anti-Semitism was increasingly visible in word and deed. The prestigious colleges that Jews had idolized and aimed for during a century of assimilation found themselves awash in anti-Semitic activities, often led by professors and administrators—and the presidents, deans, and provosts were all too often mute and inert. Jewish students were suddenly on their own.

But what did we learn from all of that?

There are "a thousand points of light" in the American Jewish community. Not only are there new schools, there are new camps, scores of programs that provide ways to travel to or study in Israel, many thoughtful efforts to address the issue of financing day school education, programs to improve supplemental education and to teach Hebrew, and a host of programs that bring young Jews together—whether for one shabbat or weekend, or to live together as residents of a new self-made Jewish community. Every JCC and local federation, many Jewish foundations, and many synagogues are trying new approaches to increasing membership and charitable support, and are inventing new programming that will reach and attract Jews who may not yet be engaged with the community. Sometimes it seems like a community in ferment, actively addressing its perceived problems.

This is accurate, but so is the conclusion that the community is declining in numbers over time. With every decade, there are more people "of Jewish background" who are not now Jews, and more children being raised outside the Jewish faith and the Jewish community in homes where one parent or even two descend from Jews. In America, one must choose to be a Jew, and never in the long history of the Jews has it been easier to make another choice. The data clearly shows how many are choosing not to live as part of the Jewish people and are choosing to raise their children outside of it.

There is a wonderful story about the Duke of Wellington, who in Britain's then highly stratified society was once asked "Your Grace, from whom are you descended?" The Duke replied "Madam, I am not a descendant. I am an ancestor." Every American Jew is a descendant—but has the choice whether to be an ancestor of more generations of Jews or of Americans "of Jewish background" who feel no attachment to the Jewish people or the Jewish state.

For that great majority of American Jews who do not practice the Jewish religion in any serious fashion, the vast powers of assimilation and intermarriage in this open and free society are eroding the ability to pass on a sense of Jewish peoplehood and collective identity to one's children.

To sustain it requires immersive experiences that connect Jews to other Jews and to the Jewish state. And I've argued here that *three such experiences are shown by data to be the most likely to succeed: Jewish day schools, Jewish camps, and time in Israel.*

If that is right, the beehive of activity in the American Jewish community may risk losing focus. Not every new program is likely to work; not every experiment will get at what seems to be the critical factor in building Jewish identity: *living as a Jew among Jews*. Of course, the basic building block for American Jews, as in every society, is the family, but the vast majority of American Jewish families do not provide the kind of immersion that Jewish family life did seventy-five or one hundred years ago.

A strong Jewish identity was natural for the children or grandchildren of immigrants living in dense Jewish neighborhoods and social networks; Jewishness was pervasive. When I was a child, we had dinner with my immigrant grandparents and all my aunts, uncles, and cousins every Sunday. Everyone lived in the same city, everyone had a kosher home, and there was plenty of Yiddish spoken. My own children and grandchildren—and their cousins and Jewish friends—have had a very different upbringing in America.

Today, most Jews live, raise, and educate their children less in the Jewish community than in the borderless American society we experience each day. So, living as a Jew among Jews does not happen naturally; *the experience must intentionally be created*. And it can be by any American Jew—for semesters or academic years, or for summers, here and in Israel.

The historian Lucy Dawidowicz once wrote that "The reward of being Jewish lies in defining oneself, not in being defined."[1] Too many American Jews are losing that reward by drifting into a new and easy definition as Americans with Jewish heritage or background (or even a religious "preference") that has little meaning for their lives. They are being defined by the open society in which they live.

But this is not inevitable; they can once again define themselves as Jews and take their place among this extraordinary people extending across the world and back thousands of years in history. This may occasionally happen after an individual search for meaning, but much more often, it will happen as a discovery made among other Jews. Those who care most about the future of American Jewry and its relationship with the Jewish state should be providing those opportunities—to be a Jew among Jews, sometimes at home or school or camp, and sometimes in the Jewish state absorbing what Dawidowicz called the "gift" of being Jewish: "in possessing one's own heritage and in affirming one's existence on one's own ground."[2]

No better goal for the American Jewish community can be described. Is it possible? If we will it, it is no dream.

Bibliography

Abelson, Raziel. "Jewishness & the Young Intellectuals." *Commentary*, April 1961. https://www.commentary.org/articles/raziel-abelson/jewishness-the-younger-intellectuals-contributors/.

Abrams, Elliott. *Faith or Fear: How Jews Can Survive in a Christian America*. New York: The Free Press, 1997.

Abrams, Samuel J., and David Bernstein. "Liberals, Progressives, Wokeness, and Israel." *Jewish Journal*, December 13, 2022. https://jewishjournal.com/commentary/opinion/354001/liberals-progressives-wokeness-and-israel/.

Aharon, Nettie, and Alex Pomson. "What's Happening at the Flagpole? Studying Camps as Institutions for Israel Education." *Journal of Jewish Education* 84, no. 4 (2018).

Alper, Becka A. "Modest Warming in U.S. Views on Israel and Palestinians." Pew Research Center, May 26, 2022. https://www.pewresearch.org/religion/2022/05/26/modest-warming-in-u-s-views-on-israel-and-palestinians/.

Anabi, Or and Tamar Hermann. "Does Iran Pose an Existential Threat? Israeli Voice Index November 2021." Israel Democracy Institute, December 8, 2021. https://en.idi.org.il/articles/36760.

AP and Times of Israel Staff. "My Nation Is in Trauma: Herzog Says Now Not the Time to Discuss 2-state Solution." *Times of Israel*, December 15, 2023. https://

www.timesofisrael.com/my-nation-is-in-trauma-herzog-says-now-not-the-time-to-discuss-2-state-solution.

Arian, Ramie. "Funding Jewish Overnight Camp." *Greenbook: A Guide to Intelligent Giving* 4, Jewish Funders Network (March 2016): 79. https://jewishcamp.org/wp-content/uploads/2017/01/Final-JFN-Greenbook-on-Jewish-Camping.pdf.

Auerbach, Jerold S. "Are We One? Menachem Begin and the Long Shadow of 1977." *Envisioning Israel: The Changing Ideas and Images of North American Jews*. Edited by Allon Gal. 319–334. Detroit and Jerusalem: Wayne State University Press, 1996.

"Bad Boy Beilin Seeks to Scrap Jewish Agency." *Forward*, July 1, 1994.

Balz, Dan. "A Changed Democratic Party Continues to Influence the Biden Presidency." *Washington Post*, May 22, 2021. https://www.washingtonpost.com/politics/sunday-take-biden-liberals-israel/2021/05/22/d6131834-bb0d-11eb-96b9-e949d5397de9_story.html.

Bar-Siman-Tov, Yaacov. "The United States and Israel Since 1948: A 'Special Relationship'?" *Diplomatic History* 22, no. 2 (Spring 1998).

Bar-Zohar, Michael. *Ben-Gurion: A Biography*. New York: Delacorte, 1979.

Bershtel, Sara, and Allan Graubard. *Saving Remnants: Feeling Jewish in America*. Berkeley: University of California Press, 1992.

"The Values & Spirit of Birthright Israel." Birthright Israel Foundation. Accessed April 7, 2024. https://birthrightisrael.foundation/approach/.

Bitton, Israel B., and Melissa L. Steinberg. "The Prosecution—or Lack Thereof—of Anti-Jewish Hate Crimes in NYC." *Americans Against Antisemitism*, July 2022. https://issuu.com/americansaa/docs/prosecutions_or_lack_thereof_of_hate_crimes_in_new.

Brecher, Frank W. "US Secretary of State Marshall's Losing Battles against President Harry S Truman's Palestine Policy, January-June 1948." *Middle Eastern Studies* 48, no. 2 (March 2012).

Breitman, Richard, and Allan J. Lichtman. *FDR and the Jews*. Cambridge: Harvard University Press, 2014.

Buie, Lisa. "Florida Jewish Schools Booming Thanks to Sunshine and School Choice Scholarships." NextSteps, April 28, 2021. https://www.reimaginedonline.org/2021/04/florida-jewish-schools-booming-thanks-to-sunshine-and-school-choice-scholarships/.

Caplan, Neil. "Early Arab-Zionist Negotiation Attempts, 1913-1931." *Futile Diplomacy- A History of Arab-Israeli Negotiations, 1913-56*. Vol. 1, London: Routledge, 2015.

Carroll, Lucy. "Falling enrolments, high fees threaten viability of Sydney's Jewish schools." *Sydney Morning Herald*, July 30, 2022. https://www.smh.com.au/national/nsw/falling-enrolments-high-fees-threaten-viability-of-sydney-s-jewish-schools-20220701-p5ay9f.html.

Charendoff, Mark. "Publisher's Note." *Sapir* 6 (Summer 2022). https://sapirjournal.org/education/2022/08/publishers-note-education/.

Chazan, Barry, Richard Juran, and Michael B. Soberman. "The Connection of Israel Education to Jewish Peoplehood." *Consortium for Applied Studies in Jewish*

Education, 2021. https://www.casje.org/sites/default/files/docs/jewishpeoplehood.pdf.

Clifford, Clark and Richard Holbrooke. "Showdown in the Oval Office." In *Counsel to the President: A Memoir*. New York: Anchor Books, 1992.

Cohen, Naomi. "Dual Loyalties: Zionism and Liberalism." *Envisioning Israel: The Changing Ideas and Images of North American Jews*. Edited by Allon Gal, 319–334. Detroit and Jerusalem: Wayne State University Press, 1996.

Cohen, Steven M., Ron Miller, Ira M. Sheskin, and Berna Torr. "Camp Works: The Long-Term Impact of Jewish Overnight Camp." *Foundation for Jewish Camp*, Spring 2011. https://jewishcamp.org/wp-content/uploads/2017/03/Camp-Works-FINAL-PDF.pdf.

Cohen, Steven M. and Ari Kelman. "Beyond Distancing: Young Adult American Jews and Their Alienation From Israel." The Jewish Identity Project of Reboot and Andrea and Charles Bronfman Philanthropies, 2007. https://www.jewishdatabank.org/content/upload/bjdb/574/N-Survey_American_Jews-2007-Beyond_Distancing.pdf.

Cohen, Steven M. and Ari Kelman. *Beyond Distancing: Young Adult American Jews and Their Alienation from Israel*. Stanford: Berman Jewish Policy Archive, 2007.

"Concurrent Resolution on Palestine, 79th Congress, 1st Session, December 17 and 19, 1945." In *Foreign Relations of the United States: Diplomatic Papers, 1945, The Near East and Africa, Volume VIII*. Edited by E. Ralph Perkins and S. Everett Gleason. Washington: United States Government Printing Office, 1969. https://history.state.gov/historicaldocuments/frus1945v08/d824.

Cooperman, Allan, Becka A. Alper, Anna Schiller, et al. "Jewish Americans in 2020." Pew Research Center, May 11, 2021.

"Core Mission." Hamilton Center, University of Florida. Accessed April 7, 2023. https://hamilton.center.ufl.edu/.

Cosgrove, Elliot J. "Amnesty, Israel, Apartheid." Park Avenue Synagogue, February 5, 2022. https://pasyn.org/sermon/amnesty-israel-apartheid.

Cox, Daniel A. "Emerging Trends and Enduring Patterns in American Family Life." *American Enterprise Institute, Survey Center on American Life*, February 9, 2022. https://www.americansurveycenter.org/research/emerging-trends-and-enduring-patterns-in-american-family-life/#_edn10.

Declaration of Independence. Provisional Government of Israel, May 14, 1948. https://m.knesset.gov.il/en/about/pages/declaration.aspx.

Deutch, Gabby. "Israel's New Diaspora Affairs Minister Visits a Jewish Community in Crisis." *Jewish Insider*, June 28, 2021. https://jewishinsider.com/2021/06/israels-new-diaspora-affairs-minister-visits-a-jewish-community-in-crisis/.

Douglas, Carly. "Jewish Education is at a Crisis Point." *Australian Jewish News*, August 5, 2021. https://www.australianjewishnews.com/jewish-education-is-at-a-crisis-point/.

Douthat, Ross. "Catholic Ideas and Catholic Realities." *First Things*, August/September 2021.

Eisenstein, Susan R. "US Birthright Participants 160% more likely to marry Jews." *Jewish News Syndicate*,

November 30, 2022. https://www.jns.org/us-birthright-participants-160-more-likely-to-marry-jews/.

Elazar, Daniel J. "Community and Polity: The Organizational Dynamics of American Jewry." In *Assimilation and Authenticity: The Problem of the American Jewish Community*. Jerusalem: Jerusalem Center for Public Affairs, 1993. https://www.jcpa.org/dje/books/cp2-ch1.htm

Fagan, Moira, and Laura Silver. "Most Israelis Express Confidence in Biden, But His Ratings Are Down From Trump's." Pew Research Center, July 11, 2022. https://www.pewresearch.org/global/2022/07/11/most-israelis-express-confidence-in-biden-but-his-ratings-are-down-from-trumps/.

Farberov, Snejana. '"Radical' Yale Professor Faces Calls to Be Fired Over Comments on Hamas Attacks." *New York Post*, October 12, 2023. https://nypost.com/2023/10/12/radical-yale-professor-faces-calls-to-be-fired-over-comments-on-hamas-attacks/.

Feferman, Dan. "Despite the Gloomy Headlines, American Jewry has Grown in Size." *Jewish People Policy Institute*, July 21, 2021. https://jppi.org.il/en/article/despite-the-gloomy-headlines-american-jewry-has-grown-in-size/?utm_source=jppinewsletter&utm_medium=e7#.Yxozry2cZm8.

Finefter-Rosenblum, Ilana, Rebecca Forgasz, and Jane Wilkinson. "The Future of Victorian Jewish Schools: A Community Consultation to Re-Assess the Ethical Responsibility of Schooling." *Monash University*, 2022. https://www.monash.edu/education/research/projects/the-future-of-victorian-jewish-schools-a-community-consultation-to-re-assess-the-ethical-responsibility-of-schooling.

Fischer, Shlomo. "One, Two, or Three Jewish Identities among Jewish Americans?" *Jewish People Policy Institute*, June 1, 2021. https://jppi.org.il/en/%D7%90%D7%97%D7%AA-%D7%A9%D7%AA%D7%99%D7%99%D7%9D-%D7%90%D7%95-%D7%A9%D7%9C%D7%95%D7%A9-%D7%96%D7%94%D7%95%D7%99%D7%95%D7%AA-%D7%99%D7%94%D7%95%D7%93%D7%99%D7%95%D7%AA-%D7%91%D7%99%D7%94%D7%93%D7%95/.

Fisher, Max. "As Israel's Dependence on U.S. Shrinks, So Does U.S. Leverage." *New York Times*, May 24, 2021. https://www.nytimes.com/2021/05/24/world/middleeast/Israel-American-support.html.

Frankovic, Kathy. "Israel and the Palestinians: Where Do America's Sympathies Lie?" *YouGov*, May 19, 2021. https://today.yougov.com/topics/international/articles-reports/2021/05/19/israel-and-palestinians-where-do-americas-sympathi.

Freedman, Dan. "The State of Holocaust Education in America." *Moment*, Winter 2022. https://momentmag.com/the-state-of-holocaust-education-in-america/.

Frydman, Adina H. "Moving Towards a Universal Gap Year: A Response to 'Can a Year in Israel Transform Your Teen?" *Times of Israel*, February 27, 2022. https://blogs.timesofisrael.com/moving-towards-a-universal-gap-year-a-response-to-can-a-year-in-israel-transform-your-teen/.

"Gallup Polls on American Sympathy Toward Israel and the Arabs/Palestinians (1967-Present)." Jewish Virtual Library. Accessed April 6, 2024. https://www.jewishvirtuallibrary.org/gallup-polls-on-american-sympathy-toward-israel-and-the-arabs-palestinians.

Garnett, Nicole Stelle. "Time for Religious Charter Schools." *City Journal*, December 7, 2022. https://www.city-journal.org/time-for-religious-charter-schools.

Gilboa, Eytan. "Trends in American Attitudes Toward Israel." In *Dynamics of Dependence: U.S.-Israeli Relations*. Edited by Gabriel Sheffer. New York: Routledge, 1987.

Gittleman, Zvi. "The Decline of the Diaspora Jewish Nation: Boundaries, Content, and Jewish Identity." *Jewish Social Studies* 4, no. 2 (Winter 1998).

Glazer, Nathan. *American Judaism*. Chicago: The University of Chicago Press, 2017.

Goldman, Shalom. *God's Sacred Tongue: Hebrew & The American Imagination*. Chapel Hill, NC: University of North Carolina Press, 2004.

Goldscheider, Calvin. *Jewish Continuity and Change*. Bloomington, IN: Indiana University Press (1981), 181.

Gordis, Daniel. *We Stand Divided*. New York: Harper Collins, 2019.

"Government Funding and Advocacy." The Jewish Education Project, 2022. https://www.jewishedproject.org/our-work/day-schools-yeshivas/government-funding-and-advocacy.

Graizbord, David L. *The New Zionists: Young American Jews, Jewish National Identity, and Israel*. Lanham, MD: Lexington Books, 2020.

Gurock, Jeffrey S. *America, American Jews, and the Holocaust*. American Jewish History. London: Routledge, 1998.

Halevi, Yossi Klein. "Jacob Birnbaum and the Struggle for Soviet Jewry." *Azure*, no. 17 (Spring 2004). https://azure.org.il/article.php?id=221&page=all.

Hamid, Shadi. "America Without God." *The Atlantic*, April 2021. https://www.theatlantic.com/magazine/archive/2021/04/america-politics-religion/618072/.

Hayes, Jana. "Oklahoma Attorney General: Law Against Religious Charter Schools May be Unconstitutional." *Oklahoman*, December 2, 2022. https://www.oklahoman.com/story/news/education/2022/12/02/oklahoma-ag-releases-opinion-on-religious-charter-schools/69695429007/.

Hecht, Shahar, Graham Wright, Sasha Volodarsky, and Leonard Saxe. "In the Shadow of War: Hotspots of Antisemitism on US College Campuses." Cohen Center for Modern Jewish Studies, Brandeis University, December 2023. https://www.brandeis.edu/cmjs/research/antisemitism/hotspots-2023-report1.html.

Hecht, Shahar, Leonard Saxe, and Graham Wright. "Birthright Israel's First Decade of Applicants: A Look at the Long-term Program Impact," *Jewish Futures Project*, Cohen Center for Modern Jewish Studies, Brandeis University (November 2020): 1–2.

Held, Daniel. "Experiments in Affordability Programs." *Prizmah*, November 13, 2022. https://prizmah.org/hayidion/affordability/experiments-affordability-programs-major-findings.

Herberg, Will. *Protestant Catholic Jew*. Chicago: University of Chicago Press, 1955.

Herf, Jeffrey. *Israel's Moment: International Support for and Opposition to Establishing the Jewish State, 1945–1949*. Cambridge: Cambridge University Press, 2022.

Hertzberg, Arthur. "Israel and American Jewry." *Commentary*, August 1967. https://www.commentary.org/articles/arthur-hertzberg/israel-and-american-jewry/.

Hillel International, "More Than One-Third of Jewish College Students Are Forced to Hide Their Jewish Identity, New Hillel Poll Finds." November 20, 2023. https://www.hillel.org/more-than-one-third-of-jewish-college-students-are-hiding-their-jewish-identity-on-campus-new-hillel-international-poll-finds/.

Hirsch, Ammiel. "The Fracturing of Liberal Judaism over Jewish Particularism." *Jerusalem Post*, May 27, 2021. https://www.jpost.com/opinion/the-fracturing-of-liberal-judaism-over-jewish-particularism-opinion-669407.

Hollinger, David. *After Cloven Tongues of Fire: Protestant Liberalism in Modern American History*. Princeton: Princeton University Press, 2013.

"Holocaust Education in the United States." *United States Holocaust Memorial Museum*. https://www.ushmm.org/teach/fundamentals/where-holocaust-education-is-required-in-the-us.

Horowitz, Bethamie. "Connections and Journeys: Assessing Critical Opportunities for Enhancing Jewish Identity." UJA-Federation of Jewish Philanthropies of New York, 2000. https://www.jewishdatabank.org/content/upload/bjdb/539/Connections%20and%20Journeys...1998_Horowitz_Main_Report.pdf.

"In U.S., Decline of Christianity Continues at Rapid Pace." Pew Research Center, October 17, 2019. https://www.pewresearch.org/religion/2019/10/17/in-u-s-decline-of-christianity-continues-at-rapid-pace/.

"Internationalization Strategy and Budget." Council for Higher Education. Accessed April 7, 2024. https://che.org.il/en/strengthening-internationalism-higher-education/.

Isaac, David. "A Breakable Alliance? Israeli Conference Spotlights Worrying Socio-Political Trends in US." *Jewish News Syndicate*, November 16, 2022. https://www.jns.org/a-breakable-alliance-israeli-conference-spotlights-worrying-socio-political-trends-in-us/.

Jacobs, Paula. "The Changing Landscape of Hebrew Education." *Tablet*, December 16, 2022. https://www.tabletmag.com/sections/community/articles/changing-landscape-hebrew-education.

"Jewish Experiential Education at Camp." Collaborative for Applied Studies in Jewish Education. https://www.casje.org/focus/jewish-experiential-education-camp.

Jewish Federations of North America. "2023 Israel Hamas War Sentiment Survey." November 7, 2023. https://cdn.fedweb.org/fed-1/1/Federations%2520Survey%2520Deck%2520-%2520security%252C%2520antisemitism%252C%2520politics.pdf.

Kagan, Robert. "Opinion | The U.S.-Europe Divide." *Washington Post*, May 26, 2002. https://www.washingtonpost.com/archive/opinions/2002/05/26/the-us-europe-divide/e0f57fc2-39ed-4255-ba8e-00c2be57b40b/.

Kampeas, Ron. "As Israel debates rage, Jewish professionals face employment repercussions." *Jewish Telegraphic Agency*, April 8, 2011. https://www.jta.org/2011/04/08/united-states/as-israel-debates-rage-jewish-professionals-face-employment-repercussions.

Kaufman, Elliot. "'Inconvenient Anti-Semites' in New York's War on Hate." *Wall Street Journal*, December 17–18, 2022. https://www.wsj.com/articles/inconvenient-anti-semites-new-york-hate-crime-kanye-jewish-black-hasidic-brooklyn-11671200214.

Kaufman, Menahem. "Envisaging Israel: the Case of the United Jewish Appeal." In *Envisioning Israel: The Changing Ideals and Images of North American Jews*. Edited by Allon Gal, 224. Detroit: Wayne State University Press, 1996.

Keinon, Herb. "Jones: Israeli-Palestinian Strife Still Core of ME Ills." *Jerusalem Post*, February 8, 2011. https://www.jpost.com/middle-east/jones-israeli-palestinian-strife-still-core-of-me-ills.

Klein, Zvika. "Rashida Tlaib: You Can't Hold Progressive Values, Back Israel's Apartheid Gov't." *Jerusalem Post*, September 21, 2022. https://www.jpost.com/diaspora/antisemitism/article-717725.

Koenig, Melissa. "Over 100 Columbia Professors Sign Letter Defending Students who Supported Hamas' 'Military

Action.'" *New York Post*, October 30, 2023. https://nypost.com/2023/10/30/metro/columbia-professors-sign-letter-defending-students-who-supported-hamas-military-action/.

Kozodoy, Neal. "In Memoriam: Lucy S. Dawidowicz." *Commentary*, May 1992. https://www.commentary.org/articles/neal-kozodoy/in-memoriam-lucy-s-dawidowicz/.

Kristol, Irving. "Why Religion Is Good for the Jews." *Commentary*, August 1994. https://www.commentary.org/articles/irving-kristol/why-religion-is-good-for-the-jews/.

Lake, Eli. "Frantz Fanon, Oracle of Decolonization." *Free Press*, October 31, 2023. https://www.thefp.com/p/frantz-fanon-decolonization-israel-hamas.

Lambert, Hannah Ray. "California Professors Blast University System for 'Unsafe' Comments about Hamas." Fox News, October 30, 2023. https://www.foxnews.com/politics/california-professors-blast-university-system-unsafe-comments-hamas.

Lansing, Robert. "The Secretary of State to President Wilson, December 13, 1917." *Papers Relating to the Foreign Relations of the United States, The Lansing Papers, 1914–1920, Volume II*. Edited by J. S. Beddie. Washington: United States Government Printing Office, 1940. https://history.state.gov/historicaldocuments/frus1914-20v02/d59.

Lapson, Ariel. "Strategic Plan for Philanthropy 2021–2025." *Samis* 10, March 11, 2021. https://samisfoundation.org/wp-content/uploads/2021/03/Samis-Foundation-Strategic-Plan-For-Philanthropy.pdf.

Liebman, Charles, and Bernard Susser. *Choosing Survival.* New York: Oxford University Press, 1999.

Liebman, Charles. "Diaspora Influence on Israel: The Ben-Gurion-Blaustein 'Exchange' and Its Aftermath." *Jewish Social Studies* 36, no. 3/4 (1974): 273–75.

Liebman, Charles. *The Ambivalent American Jew: Politics, Religion and Family in American Jewish Life.* Philadelphia: Jewish Publication Society, 1973.

Lintl, Peter, and Stefan Wolfrum. "Israel's Nation-State Law." *German Institute for International and Security Affairs SWP Comment* 41 (October 2018): 5. https://www.swp-berlin.org/en/publication/israels-nation-state-law.

Lipset, Seymour Martin. *American Pluralism and the Jewish Community.* New Brunswick: Transaction Publishers, 1990.

Lipset, Seymour Martin, and Earl Raab. *Jews and the New American Scene.* Cambridge: Harvard University Press, 1995.

Lugo, Luis, Alan Cooperman, Cary Funk, Gregory A. Smith, Erin O'Connell, and Sandra Stencel. "Nones on the Rise." Pew Research Center, October 9, 2012. https://www.pewresearch.org/religion/2012/10/09/nones-on-the-rise/.

Lugo, Luis, Alan Cooperman, Gregory A. Smith, Erin O'Connell, and Sandra Stencel. "A Portrait of Jewish Americans." Pew Research Center, October 1, 2013. https://www.pewresearch.org/religion/2013/10/01/jewish-american-beliefs-attitudes-culture-survey.

Magid, Jacob. "Support for Israel Among Young US Evangelical Christians Drops Sharply—Survey."

Times of Israel, May 25, 2021. https://www.timesofisrael.com/support-for-israel-among-young-us-evangelicals-drops-sharply-survey/.

Malloy, Tim, and Doug Schwartz. "84% Of Voters Concerned The U.S. Will Be Drawn Into Military Conflict In The Middle East, Quinnipiac University National Poll Finds; Concern About Prejudice Against Jewish People In U.S. Hits Record High." Quinnipiac University, November 2, 2023. https://poll.qu.edu/poll-release?releaseid=3882.

Malloy, Tim, and Doug Schwartz. "Mideast Conflict." In "85% of Republicans Want Candidates to Agree with Trump, Quinnipiac University National Poll Finds; Americans Support Early Cut to Federal Jobless Benefit." Quinnipiac University, May 26, 2021. https://poll.qu.edu/poll-release?releaseid=3810.

Marcia, Forest Rain. Israel's Nation State Law." The Israel Forever Foundation. Accessed April 7, 2024. https://israelforever.org/interact/blog/israels_nation_state_law/.

McKinley, William, and Wade Clark Roof. *American Mainline Religion*. New Brunswick: Rutgers University Press, 1987.

Mead, Walter Russell. *The Arc of a Covenant*. New York: Knopf, 2022.

Medoff, Rafael. *Jewish Americans and Political Participation*. Santa Barbara: ABC-CLIO, 2002.

Medoff, Rafael. *The Jews Should Keep Quiet: Franklin D. Roosevelt, Rabbi Stephen S. Wise, and the Holocaust*. New York: Jewish Publication Society, 2019.

Murphy, Caryle. "Interfaith marriage is common in U.S., particularly among the recently wed." Pew Research Center, June 2, 2015. https://www.pewresearch.org/fact-tank/2015/06/02/interfaith-marriage/.

Newport, Frank. "Millennials' Religiosity Amidst the Rise of the Nones." *Gallup*, October 29, 2019. https://news.gallup.com/opinion/polling-matters/267920/millennials-religiosity-amidst-rise-nones.aspx.

Oren, Michael. "The Second War of Independence." *Azure Online*, Winter 2007. https://azure.org.il/article.php?id=28.

"Our Principles," University of Austin. Accessed April 7, 2024. https://www.uaustin.org/our-principles.

Parker, Christopher. "Catholic, Muslim, and Jewish Schools in New York Are Lobbying 'With One Voice' for STEM Education Funding." *America*, October 6, 2022. https://www.americamagazine.org/faith/2022/10/06/interfaith-school-funding-243877.

Pergola, Sergio Dan. "The Pew 2020 survey in the context of demographic studies, and US Jewry in the global Jewish context." *Jewish People Policy Institute*, June 28, 2021. http://jppi.org.il/en/article/סקר-פ%D6%BCיו%D6%BC-pew-2020-בהקשר-הדמוגרפי-ויהדות-ארה/?utm_source=jppinewsletter&utm_medium=e6#.YNnk-C2cZBw.

Peters, Jeremy W. "Jewish Viewers Find a Refuge in Fox News." *New York Times*, November 3, 2023. https://www.nytimes.com/2023/11/03/business/media/fox-news-jews-israel.html.

Pinker, Edieal. "Projecting Religious Demographics: The Case of Jews in the United States." *Journal for the Scientific Study of Religion* 60, no. 2 (2022).

Pomson, Alex and Vardit Ringvald. "Becoming connected to Israel through Hebrew: Promising new evidence." Rosov Consulting, April 8, 2021. https://www.rosovconsulting.com/learning/news/becoming-connected-to-israel-through-hebrew-promising-new-evidence/.

"Project Atlas: Israel." Institute of International Education, August 2023. https://www.iie.org/en/Research-and-Insights/Project-Atlas/Explore-Data/Israel.

Raffel, Martin J. "A History of Israel Advocacy." *Jewish Polity and American Civil Society: Communal Agencies and Religious Movements in the American Public Sphere*. Edited by Alan Mittleman, Jonathan D. Sarna, and Robert A. Licht. Lanham, MD: Rowman & Littlefield, 2002.

Rawidowicz, Simon. "Israel: The Ever-Dying People." *Judaism* 16, no. 4 (1967).

"Religion: A Trumpet for All Israel." *Time*, October 15, 1951. https://content.time.com/time/subscriber/article/0,33009,815531,00.html.

Robertson, Nick. "Tlaib Asserts Biden is 'Supporting Genocide' in Gaza." *The Hill*, November 3, 2023. https://thehill.com/homenews/house/4293191-tlaib-asserts-biden-is-supporting-genocide-in-gaza/.

Robinson, Sofia. "Cornell Professor 'Exhilarated' by Hamas's Attacks Defends Remarks." *Cornell Daily Sun*, October 16, 2023. https://cornellsun.

com/2023/10/16/cornell-professor-exhilarated-by-hamass-attack-defends-remark/.

Rocker, Simon. "Big Rise in UK Jewish School Numbers." Jewish Chronicle, January 17, 2019. https://www.thejc.com/education/education-news/jewish-day-school-pupil-numbers-rise-by-nearly-12-per-cent-in-three-years-1.478677.

Rod, Marc. "The Supreme Court Eliminated Affirmative Action. Where Does the Jewish Community Stand?" *Jewish Insider*, June 30, 2023. https://jewishinsider.com/2023/06/supreme-court-affirmative-action-harvard-university-of-north-carolina-jewish-community/.

Roosevelt, Franklin D. "Letter from President Roosevelt to King Ibn Saud." In *Attitude of American Government Toward Palestine*. Department of State Bulletin, October 21, 1945. 623. https://avalon.law.yale.edu/20th_century/decad161.asp.

Rose, Alex. "The Unequal Cost of Jewish Education in Canada." *Canadian Jewish News*, September 4, 2019. https://thecjn.ca/perspectives/the-unequal-cost-of-jewish-education-in-canada/.

Rosenberg, Saul. "The Trouble with Reading Hebrew." *Sapir* 6, Summer 2022. https://sapirjournal.org/education/2022/08/the-trouble-with-reading-hebrew/.

Rosner, Shmuel. "Rosner's Domain: A Land of the Young." *Jewish Journal*, February 2, 2022. https://jewishjournal.com/rosnersdomain/344687/rosners-domain-a-land-of-the-young/.

Ross, Dennis. *Doomed to Succeed*. New York: Farrar, Straus and Giroux, 2015.

Saad, Lydia. "Americans Still Pro-Israel, Though Palestinians Gain Support." *Gallup*, March 17, 2022. https://news.gallup.com/poll/390737/americans-pro-israel-though-palestinians-gain-support.aspx.

Saad, Lydia. "Gallup Vault: Americans Backed 1947 Palestine Partition Plan." *Gallup*, November 29, 2017. https://news.gallup.com/vault/222974/gallup-vault-americans-backed-1947-palestine-partition-plan.aspx.

Sarna, Jonathan. *American Judaism*. New Haven: Yale University Press, 2002.

Sarna, Jonathan. "Intermarriage in America, The Jewish Experience in Historical Context." In *Ambivalent Jew: Charles Liebman in Memoriam*, Edited by Stuart Cohen and Bernard Susser. New York: Jewish Theological Seminary, 2007.

Savage, Jacob. "The Vanishing." *Tablet*, February 28, 2023. https://www.tabletmag.com/sections/news/articles/the-vanishing.

Schoenbaum, David. *The United States and the State of Israel*. Oxford: Oxford University Press, 1993.

Schoenberg, Shira. "Jewish Groups Rethinking Vouchers, Tax Credits to Religious Schools." *Jewish Telegraphic Agency*, April 18, 2012. https://www.jta.org/2012/04/18/united-states/jewish-groups-rethinking-vouchers-tax-credits-to-religious-schools.

Schwartz, Daniel B. "Pogroms, Politics, and the Association of Jewish Studies." *Jewish Review of Books*, October 16, 2023. https://jewishreviewofbooks.

com/israel/14831/daniel-schwartz-pogroms-politics-and-the-association-of-jewish-studies/.

Shain, Yossi. *The Israeli Century*. New York: Post Hill Press, 2021.

Shapira, Anita. *Ben Gurion: Father of Modern Israel*. New Haven: Yale University Press, 2014.

Sharansky, Natan, and Gil Troy. "Can a Year in Israel Transform Your Teen?" *Sapir* (Winter 2022). https://sapirjournal.org/aspiration/2022/01/can-a-year-in-israel-transform-your-teen/.

Sillman, Daniel. "Decline of Christianity Shows No Signs of Stopping." *Christianity Today*, September 13, 2022. https://www.christianitytoday.com/news/2022/september/christian-decline-inexorable-nones-rise-pew-study.html.

Sklare, Marshall. "Intermarriage and the Jewish Future." *Commentary* 37, no. 4 (1964).

Smith, Gregory A. "About Three-in-Ten U.S. Adults Are Now Religiously Unaffiliated." Pew Research Center, December 14, 2021. https://www.pewresearch.org/religion/2021/12/14/about-three-in-ten-u-s-adults-are-now-religiously-unaffiliated/.

Spiegel, Steven L. *The Other Arab-Israeli Conflict: Making America's Middle East Policy, from Truman to Reagan*. Chicago: University of Chicago Press, 1988.

"Students." Jewish Leadership Academy. Accessed April 7, 2024. https://jlamiami.org/.

Telhami, Shibley. "Is the Israel-Gaza War Changing Public Attitudes?" Brookings Institution, November 2, 2023. https://www.brookings.edu/articles/is-the-israel-gaza-war-changing-us-public-attitudes/.

Telhami, Shibley. "As Israel Increasingly Relies on US Evangelicals for Support, Younger Ones Are Walking Away: What Polls Show." Brookings Institution, May 26, 2021. https://www.brookings.edu/blog/order-from-chaos/2021/05/26/as-israel-increasingly-relies-on-us-evangelicals-for-support-younger-ones-are-walking-away-what-polls-show/.

The Editorial Board. "The School Choice Drive Accelerates." *Wall Street Journal*, January 27, 2023. https://www.wsj.com/articles/utah-school-choice-bill-iowa-education-savings-accounts-kim-reynolds-spencer-cox-11674860799.

"Trio of Jewish Groups Calls for Passage of Historic Education Tax Bill." *Orthodox Union*, June 8, 2015. https://advocacy.ou.org/trio-jewish-groups-calls-passage-historic-education-tax-credit-bill/.

Truman, Harry S. *1946–52: Years of Trial and Hope: Memoirs: Volume II*. New York: Doubleday & Co, 1955.

Truman, Harry S. "The President's News Conference." In *The Public Papers of Harry S. Truman*. National Archives of the United States. August 16, 1945. https://www.trumanlibrary.gov/library/public-papers/106/presidents-news-conference

Truman, Harry S. "Statement by the President Following the Adjournment of the Palestine Conference in London" In *The Public Papers of Harry S. Truman*. National Archives of the United States. October 4, 1946. https://www.trumanlibrary.gov/library/public-papers/227/statement-president-following-adjournment-palestine-conference-london.

Urofsky, Melvin I. *American Zionism*. Lincoln: University of Nebraska Press, 1975.

"U.S. Presidential Elections: Jewish Voting Record." Jewish Virtual Library. Accessed April 6, 2024. https://www.jewishvirtuallibrary.org/jewish-voting-record-in-u-s-presidential-elections.

Waxman, Chaim I. Weakening Ties: American Jewish Baby-Boomers and Israel." *Envisioning Israel*. Edited by Allon Gal. Detroit: Wayne State University Press, 1996.

Waxman, Dov. "How 'Israelotry' Became an American Religion." In "How the Six-Day War Transformed Religion" by Sigal Samuel. *The Atlantic*, June 5, 2017. https://www.theatlantic.com/international/archive/2017/06/how-the-six-day-war-changed-religion/528981/.

Wertheimer, Jack. *A People Divided: Judaism in Contemporary America*. Boston: Brandeis University Press, 1997.

Wertheimer, Jack. "How to Save American Jews." *Commentary*, January 1996. https://www.commentary.org/articles/jack-wertheimer/how-to-save-american-jews/.

Wertheimer, Jack. *The New American Judaism*. Princeton: Princeton University Press, 2018.

Wertheimer, Jack. "Whatever Happened to the Jewish People." *Commentary*, June 2006. https://www.commentary.org/articles/jack-wertheimer/whatever-happened-to-the-jewish-people/.

Wertheimer, Jack. "Which Americans are Most Distant From Israel?" *eJewish Philanthropy*, March 3, 2022. https://ejewishphilanthropy.com/which-american-jews-are-most-distant-from-israel/.

Windmueller, Steven. "The Undoing: Church-state separation in America." *eJewish Philanthropy*, January 14, 2022. https://ejewishphilanthropy.com/the-undoing-church-state-separation-in-america/.

Wyman, David S. *The Abandonment of the Jews: America and the Holocaust, 1941–1945*. New York: Pantheon Books, 1984.

Wyschogrod, Michael. "Faith and the Holocaust." *Judaism* 20 (Summer 1971). Quoted in Neusner, Jacob. *Stranger at Home*. Chicago: University of Chicago Press, 1981. https://www.jstor.org/stable/1202134.

Endnotes

1 Amy Teibel and The Associated Press, "UN Chief's Comment that Hamas Attack 'Did not Happen in a Vacuum' Outrages Israeli Officials," *Fortune*, October 25, 2023, https://fortune.com/2023/10/25/un-secretary-general-says-hamas-attack-did-not-happen-in-vacuum-guterres-israel/.

2 Nathan Glazer, *American Judaism* (Chicago: University of Chicago Press, 1989), 114–5.

3 Arthur Hertzberg, "Israel and American Jewry," *Commentary,* August 1967, https://www.commentary.org/articles/arthur-hertzberg/israel-and-american-jewry/.

4 Glazer, *American Judaism*

5 Allan Cooperman et al., "Jewish Americans in 2020," Pew Research Center, May 11, 2021, https://www.pewresearch.org/religion/2021/05/11/jewish-americans-in-2020/, 43, 51-2.

CHAPTER ONE

1 Allan Cooperman et al., "Jewish Americans in 2020," Pew Research Center, May 11, 2021, https://www.pewresearch. org/religion/2021/05/11/jewish-americans-in-2020/.

2 "Religion: A Trumpet for All Israel," *Time,* October 15, 1951, https://content.time.com/time/subscriber/article/0,33009,815531,00.html.

3 Thomas B. Morgan, "The Vanishing American Jew: Leaders fear threat to Jewish survival in today's 'crisis of freedom.'" *Look Magazine,* May 5, 1964.

4 Simon Rawidowicz, "Israel: the Ever-Dying People," *Judaism* 16 (1967): 431–2.

5 Cooperman et al., "Jewish Americans," 43.

6 Ibid, 51.

7 Ibid, 52.

8 Ibid, 52–3.

9 Elliott Abrams, *Faith or Fear* (New York: The Free Press, 1997), 9.

10 Cooperman et al., "Jewish Americans," 18.

11 Ibid, 19.

12 Dan Feferman, ed, "Despite the Gloomy Headlines, American Jewry has Grown in Size," *Jewish People Policy Institute,* July 21, 2021, https://jppi.org.il/en/article/ despite-the-gloomy-headlines-american-jewry-has-grown-in-size/?utm_source=jppinewsletter&utm_medium=e7#. Yxozry2cZm8.

13 Nathan Glazer, *American Judaism* (Chicago: University of Chicago Press, 1989), xxv. The full quotation is "Charles Liebman makes the interesting point that this generation is the first in two hundred years in which Orthodoxy has not declined."

14 Cooperman et al., "Jewish Americans," 9.

15 Sergio Della Pergola, "The Pew 2020 survey in the context of demographic studies, and US Jewry in the global Jewish context," *Jewish People Policy Institute,* June 28, 2021, http://jppi.org.il/en/article/סקר-פ%D6%BCיו%D6%BC-pew-2020-בהקשר-הדמוגרפי-ויהדות-ארה/?utm_source=jppinewsletter&utm_medium=e6#.YNnk-C2cZBw.

16 Jack Wertheimer, *The New American Judaism* (Princeton: Princeton University Press, 2018), 271.

17 Jonathan Sarna, *American Judaism* (New Haven: Yale University Press, 2002), 223.

18 Ibid, 283.

19 The term "descent community" comes from David Hollinger, *After Cloven Tongues of Fire: Protestant Liberalism in Modern American History* (Princeton: Princeton University Press, 2013), 156.

20 Sara Bershtel and Allen Graubard, *Saving Remnants: Feeling Jewish in America* (Berkeley: University of California Press, 1992), 11–2.

21 Cooperman et al., "Jewish Americans," 40.

22 Caryle Murphy, "Interfaith marriage is common in U.S., particularly among the recently wed," Pew Research Center, June 2, 2015, https://www.pewresearch.org/fact-tank/2015/06/02/interfaith-marriage/.

23 Daniel A. Cox, "Emerging Trends and Enduring Patterns in American Family Life," *American Enterprise Institute, Survey Center on American Life,* February 9, 2022, https:// www. americansurveycenter.org/research/emerging-trends-and-en-during-patterns-in-american-family-life/#_edn10.

24 Irving Kristol, "Why Religion Is Good for the Jews," *Commentary,* August 1994, https://www.commentary.org/articles/irving-kristol/why-religion-is-good-for-the-jews/.

25 Cooperman et al., "Jewish Americans," 41.

26 Ibid, 95.

27 Jack Wertheimer, "Which Americans are Most Distant From Israel?" *eJewish Philanthropy,* March 3, 2022, https://ejewishphilanthropy.com/which-american-jews-are-most-distant-from-israel/.

28 Jonathan Sarna, interview with author, May 18, 2022. See also Steven M. Cohen, "A Tale of Two Jewries: The 'Inconvenient Truth' for American Jews," Jewish Life Network/Steinhardt Foundation, November 2006, https:// www.bjpa.org/content/upload/bjpa/atal/ATaleOfTwo Jewries.pdf.

29 See also Edieal Pinker, "Projecting Religious Demographics: The Case of Jews in the United States," (*Journal for the Scientific Study of Religion* 60 no, 2 (2022): 244), "In theory, intermarriage can increase the population because marriages of Jewish men to non-Jewish women on average increase the number of fertile females associated with the Jewish population. The offspring of intermarried couples

are less likely to identify as Jewish when they become adults, but the two opposing effects balance each other, leading to very little impact on total population size. This finding may seem surprising, but it is not because intermarriage is not influential on individuals or an important phenomenon. Rather, our modeling assumptions, specific parameter values, other effects, and the perspective of the entire population all work together to reduce the impact of intermarriage."

30 Feferman "Despite the Gloomy Headlines, American Jewry has Grown in Size."

31 Cooperman, et al, Jewish Americans, 43–44.

32 Sergio Della Pergola, "The Pew 2020 survey in the context of demographic studies, and US Jewry in the global Jewish context," *Jewish People Policy Institute,* June 28, 2021, http://jppi.org.il/en/article/פ-סקר%D6%BCיו%D6%BC-pew-2020-בהקשר-הדמוגרפי-ויהדות-ארה/?utm_source=jppinewsletter&utm_medium=e6#.YNnk-C2cZBw.

33 Shlomo Fischer, "One, Two, or Three Jewish Identities among Jewish Americans?" Jewish People Policy Institute, June 1, 2021, https://jppi.org.il/en/%D7%90%D7%97%D7%AA-%D7%A9%D7%AA%D7%99%D7%99%D7%9D-%D7%90%D7%95-%D7%A9%D7%9C%D7%95%D7%A9-%D7%96%D7%94%D7%95%D7%99%D7%95%D7%AA-%D7%99%D7%94%D7%95%D7%93%D7%99%D7%95%D7%AA-%D7%91%D7%99%D7%94%D7%93%D7%95/.

34 Seymour Martin Lipset and Earl Raab, *Jews and the New American Scene* (Cambridge: Harvard University Press, 1995), 6–7.

35 Bethamie Horowitz, "Connections and Journeys: Assessing Critical Opportunities for Enhancing Jewish Identity," *UJA-Federation of Jewish Philanthropies of New York,* 2000, v, https://www.jewishdatabank.org/content/upload/bjdb/539/Connections%20and%20Journeys...1998_Horowitz_Main_Report.pdf.

36 Jonathan Sarna, "Intermarriage in America, The Jewish Experience in Historical Context," in Stuart Cohen and Bernard Susser, eds., *Ambivalent Jew: Charles Liebman in Memoriam* (New York: Jewish Theological Seminary, 2007), 131.

37 Benjamin Philips,"National Jewish Population Survey 1990," https://www.myjewishlearning.com/article/national-jewish-population-survey-1990/.

38 Cooperman et al., "Jewish Americans," 29–30.

39 Ibid, 31.

40 Ibid, 125.

41 Elliot Kaufman, "'Inconvenient Anti-Semites' in New York's War on Hate," *Wall Street Journal,* December 17–18, 2022, https://www.wsj.com/articles/inconvenient-anti-semites-new-york-hate-crime-kanye-jewish-black-hasidic-brooklyn-11671200214; The *Americans Against Antisemitism* report, "The Prosecution—or Lack Thereof—of Anti-Jewish Hate Crimes in NYC" can be found at https://issuu.com/americansaa/docs/prosecutions_or_lack_thereof_of_hate_crimes_in_new.

42 Cooperman et al., "Jewish Americans," 30.

43 ibid, 122.

44 Jacob Savage, "The Vanishing," *Tablet,* February 28, 2023, https://www.tabletmag.com/sections/news/articles/the-vanishing.

45 Marc Rod, "The Supreme Court eliminated affirmative action. Where does the Jewish community stand?" *Jewish Insider,* June 30, 2023, https://jewishinsider.com/2023/06/supreme-court-affirmative-action-harvard-university-of-north-carolina-jewish-community/.

46 Cooperman et al., "Jewish Americans," 32.

47 Ibid, 123.

48 Melissa Koenig, "Over 100 Columbia professors sign letter defending students who supported Hamas' 'military action,'" *New York Post,* October 30, 2023, https://nypost.

com/2023/10/30/metro/columbia-professors-sign-letter-defending-students-who-supported-hamas-military-action/.

49 Hannah Ray Lambert, "California professors blast university system for 'unsafe' comments about Hamas," Fox News, October 30, 2023, https://www.foxnews.com/politics/california-professors-blast-university-system-unsafe-comments-hamas.

50 Sofia Robinson, "Cornell Professor 'Exhilarated' by Hamas's Attacks Defends Remarks," *Cornell Daily Sun,* October 16, 2023, https://cornellsun.com/2023/10/16/cornell-professor-exhilarated-by-hamass-attack-defends-remark/.

51 Snejana Farberov, "'Radical' Yale Professor Faces Calls to be Fired Over Comments on Hamas Attacks," *New York Post,* October 12, 2023, https://nypost.com/2023/10/12/radical-yale-professor-faces-calls-to-be-fired-over-comments-on-hamas-attacks/.

52 Eli Lake, "Frantz Fanon, Oracle of Decolonization," *Free Press,* October 31, 2023, https://www.thefp.com/p/frantz-fanon-decolonization-israel-hamas.

53 Daniel B. Schwartz, "Pogroms, Politics, and the Association of Jewish Studies," *Jewish Review of Books,* October 16, 2023, https://jewishreviewofbooks.com/israel/14831/daniel-schwartz-pogroms-politics-and-the-association-of-jewish-studies/.

54 Stephanie Saul and Anemona Hartocollis, "College Presidents Under Fire After Dodging Questions About Antisemitism," *The New York Times,* December 6, 2023, https://www.nytimes.com/2023/12/06/us/harvard-mit-penn-presidents-antisemitism.html.

55 United Nations General Assembly Resolution 3379, November 10, 1975, https://www.un.org/unispal/document/auto-insert-181963/.

56 Shahar Hecht et al., "In the Shadow of War: Hotspots of Antisemitism on US College Campuses," Cohen Center for Modern Jewish Studies, Brandeis University, December 2023,

https://www.brandeis.edu/cmjs/research/antisemitism/hotspots-2023-report1.html.

57 Jewish Federations of North America, "2023 Israel Hamas War Sentiment Survey," November 7, 2023, https://cdn.fedweb.org/fed-1/1/Federations%2520Survey%2520Deck%2520-%2520security%252C%2520antisemitism%252C%2520politics.pdf.

58 Hillel International, "More Than One-Third of Jewish College Students Are Forced to Hide Their Jewish Identity, New Hillel Poll Finds," November 20, 2023, https://www.hillel.org/more-than-one-third-of-jewish-college-students-are-hiding-their-jewish-identity-on-campus-new-hillel-international-poll-finds/.

59 Jeremy W. Peters, "Jewish Viewers Find a Refuge in Fox News," *New York Times,* November 3, 2023, https://www.nytimes.com/2023/11/03/business/media/fox-news-jews-israel.html.

60 David L. Graizbord, The New Zionists: Young American Jews, Jewish National Identity, and Israel (Lanham, MD: Lexington Books, 2020), 117.

61 Ibid, 118.

62 Ibid, 133.

63 David Isaac, "A Breakable Alliance? Israeli Conference Spotlights Worrying Socio-Political Trends in US," *Jewish News Syndicate,* November 16, 2022, https://www.jns. org/a-breakable-alliance-israeli-conference-spotlights-worrying-socio-political-trends-in-us/.

64 Barry Chazan, Richard Juran, and Michael B. Soberman, "The Connection of Israel Education to Jewish Peoplehood," *Consortium for Applied Studies in Jewish Education* 4 (2013), accessed March 24, 2024, https://www.casje.org/sites/default/files/docs/jewishpeoplehood.pdf.

CHAPTER TWO

1 Raziel Abelson, "Jewishness & the Younger Intellectuals," *Commentary* (April 1961), https://www.commentary.org/articles/raziel-abelson/jewishness-the-younger-intellectuals-contributors/.

2 Sarna, *American Judaism,* 283.

3 Marshall Sklare, "Intermarriage and the Jewish Future," *Commentary* 37, no. 4 (1964): 46.

4 *American Pluralism and the Jewish Community,* ed. Seymour Martin Lipset (New Brunswick, NJ: Transaction Publishers, 1990), 3.

5 Lipset and Raab, *Jews and the New American Scene,* 47.

6 Sarna, *American Judaism,* 161.

7 Will Herberg, *Protestant Catholic Jew* (Chicago: University of Chicago Press, 1955).

8 Daniel J. Elazar,"Community and Polity: The Organizational Dynamics of American Jewry, Chapter 1," in *Assimilation and Authenticity: The Problem of the American Jewish Community* (Jerusalem: Jerusalem Center for Public Affairs, 1993), https://www.jcpa.org/dje/books/cp2-ch1.htm.

9 Graizbord, *The New Zionists,* 22.

10 Ibid, 21–22.

11 Charles Liebman, *The Ambivalent American Jew: Politics, Religion and Family in American Jewish Life* (Philadelphia: Jewish Publication Society, 1973), 75.

12 Graizbord, The New Zionists, 22–23.

13 Steven M. Cohen and Ari Kelman, *Beyond Distancing: Young Adult American Jews and Their Alienation from Israel* (Stanford: Berman Jewish Policy Archive, 2007), 21, https:// www.jewishdatabank.org/content/upload/bjdb/574/N-Survey_American_Jews-2007-Beyond_Distancing.pdf.

14 Luis Lugo et al., "'Nones' on the Rise," Pew Research Center, October 9, 2012, https://www.pewresearch.org/religion/2012/10/09/nones-on-the-rise/.

15 Gregory A. Smith, "About Three-in-Ten U.S. Adults Are Now Religiously Unaffiliated," Pew Research Center, December 14, 2021, https://www.pewresearch.org/religion/2021/12/14/about-three-in-ten-u-s-adults-are-now-religiously-unaffiliated/.

16 Daniel Silliman, "Decline of Christianity Shows No Signs of Stopping," *Christianity Today,* September 13, 2022, https:// www.christianitytoday.com/news/2022/september/christian-decline-inexorable-nones-rise-pew-study.html.

17 Chaim I. Waxman, "Weakening Ties: American Jewish Baby-Boomers and Israel," in *Envisioning Israel,* ed. Allon Gal (Detroit: Wayne State University Press, 1996), 391.

18 Ross Douthat, "Catholic Ideas and Catholic Realities," *First Things,* August 2021, 35.

19 Shadi Hamid, "America Without God," *The Atlantic,* April 2021, https://www.theatlantic.com/magazine/archive/2021/04/america-politics-religion/618072/.

20 Bernard Susser and Charles Liebman, *Choosing Survival* (New York: Oxford University Press, 1999), 68–9.

21 Wertheimer, *A People Divided: Judaism in Contemporary America* (Boston: Brandeis University Press, 1997), 191.

22 Wade Clark Roof and William McKinney, *American Mainline Religion* (New Brunswick, NJ: Rutgers University Press, 1987), 67.

23 Ammiel Hirsch, "The Fracturing of Liberal Judaism over Jewish Particularism," *Jerusalem Post,* May 27, 2021, https://www.jpost.com/opinion/the-fracturing-of-liberal-judaism-over-jewish-particularism-opinion-669407.

24 Elliott Abrams, Faith or Fear (New York: Free Press, 1997), 1.

25 Ibid, 186, 193, 197.

26 Ibid, 184.

27 Ibid, 184–185.

28 Cooperman et al., "Jewish Americans," 218.

29 Graizbord, *The New Zionists,* 24.

30 Jack Wertheimer, "How To Save American Jews," *Commentary* (January 1996), https://www.commentary. org/articles/jack-wertheimer/how-to-save-american-jews/.

31 Zvi Gitelman, "The Decline of the Diaspora Jewish Nation: Boundaries, Content, and Jewish Identity," *Jewish Social Studies* 4, no. 2 (Winter, 1998): 122.

32 Graizbord, *The New Zionists,* 273–4.

33 Lipset & Raab, *Jews and the New American Scene,* 65.

34 Jack Wertheimer, *The New American Judaism,* 270.

35 Yossi Klein Halevi, "The Tragedy of the Wall," *Times of Israel,* June 26, 2017, https://blogs.timesofisrael.com/the-tragedy-of-the-western-wall/.

36 Jack Wertheimer in "Whatever Happened to the Jewish People," *Commentary* (June 2006), 37, https://www.commentary.org/articles/jack-wertheimer/whatever-happened-to-the-jewish-people/.

37 Glazer, *American Judaism,* 142-144.

CHAPTER THREE

1 Shalom Goldman, *God's Sacred Tongue: Hebrew & The American Imagination* (Chapel Hill: University of North Carolina Press 2004), 208.

2 Robert Lansing, "The Secretary of State to President Wilson, December 13, 1917," in *Papers Relating to the Foreign Relations of the United States, The Lansing Papers, 1914–1920, Volume II,* ed. J. S. Beddie (Washington: United States Government Printing Office, 1940), https://history.state.gov/historicaldocuments/frus1914-20v02/d59.

3 Rafael Medoff, *Jewish Americans and Political Participation: A Reference Handbook* (Santa Barbara, CA: ABC-CLIO, 2002), 216.

4 Walter Russell Mead, *The Arc of A Covenant* (New York: Knopf, 2022), 42.

5 David S. Wyman, *The Abandonment of the Jews: America and the Holocaust,* 1941–1945 (New York: Pantheon Books, 1984).

6 Richard Breitman and Allan J. Lichtman, *FDR and the Jews* (Cambridge, MA: Harvard University Press, 2013).

7 Rafael Medoff, *The Jews Should Keep Quiet: Franklin D. Roosevelt, Rabbi Stephen S. Wise, and the Holocaust* (New York: Jewish Publication Society, 2019).

8 Franklin D. Roosevelt, "Letter From President Roosevelt to King Ibn Saud, April 5, 1945," in *Attitude of American Government Toward Palestine,* Department of State Bulletin, October 21, 1945, 623. https://avalon.law.yale.edu/20th_century/decad161.asp.

9 Harry S. Truman,"The President's News Conference," in *The Public Papers of Harry S. Truman,* National Archives of the United States, August 16, 1945, https://www.trumanlibrary.gov/library/public-papers/106/presidents-news-conference.

10 Harry S. Truman, *1946–52: Years of Trial and Hope: Memoirs: Volume II* (New York: Doubleday & Co, 1955), 140.

11 "37 Governors Join in Palestine Plea," *New York Times,* July 5, 1945, https://www.nytimes.com/1945/07/05/archives/37-governors-join-in-palestine-plea.html.

12 Harry S. Truman, "Statement by the President Following the Adjournment of the Palestine Conference in London," in *The Public Papers of Harry S. Truman,* National Archives of the United States, October 4, 1946, https://www.trumanlibrary.gov/library/public-papers/227/statement-president-following-adjournment-palestine-conference-london.

13 "Concurrent Resolution on Palestine, 79th Congress, 1st Session, December 17 and 19, 1945," in *Foreign Relations of the United States: Diplomatic Papers, 1945, The Near East and Africa, Volume VIII,* eds. E. Ralph Perkins and S. Everett Gleason (Washington, DC: United States

Government Printing Office, 1969), https://history.state.gov/historicaldocuments/frus1945v08/d824.

14 Jeffrey Herf, *Israel's Moment: International Support for and Opposition to Establishing the Jewish State, 1945–1949* (Cambridge, MA: Cambridge University Press, 2022), 461.

15 Ibid, 251.

16 Ibid, 263–4.

17 Ibid, 11.

18 Clark Clifford and Richard Holbrooke, "Showdown in the Oval Office," in *Counsel to the President: A Memoir* (New York: Anchor Books, 1992).

19 Herf, *Israel's Moment,* 453.

20 Frank W. Brecher, *American Diplomacy and the Israeli War of Independence,* (Jefferson, N.C: McFarland & Company, 2013), 11.

21 Herf, *Israel's Moment,* 332, 451.

22 Mead, *The Arc of a Covenant,* 43.

23 Steven L. Spiegel, *The Other Arab-Israeli Conflict: Making America's Middle East Policy, from Truman to Reagan* (Chicago: University of Chicago Press, 1988), 51.

24 Michael Oren, "The Second War of Independence," *Azure Online,* Winter 2007, https://azure.org.il/article.php?id=28.

25 Yaacov Bar-Siman-Tov, "The United States and Israel Since 1948: A 'Special Relationship?'" *Diplomatic History* 22, no. 2 (Spring 1998): 233.

26 Spiegel, *The Other Arab-Israeli Conflict: Making America's Middle East Policy, from Truman to Reagan*, 45; David Schoenbaum, The United States and the State of Israel (Oxford: Oxford University Press, 1993), 85.

27 Spiegel, *The Other Arab-Israeli Conflict,* 52.

28 Turki al-Hamad, "Israel and the Arab world: From illusion to realism," AlArabiya News, August 25, 2020.

29 See Bernard Lewis, "The Anti-Zionist Resolution," *Foreign Affairs,* October 1976, https://www.foreignaffairs.com/articles/israel/1976-10-01/anti-zionist-resolution.

30 Herb Keinon, "Jones: Israeli-Palestinian strife still core of ME ills," *Jerusalem Post,* February 8, 2011, https:// www. jpost.com/middle-east/jones-israeli-palestinian-strife-still-core-of-me-ills.

31 Mead, *The Arc of the Covenant,* 524.

32 Dennis Ross, *Doomed to Succeed* (New York: Farrar, Straus and Giroux, 2015), 393.

33 Herzl, Theodor, *The Complete Diaries of Theodor Herzl,* Raphael Patai, ed., (New York and London: Herzl Press and Thomas Yoseloff, 1961), vol. 1, 378.

34 Neil Caplan, *Futile Diplomacy, Volume 1: Early Arab-Israeli Negotiation Attempts,* 1913–31 (London: Routledge, 2015), 7.

35 Max Fisher, "As Israel's Dependence on U.S. Shrinks, So Does U.S. Leverage," *New York Times,* May 24, 2021, https://www.nytimes.com/2021/05/24/world/middleeast/Israel-American-support.html.

36 Lydia Saad, "Gallup Vault: Americans Backed 1947 Palestine Partition Plan," *Gallup,* November 29, 2017, https://news.gallup.com/vault/222974/gallup-vault-americans-backed-1947-palestine-partition-plan.aspx.

37 Eytan Gilboa, "Trends in American Attitudes Toward Israel," in Gabriel Sheffer, ed., *Dynamics of Dependence: U.S.-Israeli Relations* (New York: Routledge, 1987), 40–43.

38 "Gallup Polls on American Sympathy Toward Israel and the Arabs/Palestinians (1967-Present)," Jewish Virtual Library, accessed April 6, 2024, https://www.jewishvirtuallibrary.org/gallup-polls-on-american-sympathy-toward-israel-and-the-arabs-palestinians.

39 Kathy Frankovic, "Israel and the Palestinians: Where Do America's Sympathies Lie?" *YouGov,* May 19, 2021, https:// today.yougov. com/topics/international/ articles reports/2021/05/19/israel-and-palestinians-where-do-americas-sympathi.

40 Tim Malloy and Doug Schwartz, "Mideast Conflict" in "85% of Republicans Want Candidates to Agree with Trump, Quinnipiac University National Poll Finds; Americans Support Early Cut to Federal Jobless Benefit," Quinnipiac University, May 26, 2021, https://poll.qu.edu/poll-release?releaseid=3810.

41 Dan Balz, "A Changed Democratic Party Continues to Influence the Biden Presidency," *Washington Post*, May 22, 2021, https://www.washingtonpost.com/politics/sunday-take-biden-liberals-israel/2021/05/22/d6131834-bb0d-11eb-96b9-e949d5397de9_story.html.

42 Becka A. Alper, "Modest Warming in U.S. Views on Israel and Palestinians," Pew Research Center, May 26, 2022, https://www.pewresearch.org/religion/2022/05/26/modest-warming-in-u-s-views-on-israel-and-palestinians/.

43 Laura Silver and Moira Fagan, "Most Israelis Express Confidence in Biden, but His Ratings Are Down From Trump's," Pew Research Center, July 11, 2022, https://www.pewresearch.org/global/2022/07/11/most-israelis-express-confidence-in-biden-but-his-ratings-are-down-from-trumps/.

44 Lydia Saad, "Americans Still Pro-Israel, Though Palestinians Gain Support," *Gallup*, March 17, 2022, https://news.gallup.com/poll/390737/americans-pro-israel-though-palestinians-gain-support.aspx.

45 Samuel J. Abrams and David Bernstein, "Liberals, Progressives, Wokeness, and Israel," *Jewish Journal*, December 13, 2022, https://jewishjournal.com/commentary/opinion/354001/liberals-progressives-wokeness-and-israel/.

46 Ibid.

47 See for example: Shibley Telhami, "Is the Israel-Gaza War Changing Public Attitudes?" Brookings Institution, November 2, 2023, https://www.brookings.edu/articles/is-the-israel-gaza-war-changing-us-public-attitudes/.

48 Tim Malloy and Doug Schwartz, "84% Of Voters Concerned the U.S. Will Be Drawn into Military Conflict in the Middle East, Quinnipiac University National Poll Finds; Concern About Prejudice Against Jewish People In U.S. Hits Record High," Quinnipiac University, November 2, 2023, https://poll.qu.edu/poll-release?releaseid=3882.

49 Zvika Klein, "Rashida Tlaib: You Can't Hold Progressive Values, Back Israel's Apartheid Gov't," *Jerusalem Post,* September 21, 2022, https://www.jpost.com/diaspora/antisemitism/article-717725.

50 Nick Robertson, "Tlaib Asserts Biden is 'Supporting Genocide' in Gaza," The Hill, November 3, 2023, https://thehill.com/homenews/house/4293191-tlaib-asserts-biden-is-supporting-genocide-in-gaza/.

51 Pew Research Center, "Voting patterns in the 2022 elections," https://www.pewresearch.org/politics/2023/07/12/voting-patterns-in-the-2022-elections/. See also "Republican Share of Jewish Vote Rises to 33% in Midterms, Exit Poll Shows," *Jewish News Syndicate,* November 11, 2022, https://www.jns.org/republican-share-of-the-jewish-vote-rises-to-33-in-midterms-exit-poll-shows/.

52 "U.S. Presidential Elections: Jewish Voting Record," Jewish Virtual Library, accessed April 6, 2024, https://www.jewishvirtuallibrary.org/jewish-voting-record-in-u-s-presidential-elections.

53 Mead, *The Arc of the Covenant,* 501–2.

54 Ibid, 440.

55 Jacob Magid, "Support for Israel Among Young US Evangelical Christians Drops Sharply—Survey," *Times of Israel,* May 25, 2021, https://www.timesofisrael.com/support-for-israel-among-young-us-evangelicals-drops-sharply-survey/.

56 Shibley Telhami, "As Israel Increasingly Relies on US Evangelicals for Support, Younger Ones Are Walking Away: What Polls Show," Brookings Institution, May 26, 2021,

https://www.brookings.edu/blog/order-from-chaos/2021/05/26/as-israel-increasingly-relies-on-us-evangelicals-for-support-younger-ones-are-walking-away-what-polls-show/.

57 Frank Newport, "Millennials' Religiosity Amidst the Rise of the Nones," *Gallup,* October 29, 2019, https://news.gallup. com/opinion/polling-matters/267920/millennials-religiosity-amidst-rise-nones.aspx.

58 "In U.S., Decline of Christianity Continues at Rapid Pace," Pew Research Center, October 17, 2019, https://www.pewresearch.org/religion/2019/10/17/in-u-s-decline-of-christianity-continues-at-rapid-pace/.

59 Mead, The Arc of the Covenant, 585.

CHAPTER FOUR

1 Melvin I. Urofsky, American Zionism from Herzl to the Holocaust (Lincoln, NE: University of Nebraska Press, 1975), 92.

2 Jonathan Sarna, *American Judaism,* 202.

3 Urofsky, *American Zionism,* 95.

4 Daniel Gordis, *We Stand Divided* (New York: Harper Collins, 2019), 48

5 Martin J. Raffel, "A History of Israel Advocacy" in *Jewish Polity and American Civil Society: Communal Agencies and Religious Movements in the American Public Sphere,* eds. Alan Mittleman, Jonathan D. Sarna, and Robert A. Licht (Lanham, MD: Rowman & Littlefield, 2002), 105.

6 Urofsky, *American Zionism,* 97.

7 "Zionism a Fallacy, Says Morgenthau," *New York Times,* June 27, 1921, 4, https://www.nytimes.com/1921/06/27/archives/zionism-a-fallacy-says-morgenthau-wrong-in-principle-impossible-of.html.

8 Urofsky, *American Zionism,* 33.

9 Gordis, *We Stand Divided,* 87.

10 Urofsky, *American Zionism,* 257.

11 Ibid, 128–9.
12 Ibid, 297.
13 Ibid, 420–422.
14 Ibid, 429.
15 Declaration Adopted by the Biltmore Conference, May 11, 1942,https://www.jewishvirtuallibrary.org/the-biltmore-conference-1942.
16 Quoted in Henry L. Feingold, "Who Shall Bear Guilt for the Holocaust: The Human Dilemma," in Jeffery S. Gurock, ed., *America, American Jews, and the Holocaust: American Jewish History,* (London: Routledge, 1998), 275.
17 Anita Shapira, *Ben Gurion: Father of Modern Israel* (New Haven, CT: Yale University Press, 2014), 120.
18 Michael Bar-Zohar, *Ben Gurion: A Biography,* (New York: Delacorte, 1979), 104.
19 Charles S. Liebman, "Diaspora Influence on Israel: The Ben-Gurion–Blaustein 'Exchange' and Its Aftermath," Jewish Social Studies, Vol. 36, Nos. 3/4 (July–October 1974): 273, https://www.jstor.org/stable/4466837.
20 Ibid, 275.
21 Ibid, 275.
22 Ibid, 277.
23 Bar-Zohar, Ben-Gurion, 105.
24 Gordis, *We Stand Divided,*103–104.
25 Glazer, *American Judaism,* 114–116.
26 Sarna, *American Judaism,* 335.
27 Menahem Kaufman, "Envisaging Israel: The Case of the United Jewish Appeal," in *Envisioning Israel: The Changing Ideals and Images of North American Jews,* ed. Allon Gal (Detroit: Wayne State University Press, 1996), 224.
28 Ibid, 232.
29 Ibid, 235.
30 Dov Waxman, "How 'Israelotry' Became an American Religion," in "How the Six-Day War Transformed Religion" by Sigal Samuel, *The Atlantic,* June 5, 2017, https:// www.

theatlantic.com/international/archive/2017/06/ how-the-six-day-war-changed-religion/528981/.

31 Hertzberg, "Israel and American Jewry."

32 "Holocaust Education in the United States," United States Holocaust Memorial Museum, https://www.ushmm.org/teach/fundamentals/where-holocaust-education-is-required-in-the-us.

33 Dan Freedman, "The State of Holocaust Education in America," *Moment,* January 24, 2022, https://momentmag.com/the-state-of-holocaust-education-in-america/.

34 Yossi Klein Halevi, "Jacob Birnbaum and the Struggle for Soviet Jewry," *Azure,* no. 17 (Spring 2004), https://azure.org.il/article.php?id=221&page=all.

35 Cooperman et al., "Jewish Americans," 65.

36 Michael Wyschogrod, "Faith and the Holocaust," *Judaism* 20 (Summer 1971): 286–94, quoted in Jacob Neusner, "The Implications of the Holocaust," *Journal of Religion* 53, no. 3 (July 1973): 300–301, https://www.jstor.org/stable/1202134.

37 *The National Jewish Population Survey 2000-1,* United Jewish Communities, https://cdn.fedweb.org/fed-34/136/National-Jewish-Population-Study.pdf

38 Cooperman et al., "Jewish Americans," 138.

39 Ibid, 36.

40 Philissa Cramer, "Dozens of US rabbinical students sign letter calling for American Jews to hold Israel accountable for its human rights abuses," Jewish Telegraphic Agency, May 14, 2021, https://www.jta.org/2021/05/14/united-states/dozens-of-us-rabbinical-students-sign-letter-calling-for-american-jews-to-hold-israel-accountable-for-its-human-rights-abuses

41 Ibid, 156.

42 Ron Kampeas, "As Israel Debates Rage, Jewish Professionals Face Employment Repercussions," *Jewish Telegraphic Agency,* April 8, 2011, https://www.jta.org/2011/04/08/

united-states/as-israel-debates-rage-jewish-professionals-face-employment-repercussions.

43 Steven M. Cohen and Ari Y. Kelman, "Beyond Distancing: Young Adult American Jews and Their Alienation From Israel," The Jewish Identity Project of Reboot and Andrea and Charles Bronfman Philanthropies, 2007, 3, https://www.jewishdatabank.org/content/upload/bjdb/574/N-Survey_American_Jews-2007-Beyond_Distancing.pdf.

44 Ibid.

45 Naomi Cohen, "Dual Loyalties: Zionism and Liberalism," in *Envisioning Israel,* 321–2.

46 Ibid, 322.

47 Jerold S. Auerbach, "Are We One? Menachem Begin and the Long Shadow of 1977," in *Envisioning Israel,* 339–41.

48 AP and TOI Staff, "'My Nation Is in Trauma': Herzog Says Now Not the Time to Discuss 2-State Solution," *Times of Israel,* December 15, 2023, https://www.timesofisrael.com/my-nation-is-in-trauma-herzog-says-now-not-the-time-to-discuss-2-state-solution.

49 Gordis, *We Stand Divided,* 38.

50 Ibid, 132–133.

51 Yossi Shain, *The Israeli Century* (Nashville: Post Hill Press, 2021), 412.

52 Robert Kagan, "Opinion | The U.S.-Europe Divide," *Washington Post,* May 26, 2002, https://www. washington post.com/archive/opinions/2002/05/26/ the-us-europe-divide/e0f57fc2-39ed-4255-ba8e-00 c2be57b40b/.

53 "April 2022 National Survey of Jewish Voters," Jewish Electoral Institute, Aoril 13, 2022, https://www.jewishelectorateinstitute.org/2022-national-survey-of-jewish-voters/.

54 Or Anabi and Tamar Hermann, "Does Iran Pose an Existential Threat? Israeli Voice Index November 2021," Israel Democracy Institute, December 8, 2021, https://en.idi.org.il/articles/36760.

55 Cohen and Kelman, *Beyond Distancing,* 13.
56 Ibid, 20.
57 Wertheimer, "Which Americans are Most Distant From Israel?"
58 Steven M. Cohen, "Why Are Today's Non-Orthodox Jews More Detached From Israel?" in *Twenty-Five Essays about the Current State of Israeli-American Jewish Relations,* AJC Global Jewish Advocacy, June 2018, 18, https://www.ajc.org/sites/default/files/pdf/2018-06/Twenty-Five%20Essays%20about%20the%20Current%20State%20of%20Israeli-American%20Jewish%20Relations.pdf.
59 Cohen and Kelman, *Beyond Distancing,* 21.
60 Wertheimer, "Which Americans are Most Distant From Israel?"
61 Graizbord, *The New Zionists,* 79.
62 Wertheimer, "Which Americans are Most Distant From Israel?"
63 Ibid.
64 Shain, *The Israeli Century,* 79.
65 Graizbord, *The New Zionists,* 4.
66 Ibid, 24.
67 Ibid, 26.
68 Ibid, 273.
69 Natan Sharansky and Gil Troy, "Can a Year in Israel Transform Your Teen?" Sapir 4 (Winter 2022): January 27, 2022, https://sapirjournal.org/aspiration/2022/01/ can-a-year-in-israel-transform-your-teen/.
70 Rabbi Ammiel Hirsh, interview with author, February 9, 2022.
71 Shmuel Rosner, "Rosner's Domain: A Land of the Young," *Jewish Journal,* February 2, 2022, https://jewishjournal.com/rosnersdomain/344687/rosners-domain-a-land-of-the-young/.
72 Elliot J. Cosgrove, "Amnesty, Israel, Apartheid," Park Avenue Synagogue, February 5, 2022, https://pasyn.org/sermon/amnesty-israel-apartheid.

CHAPTER FIVE

1 Calvin Goldscheider, "Ethnicity, American Judaism, and Jewish Cohesion," in Calvin Goldscheider and Jacob Neusner, eds, *Social Foundations of Judaism* (Englewood Cliffs, N.J.: Prentice Hall, 1990), 209.
2 Rabbi Ammiel Hirsh, interview with author, February 9, 2022.
3 Wertheimer, "How to Save American Jews."
4 Ibid.
5 Mark Charendoff,"Publisher's Note," *Sapir* 6 (Summer 2022): 7, https://sapirjournal.org/education/2022/08/publishers-note-education/.
6 Danielle Alexander," interview with author, September 9, 2022.
7 Ibid.
8 Charendoff, "Publisher's Note," 7.
9 Gordis, *We Stand Divided,* 165.
10 John Ruskay, interview with author, March 28, 2022.
11 Alex Pomson and Vardit Ringvald, "Becoming Connected to Israel through Hebrew: Promising New Evidence," Rosov Consulting, April 8, 2021, https://www.rosovcon-sulting.com/learning/news/becoming-connected-to-israel-through-hebrew-promising-new-evidence/.
12 Ibid.
13 Saul Rosenberg, "The Trouble with Reading Hebrew," *Sapir* 6 (Summer 2022): 50–57, https://sapirjournal.org/education/2022/08/the-trouble-with-reading-hebrew/.
14 Ibid, 53–54.
15 Ibid, 55.
16 Ibid, 56.
17 Paula Jacobs, "The Changing Landscape of Hebrew Education," *Tablet,* December 15, 2022, https://www.tabletmag.com/sections/community/articles/changing-landscape-hebrew-education.

18 Luis Lugo et al., "A Portrait of Jewish Americans," Pew Research Center, October 1, 2013, 16, https://www.pewresearch.org/religion/2013/10/01/jewish-american-beliefs-attitudes-culture-survey.
19 Alex Pomson and Jack Wertheimer, *Inside Jewish Day Schools* (Waltham: Brandeis University Press, 2022), 255.
20 Ibid, 268.
21 Ibid, 258.
22 Ibid, 262.
23 Ariel Lapson, "Strategic Plan for Philanthropy 2021–2025," Samis Foundation, 10, https://samisfoundation.org/wp-content/uploads/2021/03/Samis-Foundation-Strategic-Plan-For-Philanthropy.pdf.
24 "Students," Jewish Leadership Academy, accessed April 7, 2024, https://jlamiami.org/.
25 Rabbi Gil Perl, interview with author, May 2, 2022.
26 Ibid.
27 Rabbi Harry Pell, interview with author, May 18, 2022.
28 Pomson and Wertheimer, *Inside Jewish Day Schools,* 273.
29 Lapson, "Strategic Plan for Philanthropy," 10.
30 Ibid, 10–11.
31 Connie Kanter,conversation with author,September 16,2022.
32 Ibid.
33 Ibid.
34 Kari Saratovsky, interview with author, March 28, 2022.
35 Kanter, conversation with author, September 16, 2022.
36 Daniel Held, "Experiments in Affordability Programs," *Prizmah,* November 13, 2022, https://prizmah.org/hayidion/affordability/experiments-affordability-programs-major-findings.
37 Ibid.
38 Ibid.
39 Ibid.
40 Daniel Held, interview with author, October 20, 2022.

41 Alex Rose, "The Unequal Cost of Jewish Education in Canada," *Canadian Jewish News,* September 4, 2019, https://thecjn.ca/perspectives/the-unequal-cost-of-jewish-education-in-canada/.

42 Simon Rocker, "Big Rise in UK Jewish School Numbers," *Jewish Chronicle,* January 17, 2019, https://www.thejc.com/education/education-news/jewish-day-school-pupil-numbers-rise-by-nearly-12-percent-in-three-years-1.478677.

43 Ilana Finefter-Rosenbluh, Rebecca Forgasz, and Jane Wilkinson, "The Future of Victorian Jewish Schools: A Community Consultation to Re-Assess the Ethical Responsibility of Schooling," Monash University, 2022, https://www.monash.edu/education/research/projects/the-future-of-victorian-jewish-schools-a-community-consultation-to-re-assess-the-ethical-responsibility-of-schooling.

44 Carly Douglas, "Jewish Education is at a Crisis Point," *Australian Jewish News,* August 5, 2021, https://www.australianjewishnews.com/jewish-education-is-at-a-crisis-point/.

45 Lucy Carroll, "Falling Enrolments, High Fees Threaten Viability of Sydney's Jewish schools," *Sydney Morning Herald,* July 30, 2022, https://www.smh.com.au/national/nsw/falling-enrolments-high-fees-threaten-viability-of-sydney-s-jewish-schools-20220701-p5ay9f.html.

46 Steven Windmueller, "The Undoing: Church-State Separation in America," *eJewish Philanthropy,* January 14, 2022, https:// ejewishphilanthropy.com/the-undoing-church-state-separation-in-america/.

47 Shira Schoenberg, "Jewish Groups Rethinking Vouchers, Tax Credits to Religious Schools," *Jewish Telegraphic Agency,* April 18, 2012, https://www.jta.org/2012/04/18/ united-states/jewish-groups-rethinking-vouchers-tax-credits-to-religious-schools.

48 Roslyn Singer, "Trio of Jewish Groups Calls for Passage of Historic Education Tax Credit Bill," Orthodox Union, June

8, 2015, https://advocacy.ou.org/trio-jewish-groups-calls-passage-historic-education-tax-credit-bill/.

49 Nicole Stelle Garnett, "Time for Religious Charter Schools," *City Journal,* December 7, 2022, https://www.city-journal.org/time-for-religious-charter-schools.

50 "Government Funding and Advocacy,"The Jewish Education Project, 2022, https://www.jewishedproject.org/our-work/day-schools-yeshivas/government-funding-and-advocacy.

51 Christopher Parker, "Catholic, Muslim and Jewish Schools in New York Are Lobbying 'With One Voice' for STEM Education Funding," *America,* October 6, 2022, https://www.americamagazine.org/faith/2022/10/06/interfaith-school-funding-243877.

52 Jana Hayes, "Oklahoma Attorney General: Law Against Religious Charter Schools May be Unconstitutional," *Oklahoman,* December 2, 2022, https://www.oklahoman.com/story/news/education/2022/12/02/oklahoma-ag-releases-opinion-on-religious-charter-schools/69695429007/.

53 Lisa Buie, "Florida Jewish Schools Booming Thanks to Sunshine and School Choice Scholarships," NextSteps, April 28, 2021, https://www.reimaginedonline.org/2021/04/florida-jewish-schools-booming-thanks-to-sunshine-and-school-choice-scholarships/.

54 The Editorial Board, "The School Choice Drive Accelerates," *Wall Street Journal,* January 28, 2023, https://www.wsj. com/articles/utah-school-choice-bill-iowa-education-savings-accounts-kim-reynolds-spencer-cox-11674860799.

55 Lapson, "Strategic Plan for Philanthropy," 10.

56 Annie Ma, "How the Presidents of Harvard, Penn and MIT Testified to Congress on Antisemitism," *Associated Press,* December 12, 2023, https://apnews.com/article/harvard-penn-mit-president-congress-intifada-193a1c81e9ebcc15c5dd68b71b4c6b71.

57 "Our Principles," University of Austin, accessed April 7, 2024, https://www.uaustin.org/our-principles.

58 "Core Mission," Hamilton Center, University of Florida, accessed April 7, 2023, https://hamilton.center.ufl.edu/.

59 Rabbi Dan Fink, interview with author, February 10, 2022.

60 John Ruskay, interview with author, March 28, 2022.

61 Rabbi David Ellenson, interview with author, January 26, 2022.

62 Steve Hoffman, interview with author, March 21, 2022.

63 Steven Cohen et al., "Camp Works: The Long-Term Impact of Jewish Overnight Camp," *Foundation for Jewish Camp,* https://jewishcamp.org/wp-content/uploads/2017/03/Camp-Works-FINAL-PDF.pdf.

64 Ibid.

65 Ramie Arian, "Funding Jewish Overnight Camp," *Greenbook: A Guide to Intelligent Giving* 4, Jewish Funders Network (March 2016): 79, https://jewishcamp. org/wp-content/uploads/2017/01/Final-JFN-Greenbook-on-Jewish-Camping.pdf.

66 Cohen et al., "Camp Works," 12. Other studies have reached a different conclusion. For example, Nettie Aharon and Alex Pomson ("What's Happening at the Flagpole? Studying Camps as Institutions for Israel Education, *Journal of Jewish Education* 84, no. 4 (2018): 337–358) studied camps in Canada and found that "relative to other immersive experiences where young people encounter Israel, such as day school, and even more so when compared to experiencing Israel itself in the course of a trip, camp has much less additional impact on Israel engagement" (352). Nevertheless, the study did find that "participating in camp is associated with an additive increase in campers' Israel engagement" that is "statistically significant" (349).

67 Cohen et al., "Camp Works," 14.

68 Ibid, 13.

69 Graizbord, *The New Zionism,* 86–87.

70 Arian, "Funding Jewish Overnight Camp," 8.
71 Ibid, 7.
72 Jeremy Fingerman, interview with author, March 14, 2022.
73 Arian, "Funding Jewish Overnight Camp," 13–14.
74 Ibid, 16.
75 Collaborative for Applied Studies in Jewish Education, "Jewish Experiential Education at Camp," https://www.casje.org/focus/jewish-experiential-education-camp.
76 Arian, "Funding Jewish Overnight Camp," 29.
77 Richard Joel, interview with author, January 24, 2022.
78 Rabbi Ethan Linden, interview with author, February 25, 2022.
79 "Our Story," RootOne, accessed April 7, 2024, https://rootone.org/about-us/.
80 Graham Wright, Shahar Hecht, and Leonard Saxe, "Birthright Israel's First Decade of Applicants: A Look at the Long-term Program Impact," Jewish Futures Project, Cohen Center for Modern Jewish Studies, Brandeis University, November 2020, 1, https://www.brandeis.edu/cmjs/birthright/jewish-futures/jewish-futures-2018.html.
81 Ibid, 1–2.
82 Ibid, 14.
83 Susan R. Eisenstein, "US Birthright Participants 160% more likely to marry Jews," *Jewish News Syndicate,* November 18, 2022. https://www.jns.org/us-birthright-participants-160-more-likely-to-marry-jews/.
84 Wright, Hecht, and Saxe, "Birthright Israel's First Decade of Applicants," 14–15.
85 Ibid, 19.
86 Ibid, 20.
87 Sharansky and Troy, "Can a Year in Israel Transform Your Teen?"
88 Adina H. Frydman, "Moving Towards a Universal Gap Year: A Response to 'Can a Year in Israel Transform Your Teen?'" *Times of Israel,* February 27, 2022, https://blogs.

timesofisrael.com/moving-towards-a-universal-gap-year-a-response-to-can-a-year-in-israel-transform-your-teen/.

89 Ibid.

90 Ibid.

91 "The Values & Spirit of Birthright Israel," Birthright Israel Foundation, accessed April 7, 2024, https://birthrightisrael.foundation/approach/.

92 Sharansky and Troy, "Can a Year in Israel Transform Your Teen?"

93 "Project Atlas: Israel" Institute of International Education, August 2023, https://www.iie.org/en/Research-and-Insights/Project-Atlas/Explore-Data/Israel.

94 "Internationalization Strategy and Budget," Council for Higher Education, accessed April 7, 2024, https://che.org.il/en/strengthening-internationalism-higher-education/.

95 Raoul Wootliff, "Final Text of Jewish Nation-State Law, Approved by the Knesset Early on July 19," *Times of Israel,* July 18, 2018, https://www.timesofisrael.com/ final-text-of-jewish-nation-state-bill-set-to-become-law/.

96 Peter Lintl and Stefan Wolfrum, "Israel's Nation-State Law," *German Institute for International and Security Affairs SWP Comment* 41 (October 2018): 5, https://www.swp-berlin. org/en/publication/israels-nation-state-law.

97 Forest Rain Marcia, "Israel's Nation State Law," The Israel Forever Foundation, accessed April 7, 2024, https://israel-forever.org/interact/blog/israels_nation_state_law/.

98 Declaration of Independence, Provisional Government of Israel, May 14, 1948, https://m.knesset.gov.il/en/about/pages/declaration.aspx.

99 "Bad Boy Beilin Seeks to Scrap Jewish Agency," *Forward,* July 1, 1994, 1.

100 Gabby Deutch, "Israel's New Diaspora Affairs Minister Visits a Jewish Community in Crisis," *Jewish Insider,* June 28, 2021, https://jewishinsider.com/2021/06/israels-

new-diaspora-affairs-minister-visits-a-jewish-community-in-crisis/.

101 Cooperman et al., "Jewish Americans," 103.

CONCLUSION

1 Neal Kozodoy, "In Memoriam: Lucy S. Dawidowicz," *Commentary*, May 1992, https://www.commentary.org/articles/neal-kozodoy/in-memoriam-lucy-s-dawidowicz/.

2 Ibid.

Acknowledgments

This book was written at the Council on Foreign Relations (CFR), where I have been a senior fellow since 2009 (except for 2019–2020, when I returned to the State Department). I am grateful to my colleagues at CFR, to Director of Studies James Lindsay, and to Michael Froman and Richard Haass, who served as the Council's presidents during the years when this book was researched and written. They have made the Council a wonderful haven for scholarship and writing, and I have benefitted greatly from their friendship and support. Many thanks to Michael Weiner for the excellent preliminary research for this book, and to Ezra Hess for his help in the final days. Special thanks to Gideon Weiss, my research assistant at the Council throughout most of the research and writing, who was dedicated to the subject matter and the completion of the work and who was a thoughtful participant in all the interviews and scores of our own conversations on this subject matter.

While developing and researching this book, I was able to speak with a number of key leaders and scholars of the American Jewish community. They graciously gave me their time, answered my questions, and discussed the important work they are doing on behalf of America's (and Canada's) Jews. In particular, I wish to thank Danielle Alexander of JTEEN and Kehillah High in Houston, Alan Cooperman of Pew Research Center, Rabbi Elliot Cosgrove of Park Avenue

Synagogue, the late Rabbi David Ellenson of Hebrew Union College, Jeremy J. Fingerman of the Foundation for Jewish Camp, Dr. Daniel Held of United Jewish Appeal (UJA) of Greater Toronto, Rabbi Ammiel Hirsch of the Stephen Wise Free Synagogue, Steven H. Hoffman (formerly) of the Jewish Federation of Cleveland, Dr. Richard Joel of Yeshiva University, Connie Kanter of the Samis Foundation, Rabbi Ethan Linden of the Shalom Hartman Institute, Rabbi Harry Pell of the Leffell School, Rabbi Gil S. Perl of the Jewish Leadership Academy, Dr. John Ruskay of the Jewish People Policy Institute and (formerly) UJA-Federation of New York, Kari Saratovsky (formerly) of the Jewish Federation of Greater Houston, Professors Jonathan Sarna and Leonard Saxe of Brandeis University, Barry Shrage (formerly) of the Combined Jewish Philanthropies of Greater Boston, and Professor Jack Wertheimer of the Jewish Theological Seminary of America. Special thanks to Dr. Steven M. Cohen, for our discussions of American Jewish life, his invaluable writings, and his help in understanding and utilizing the Pew data.

I would also like to thank The Paul E. Singer Foundation, Roger Hertog, and James and Merryl Tisch for their support throughout the writing of this book.

Many other friends and colleagues assisted me in thinking through the ideas presented here, suggesting and connecting me to sources, and providing their own analyses. Needless to say, what is written here represents my ideas alone, and none of the people mentioned above bear any responsibility for the conclusions I have reached.